Essential Knowledge and Skills for
Essay Writing

Frameworks for Writing
Series Editor: Martha C. Pennington, SOAS and Birkbeck University of London

The series offers books focused on writing and the teaching and learning of writing in educational and real-life contexts. The hallmark of the series is the application of approaches and techniques to writing and the teaching of writing that go beyond those of English literature to draw on and integrate writing with other disciplines, areas of knowledge, and contexts of everyday life. The series entertains proposals for textbooks as well as books for teachers, teacher educators, parents, and the general public. The list includes teacher reference books and student textbooks focused on innovative pedagogy aiming to prepare teachers and students for the challenges of the twenty-first century.

Published:

Academic Writing Step by Step: A Research-based Approach
Christopher N Candlin, Peter Crompton and Basil Hatim

Arting and Writing to Transform Education: An Integrated Approach for Culturally and Ecologically Responsive Pedagogy
Meleanna Aluli Meyer, Mikilani Hayes Maeshiro, and Anna Yoshie Sumida

Creativity and Discovery in the University Writing Class: A Teacher's Guide
Edited by Alice Chik, Tracey Costley, and Martha C. Pennington

Creativity and Writing Pedagogy: Linking Creative Writers, Researchers, and Teachers
Edited by Harriet Levin Millan and Martha C. Pennington

Digital L2 Writing Literacies: Directions for Classroom Practice
Ana Oskoz and Idoia Elola

English Composition Teacher's Guidebook: How to Survive (and Even Thrive) as an Adjunct or Part-time Instructor
Tom Mulder

Exploring College Writing: Reading, Writing, and Researching across the Curriculum
Dan Melzer

Investigative Creative Writing: Teaching and Practice
Mark Spitzer

Reflective Writing for Language Teachers
Thomas S. C. Farrell

Tend Your Garden: Nurturing Motivation in Young Adolescent Writers
Mary Anna Kruch

The "Backwards" Research Guide for Writers: Using Your Life for Reflection, Connection, and Inspiration
Sonya Huber

The College Writing Toolkit: Tried and Tested Ideas for Teaching College Writing
Edited by Martha C. Pennington and Pauline Burton

Understanding the Paragraph and Paragraphing
Iain McGee

Writing Poetry through the Eyes of Science: A Teacher's Guide to Scientific Literacy and Poetic Response
Nancy S. Gorrell, with Erin Colfax

Writing the Pandemic: An Instructor's Reflections on a New Era in Education
Tom Mulder

Essential Knowledge and Skills for Essay Writing

A Practical Guide for ESL and EFL Undergraduates

Neil Evan Jon Anthony Bowen

SHEFFIELD UK   BRISTOL CT

Published by Equinox Publishing Ltd.

UK: Office 415, The Workstation, 15 Paternoster Row, Sheffield, South Yorkshire S1 2BX
USA: ISD, 70 Enterprise Drive, Bristol, CT 06010

www.equinoxpub.com

First published 2023

© Neil Evan Jon Anthony Bowen 2023

All rights reserved. No part of this publication may be reproduced or transmitted in any form or by any means, electronic or mechanical, including photocopying, recording or any information storage or retrieval system, without prior permission in writing from the publishers.

British Library Cataloguing-in-Publication Data

A catalogue record for this book is available from the British Library.

ISBN-13 978 1 80050 366 3 (hardback)
         978 1 80050 367 0 (paperback)
         978 1 80050 368 7 (ePDF)
         978 1 80050 381 6 (ePub)

Library of Congress Cataloging-in-Publication Data

Names: Bowen, Neil Evan Jon Anthony, author.
Title: Essential knowledge and skills for essay writing : a practical guide
  for ESL and EFL undergraduates / Neil Evan Jon Anthony Bowen.
Description: Sheffield, South Yorkshire ; Bristol, CT : Equinox Publishing
  Ltd, 2023. | Series: Frameworks for writing | Includes bibliographical
  references and index. | Summary: "Designed for intermediate and advanced
  users of English, this book offers an integrated approach to essay
  writing by focusing on both the processes and products of writing. This
  book will help students acquire essential knowledge alongside
  transferable and functional skills-both of which can be applied across
  areas of study and in future writing projects"-- Provided by publisher.
Identifiers: LCCN 2023001275 (print) | LCCN 2023001276 (ebook) | ISBN
  9781800503663 (hardback) | ISBN 9781800503670 (paperback) | ISBN
  9781800503687 (pdf) | ISBN 9781800503816 (epub)
Subjects: LCSH: English language--Rhetoric--Problems, exercises, etc. |
  Essay--Authorship--Problems, exercises, etc. | English language--Study
  and teaching--Foreign speakers.
Classification: LCC PE1413 .B68 2023 (print) | LCC PE1413 (ebook) | DDC
  808.06/6--dc23/eng/20230509
LC record available at https://lccn.loc.gov/2023001275
LC ebook record available at https://lccn.loc.gov/2023001276

Typeset by S.J.I. Services, New Delhi

Contents

Acknowledgements	ix
Series Editor's Preface	xi
Copyright Permissions	xiii
Introduction	1

UNIT 1. ESSAY WRITING BASICS — 10

1.1. CLAUSES AND SENTENCES — 11

1.1.1. Independent Clauses	11
1.1.2. Dependent Clauses	17
1.1.3. Complex Sentences	18
1.1.4. Advanced Punctuation	22

1.2. COMMON PROBLEMS AT THE SENTENCE LEVEL — 28

1.2.1. Tense Consistency	28
1.2.2. Verb Agreement	29
1.2.3. Subject–Verb Separation	31
1.2.4. Avoiding Wordiness and Conflicting Ideas	31

1.3. THE STRUCTURE OF A PARAGRAPH — 35

1.3.1. Topic Sentences	37
1.3.2. Supporting Sentences	43
1.3.3. Concluding Sentences	44

1.4. THE STRUCTURE OF AN ESSAY — 46

1.4.1. Introductory Paragraph	47
1.4.2. Body Paragraphs	49
1.4.3. Concluding Paragraphs	55

1.5. UNDERSTANDING THE WRITING PROCESS — 57

1.5.1. Writing the First Draft	58
1.5.2. Writing the Second Draft	61
1.5.3. The Stages of the Writing Process	62

APPENDIX 1A. UNIT 1 ANSWER KEY — 65

vi ESSENTIAL KNOWLEDGE AND SKILLS FOR ESSAY WRITING

UNIT 2. DESCRIPTIVE WRITING   75

2.1. KEY SKILLS   77

2.1.1. Using All Five Senses   77
2.1.2. Figurative Language   79
2.1.3. Enhancing, Elaborating, and Extending Details   86

2.2. DESCRIBING THINGS AND PLACES   91

2.2.1. Using Vivid Words   92
2.2.2. Sequencing Descriptions of Things   95
2.2.3. Describing a Place Paragraph   98

2.3. DESCRIBING PEOPLE   100

2.3.1. Describing Faces, Body Shapes, and Clothes   101
2.3.2. Describing Personality or Character   105
2.3.3. Sequencing Descriptions of People   109
2.3.4. Describing a Person Paragraph   111

2.4. DESCRIBING PROCESSES   114

2.4.1. Informational (Explanatory or Analytical) Writing   115
2.4.2. Sequencing Explanations   115
2.4.3. Writing an Explanatory Essay   117
2.4.4. Instructional (Directional) Writing   120
2.4.5. Sequencing Instructions   122
2.4.6. Writing an Instructional Essay   124

2.5. WRITING A DESCRIPTIVE ESSAY   127

2.5.1. Writing the First Draft   127
2.5.2. Writing the Second Draft   129

APPENDIX 2A. SCORING RUBRIC FOR DESCRIPTIVE WRITING   132

APPENDIX 2B. UNIT 2 ANSWER KEY   133

UNIT 3. NARRATIVE WRITING   137

3.1. KEY SKILLS   140

3.1.1. Narrative Perspective   141
3.1.2. Dialogue   145
3.1.3. Strong, Vivid Verbs   148
3.1.4. Golden Details   151

CONTENTS   vii

3.2. ELEMENTS OF A STORY   153

3.2.1. Choosing a Good Topic   153
3.2.2. Opening the Story   155
3.2.3. Middle of the Story   162
3.2.3. Closing the Story   164

3.3. ELEMENTS OF A PLOT   166

3.3.1. Characters   166
*3.3.2. Rhetorical Structure: The Rise and Fall of a
Narrative*   172
3.3.3. Elements that Help Drive a Plot Forward   177

3.4. WRITING A NARRATIVE ESSAY   182

3.4.1. Writing the First Draft   182
3.4.2. Writing the Second Draft   185

APPENDIX 3A. SCORING RUBRIC FOR NARRATIVE WRITING   188

APPENDIX 3B. UNIT 3 ANSWER KEY   189

UNIT 4. EXPOSITORY WRITING   193

4.1. KEY SKILLS   195

*4.1.1. Elaborating, Enhancing, and Extending upon
Details*   195
4.1.2. Connecting Ideas: Transitions   197
*4.1.3. Rhetorical Structure: Block Method or Point-by-
Point Method*   197

4.2. COMPARE/CONTRAST   202

4.2.1. General Guidelines for Compare/Contrast Writing   202
4.2.2. Sequencing a Compare/Contrast Essay   207
4.2.3. Writing a Compare/Contrast Essay   209
4.2.4. Writing about Advantages and Disadvantages   212

4.3. CLASSIFICATION   214

4.3.1. General Guidelines for Classificatory Writing   215
4.3.2. Sequencing a Classification Essay   219
4.3.3. Rhetorical Structure   221
4.3.4. Writing a Classification Essay   222

viii   ESSENTIAL KNOWLEDGE AND SKILLS FOR ESSAY WRITING

4.4. CAUSE-EFFECT — 225

4.4.1. General Guidelines for Cause-Effect Writing — 226
4.4.2. Sequencing a Cause-Effect Essay — 230
4.4.3. Rhetorical Structure — 232
4.4.4. Writing a Cause-Effect Essay — 236

APPENDIX 4A. SCORING RUBRIC FOR EXPOSITORY WRITING — 240

APPENDIX 4B. UNIT 4 ANSWER KEY — 241

UNIT 5. ARGUMENT/OPINION WRITING — 246

5.1. KEY SKILLS — 249

5.1.1. Modal Verbs, Modal Adjuncts, and Comment Adjuncts — 249
5.1.2. General Guidelines for Writing an Argument/Opinion Essay — 254
5.1.3. Referencing — 266
5.1.4. Methods of Argument — 271

5.2. THE TOULMIN METHOD — 274

5.2.1. Elements of the Toulmin Model — 274
5.2.2. Putting the Toulmin Method into Action — 282
5.2.3. Sequencing a Toulmin Argument — 288
5.2.4. Rhetorical Structure of a Toulmin-Based Essay — 290

5.3. WRITING AN ARGUMENT ESSAY — 291

5.3.1. Writing the First Draft — 291
5.3.2. Writing the Second Draft — 297

APPENDIX 5A. SCORING RUBRIC FOR ARGUMENT WRITING — 300

APPENDIX 5B. UNIT 5 ANSWER KEY — 301

References — 308

Sources for Images — 314

Author Index — 318

Subject Index — 320

Acknowledgements

I am grateful to many people who have helped me develop the knowledge necessary to write this book. I would especially like to thank all my students, past and present, who have taken writing classes with me. They have been incredibly supportive and taught me just as much as I've taught them. A special thanks goes out to those whose essay extracts I include in this book, particularly Pitcha (Pete) and Iwarin (Aifon).

I would also like to thank Professors Tess Fitzpatrick and Alison Wray. Without their early encouragement and support, I would not be where I am today. The same level of appreciation goes to my former PhD supervisor, Lise Fontaine. When I decided to publish this book, Lise was the first person I emailed. I am forever grateful for all the advice and support she has given me over the years.

There are numerous other colleagues to thank, including Professors Tom Bartlett and Luuk Van Waes. Luuk is especially owed a heartfelt thank you, because without his continual support and innovative Inputlog program, many of my research projects that underpin this book would not have come about. His unwavering enthusiasm, professionalism, and level of commitment to research continues to inspire me.

I want to thank my colleagues at Thammasat University, especially Associate Professors Saneh Thongrin and Dumrong Adunyarittigun, who continue to counsel and mentor me through the complexities of higher education in Thailand, and Associate Professors Varisa Osatananda and Supawhat Pookcharoen. I also wish to acknowledge that the development of this textbook was funded by a Textbook Project Grant from the Faculty of Liberal Arts, Thammasat University, 2022.

Last but not least, my appreciation goes out to Derek Hopper and Stephen Louw for their thoughtful comments on earlier chapters, and Nathan Thomas for continually questioning my use of punctuation. I also give a special thank-you to Equinox's Frameworks for Writing Series Editor, Professor Martha Pennington, whose attention to detail and knowledge of English language teaching has undoubtedly increased the quality of this book. She is a consummate professional and has been a joy to work with.

—Neil Bowen
September 2022

Series Editor's Preface

Essential Knowledge and Skills for Essay Writing is a modern writing textbook geared for intermediate and advanced learners of English. With this audience in mind, the author has developed content and activities in a composite process-genre approach which teaches the four types of knowledge needed for the development of writing expertise: formal knowledge, rhetorical knowledge, subject knowledge, and process knowledge. Unit 1 presents an overview of sentence structure, paragraph structure, essay structure, and the writing process. On this foundation, the other four units address key types of essay writing. Unit 2 covers descriptive writing while Unit 3 centers on narrative writing. Unit 4 focuses on expository writing, including compare/contrast, classification, and cause-effect essays. The book culminates in Unit 5 with a final tour-de-force presentation and essay assignment on argument/opinion writing.

The book is authoritative and up-to-date as well as eminently teachable, having been organized into five meaty units and trialed with multiple classes of English language learners by the author, an experienced writing teacher who has also published extensively in the field. Frequent exercises and illustrations, including student writing samples, help to reinforce the content and instructional goals; and use of color, images, boxed material, and answer keys make it an especially attractive and user-friendly book. In addition to a general overview of writing processes and genres that is suitable for all undergraduates, the book features writing by Thai students that gives it intercultural relevance and fresh perspectives on and for students learning English in a global context.

Having worked with Neil Bowen as he perfected this book, I can attest to his expertise, his meticulousness, and his knowledge of and attention to audience in bringing the project to completion. He has as a result produced a writing textbook of unusual quality and excellence that I am excited to recommend to all colleagues teaching ESL and EFL the world over.

—Martha C. Pennington
Series Editor, Frameworks for Writing

Copyright Permissions

Table extracts from *Introduction to Functional Grammar* by M. A. K. Halliday and C. M. I. M. Matthiessen (2014). Reproduced by permission of Taylor and Francis Group, LLC, a division of Informa plc. Copyright (© 2014).

"Slip or Trip?" extracts from *Crime and Puzzlement 2: More Solve-Them-Yourself Picture Mysteries* by Lawrence Treat (1982), illustrated by Kathleen Borowik, page 10. Copyright © 1982 by Lawrence Treat. Illustrations copyright © 1982 by Kathleen Borowik. Reprinted with the permission of The Permissions Company, LLC on behalf of David R Godine, Publisher, Inc., www.godine.com (© 1982).

Introduction

Background to This Book

In many ways, this book is the sum of my educational experiences and professional life so far. I did not set foot on a university campus until I was 31 years old. I spent the first fifteen years of my professional life as an engineer, which I was very successful at: I was the British Mechatronics Champion (twice) and the European Skills Olympics Champion, and I came seventh in the World Skills Olympics; I even received an award from Queen Elizabeth II. Yet, when I began my bachelor's degree in Language Studies and Teaching English as a Foreign Language, many of my first-semester essays came back with low scores. The theory and content were not that difficult for me to learn, and I excelled in the exams, so I was very puzzled by these low-scoring essays. I soon learned that I was still writing like an engineer, and that my lecturers expected or wanted to see a very different kind of writing. Through trial and error, I adapted my writing style, and I returned to being a 4.0 GPA student. Now, I am very aware of how writing across the curriculum is a valuable yet often occluded skill.

The need for this book evolved from my experiences of teaching writing in a wide range of university settings, with both first- and second-language English undergraduates. Specifically, I frequently found myself using two or three books in one class to cover the range of topics and skills my students needed. Even with such an eclectic approach, I still had to supplement the books' contents with a substantial number of practical exercises and handouts. This was especially evident when working with English as a second or foreign language (ESL/EFL) undergraduates. When teaching in an internationalized university setting, students often have varying levels of English ability and vastly different experiences of writing in English. Hence, the range of additional language support and explanation they need goes beyond that of many current textbooks. However, drawing on multiple textbooks was simply not practical in my context for two reasons. First, many of my students do not have the financial means to buy two or three books for a single course. Second, when using multiple books and three to four handouts each week, my students often complained that they lost track of what it was they were supposed to be doing, and so they frequently asked me to compile everything into one document. Clearly, I could not just compile the relevant contents in such a way as this would be plagiarism and break copyright laws. For these reasons, I decided to compile my own contents into the book you see before you.

The contents I have chosen to present in this book have evolved from over thirty undergraduate courses on writing in English that I have taught and developed in the United Kingdom and Thailand. These have included courses for first-language English under-graduates, ESL and EFL students, and undergraduates studying in English-medium instruction programs (commonly referred as EMI), in which English is not their first language, but they none-theless receive most of their instruction and assessment through English. Drawing on these experiences, and informed by my research interests—which bring process and product approaches to writing together (e.g., Bowen, 2019; Bowen & Thomas, 2021; Bowen & Van Waes, 2020; Bowen et al., 2022), I consolidated my key exercises, handouts, teaching approaches, and thoughts on writ-ing into this book. The result is what I call *a composite approach to writing*—a process-genre approach that focuses on the formal aspects of language where relevant. As noted by key scholars in the field (e.g., Huang & Zhang, 2020; Racelis & Matsuda, 2013), such a textbook has been conspicuously absent for quite some time.

Although the core rationale for this book evolved from its neces-sity in my current position—as a university lecturer in Thailand—I have tailored its contents and exercises to appeal to a broad range of students. For instance, since the essay extracts come from some of my most recent Thai students, students from other countries may find themselves encountering hard to pronounce names, such as Pannaporn Wongbuakaew and Bandhita Srinualnad. They may also find themselves confronted with unfamiliar topics such as political unrest in Thailand or uniquely Thai opinions on Western media. Conversely, Thai students will encounter decidedly Western topics such as Flat Earth Conspiracy and numerous examples of classic American and European literature. This is nothing new for EFL/ESL learners as the content in many English language learning textbooks are decidedly Anglo-Western (Keles & Yazan, 2020). Nevertheless, it was my hope that by including a more diverse range of content, students using this book will embrace the notion of a more connected world, where we all strive to become global citizens, rather than divided nations, races, or interest groups.

To the Student

This book is primarily for intermediate and advanced users of English who are undergraduate students. Its content and layout are based on four types of knowledge, each of which is essential to mastering the skill of writing. These four types of knowledge are *formal knowledge*, *rhetorical knowledge*, *subject knowledge*, and *process knowledge*. This book will help you develop these four types of knowledge in tandem with the skills you need for writing at a higher level.

You will be introduced to the basic elements of writing—sentences and paragraphs—and then, in subsequent units, to various types of writing, including descriptive, narrative, expository, and argument/opinion writing. Each unit begins with a "product approach" to writing, wherein you learn to recognize and evaluate texts at micro and macro levels. The *micro level* is that of words and sentences, whereas the *macro level* is that of paragraphs and whole essays. Key language features (*formal knowledge*) and organizational elements (*rhetorical knowledge*)—such as figurative language, thesis statements, supporting details, and transitional words and phrases—are worked into each unit via short exercises. These exercises are based on real-world examples and extracts from student essays, and can be done individually or in groups, at home or in the classroom.

Once key language features and organizational elements are in place, you will then learn about generating ideas (*subject knowledge*) using critical questions, collaborative discussions, and visualization strategies. At the end of each unit, you will be challenged to write longer essays, and will be introduced to various strategies and reflective exercises (*process knowledge*), such as collaborative revision through detailed peer-review questions. Overall, the book will help you acquire essential knowledge and, ultimately, transferable and functional writing skills that you can apply in other classes and future writing projects.

To the Teacher

This book offers an integrated approach to essay writing, focusing on both the processes behind writing and the products of writing. Its content and layout are based on four main tenets, each of which is a known predictor when it comes to the quality of a finished piece of writing. These four tenets are **rhetorical knowledge**, **subject knowledge**, **process knowledge**, and **formal knowledge**. The relationship between them is shown in Figure 1.

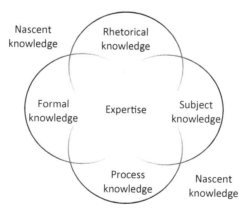

Figure 1. Integration of knowledge types needed for writing (adapted from Tardy, 2009)

Although this model is admittedly heuristic, it provides a useful overview of knowledge types that relate to the mastery of higher-level writing. Rhetorical knowledge "captures an understanding of the genre's intended purposes and an awareness of the dynamics of persuasion within a socio-rhetorical context" (Tardy, 2009, p. 21). Formal knowledge refers to the lexical, grammatical, and structural conventions of a genre, as well as the modes and media through which meaning is transmitted. However, within formal knowledge a clear distinction can be made between discourse organization (stages or moves) and lexicogrammatical patterns (registers). This distinction is the premise behind the first two tenets of this book's approach. Namely, that certain micro/macro-genres have evolved to perform specific functions in specific contexts, and that these genres (rhetorical knowledge) are composed of recognizable, and thus teachable, language choices and configurations (formal knowledge). In other words, while there are many types of essays (macro-genres) that students encounter at undergraduate level (Gardner & Nesi, 2013), many of these are thought to be amalgams of smaller, purposeful micro-genres (Martin & Rose, 2008). Fundamentally, if a student can master these micro-genres, then they can combine them to form many of the recognizable essay types they will be called upon to produce. For instance, once a student can write an introductory paragraph that consists of a hook, supporting details, and a thesis statement, then this rhetorical configuration can be transferred across essay types, as its functional basis remains the same.

However, being able to (re)construct a recognizable genre is not as simple as possessing sufficient formal and rhetorical knowledge. A writer also needs to consider the other two circles in Figure 1: subject knowledge and process knowledge.

Subject (or subject-matter) knowledge refers to content knowledge, which is one of the strongest predictors of text quality (Crossley, 2020). Subject knowledge and working memory are intricately linked, and both are strong predictors of text quality. Moreover, it may well be that their respective impacts vary across genres. For example, subject knowledge may have a stronger effect on the writing of descriptions than expositions, as descriptions are relatively simple in terms of overall structure and so, for those reading or assessing such texts, working memory may be freed up, making it easier for them to present or extract propositional meanings. Argument/Opinion Essays, on the other hand, make greater use of cohesive ties and logic-based links that span longer stretches of text incorporating unconventional grammatical patterns, which place more demands on working memory—for both producer and receiver. Consequently, subject matter may be harder to present or extract when writing or reading these texts.

For these reasons, when teaching writing, it is important to pay just as much attention to the topics we ask students to write about as to the language we expect them to produce. This is the third tenet of this book: the importance of interesting and relevant writing topics and prompts that can also minimize effects related to subject knowledge. Thus, there is considerable space devoted to topic selection and idea generation in each unit of this book.

The last tenet of the book refers to process knowledge, which encompasses cognitively based strategies and activities that a writer makes use of during the writing process. This tenet is based on the belief that writing can be likened to other complex skills, such as playing chess or a musical instrument (Galbraith & Baaijen, 2018). While some people may have an innate ability to write masterful prose, or scientific monologues that flow gracefully from page to page, the majority of us need some instruction and considerable practice to master the skill of writing. Therefore, a focus on the main cognitive processes involved in writing—planning, outlining, text production, reviewing, and revising (Hayes, 2012)—runs throughout each unit where possible, and helps put the other three tenets into practice.

Organization of Each Unit

As the first two tenets of the book are based on the premise that we cannot write *model texts*[1] unless we know what a model text looks and reads like, each chapter begins with a product approach to writing. Following this approach, the student is introduced to each genre in functional terms (Martin & Rose, 2008), which means they learn to recognize and evaluate the purposes of texts at micro (word and sentence) and macro (paragraph and essay) levels from a reader's perspective. This approach is based on the notion of genre, in which typified text-types present recurrent patterns of language choices in recognizable sequences. This is not because there is only one way to write, but because functional constraints have led to certain text-types evolving into efficient communicative devices (Bazerman, 1997; Martin & Rose, 2008; Swales, 1990). Therefore, at the start of each unit, students are introduced to the distinctive structures and features of various model texts, many of which are essays produced by students who have studied with the author. Thus, not only do students get to see each text in action, but they also get to see what is possible from students at their level who have used the contents of this book to improve their writing.

Once the student is made aware of what a model text contains and does, each unit then switches to a more pragmatic approach. Now the student is introduced to the basic elements of writing each genre: a switch from receptive to productive knowledge. Elements such as thesis statements, supporting details, transitional devices, and rhetorical devices are worked into each unit via short exercises that can be done individually or in groups, at home or in the classroom. A range of key skills important to each genre are also introduced at this stage, such as the use of figurative language in descriptions, dialogue in narratives, and evidence in argument writing to support warrants. Each unit also introduces students to the subtle differences in how these essays are organized in terms of rhetorical moves and the sequencing of information.

Once the key language features (formal knowledge) and organizational patterns/moves (rhetorical knowledge) are in place, each unit then moves on to tenets three and four: subject matter and process knowledge. Students work on generating ideas using critical questions, collaborative discussions, and visualization strategies. They also learn the importance of planning and using various outlining techniques. After some practice writing longer texts, they are then introduced to various strategies and reflective exercises that can assist them in developing their essays, such as collaborative revision using detailed peer review exercises. At the end of each unit, students are challenged to write longer essays that bring together all the types of knowledge covered in that unit.

This book covers the micro- and macro-genres that are most widely used in university settings across major subjects or fields and curriculums. It takes students from sentences to paragraphs to essays in terms of the following types of writing:

- Descriptions of people, places, and processes.
- Narratives that incorporate both a story and a plot.
- Expositions of compare/contrast, classificatory, and cause–effect relationships.
- Argument/opinion essays that include claims, grounds, warrants, and backing.

While the book is primarily aimed at intermediate to advanced ESL/EFL students, it can be used by any student who has a good grasp of the English language, which, of course, includes first-language English students as well.

Upon completion of the book, students should be able to demonstrate the following skills and knowledge:

- Use various sentence forms to modulate style and employ correct grammar.
- Apply principles of clarity and coherence to their writing in terms of sentences, paragraphs, and larger rhetorical structures.
- Compose effective descriptive, narrative, expository, and argument/opinion essays that respond to specific rhetorical situations using appropriate style, structure, conventions, and voice.

- Collect, generate, and express ideas and information in written form with clarity and precision.
- Revise written texts effectively and respond to the written work of peers in a critical, yet helpful manner.

Notes

1 I use the term *model text* to refer to those texts that accomplish the goal their author has set out for them, be it an enthralling story or a detailed description of a person.

Unit 1
ESSAY WRITING BASICS

Unit Goals

Upon completing this unit, you should be able to demonstrate the following knowledge and skills:

- Understand the fundamentals of writing sentences.
- Recognize and organize the main elements of a paragraph.
- Write a paragraph motivated by a topic sentence.
- Structure a five-paragraph essay.
- See writing as a recursive process made up of stages.

Definition

The word **essay** was originally a loanword from French (*essai*), which was first popularized in middle French by Michel de Montaigne in his collection of essays (1580/2006). Later in the same century, the word made its way into the English language through the writings of Sir Francis Bacon (1597/2009). In its original French form, *essai* signified "an effort" or "an attempt." De Montaigne used the concept to reflect on himself and many diverse subjects, from cannibals to love and friendship. In modern English, the term *essay* has come to mean *the presentation of one's point of view through a written composition of moderate length*. In this book, I use the term in this way, and I take the definition to encompass a formal or informal piece of writing that is loosely structured but has an introduction, a body, a conclusion, and an

ESSAY WRITING BASICS   11

overall purpose. In this book, the purpose ranges from description (Unit 2) to narrative (Unit 3), to exposition (Unit 4), and finally to argument (unit 5).

Before diving into essay writing, this unit starts with some back-to-basics reminders. It will (re)familiarize you with the building blocks of writing: sentences. It then moves on to explore the elements of a stand-alone paragraph, focusing on topic sentences and supporting sentences. In the penultimate section, it looks at general-purpose introductions and

> **Sentence** *A word, phrase, clause, or a group of clauses or phrases forming a complete thought or syntactic unit.*
>
> *In writing, sentences begin with a capital letter and end with appropriate punctuation.*

conclusions, and considers how they can be applied to larger texts, such as five-paragraph essays. The unit concludes by examining the writing process, outlining it in terms of seven stages that you can cycle through to help improve your writing and create better essays.

1.1. CLAUSES AND SENTENCES

This section begins with independent clauses and looks at some common problems that student writers have with this unit of language; namely, the creation of fragments (incomplete thoughts) and when to use the passive voice.

1.1.1. Independent Clauses

In English, an ***independent clause*** is group of words that contains, at a minimum, a *subject* and *verb* and can stand alone as a sentence (i.e., it expresses a complete thought). If one or more necessary element is missing, then you have a ***fragment***—an incomplete thought or syntactic unit. For instance, if you use a ditransitive verb (a verb that requires two objects) but include only one object, then you have a fragment, such as in the following example:

12 ESSENTIAL KNOWLEDGE AND SKILLS FOR ESSAY WRITING

> → Sarah gave Tom.

In this example, the recipient of the process of giving (*Tom*) is stated, but not what is being given (the object directly affected by the process: the goal in functional terms). The reader is left thinking, "What did Sarah give to Tom?"

Now, consider the complete sentence given below, which contains a transitive verb. This means that it requires a subject and one direct object to represent a complete thought:

> → June studies Critical Writing at Thammasat University.

The example above includes a subject (*June*), a main transitive verb (*studies*), and the direct object (*Critical Writing*) that the transitive verb requires. This combination of elements makes an independent clause—a complete thought. This independent clause is also written in the ***active voice***—the subject comes before the main verb. Thus, it follows one of the seven canonical sentence patterns of English. Specifically, it follows the pattern S^V^O^C (subject^verb^object^complement).

The corresponding ***passive voice*** sentence for the above clause would be as follows:

> → Critical Writing is studied by June at Thammasat University.

You should use the active voice wherever possible because it is easier to understand and closer to the way people speak. It also takes up fewer words than the passive voice—an important consideration when you have a tight word limit.

In the *active voice*, the person or thing that carries out an action or process (the doer—actor, behaver, sayer, etc.) is also the grammatical *subject* of the clause, and it is placed before the verb, as follows:

> → Anna [S] posts [V] Instagram stories [O] every day [C] – 6 words

To transform the above sentence into the *passive voice*, the subject (*Anna*; doer of the verb, or actor) is placed after the verb, which is turned into a verb phrase containing a form of *to be* and is connected via the preposition *by*. The object (or goal = *Instagram stories*), meanwhile, is moved to before the verb phrase, as shown below.

| → Instagram stories [O] are posted [V] by Anna [S] every day [C] – 8 words |

In the above example, the active verb *posts* is replaced by the passivized form *are posted* (simple present passive construction = *be* + verb^past participle). Whenever the grammatical subject comes after a verb phrase of the form *be* + verb^past participle, that is passive voice.

The only time you should use the passive is for one of the reasons given below.

USE THE PASSIVE WHEN THE SUBJECT IS UNKNOWN

| → My car was stolen yesterday (by whom?). |

In this instance, the passive voice emphasizes the stolen item— the direct object (or goal) of a physical process of stealing. If you knew who stole the car (subject; actor), it may not be such a problem.

USE THE PASSIVE WHEN THE SUBJECT IS IRRELEVANT

| → The rat was placed into a T-shaped maze. |

Who places the rat into the maze? Scientists, duh. However, that is less important than the experiment the scientists are conducting. The focus is on the experiment and the experimental animal (the rat). Therefore, passive voice is typically used.

USE THE PASSIVE WHEN YOU WANT TO GIVE THE OBJECT THEMATIC PROMINENCE

It is often useful to change the order of *subject* and *object* to establish a particular order and flow of information between clauses (see Bowen & Thomas, 2020), especially when changing topics, such as in the following example:

14 ESSENTIAL KNOWLEDGE AND SKILLS FOR ESSAY WRITING

> (i) Increasing the flow of water would mean replacing all the pipes.
>
> (ii) However, this *[replacing the pipes]* can be avoided by using bigger pumps.
>
> (iii) Bigger pumps are also cheaper and more efficient.

In the example above, the writer switches between two topics: *increasing the flow of water* in (i) to *bigger pumps* in (iii). They do this by using a passive construction to manipulate what they place at the start of sentence (ii). The type of relationship between the content at the end of clause (i) and the content at the start of clause (ii) is called a ***linear theme***. In this type of pattern, information that is introduced toward the end of one sentence is further developed as the subject and theme of the sentence that follows. The themes then progress in a straight line of development from one sentence to the next. This organizational pattern is very easy for a reader to follow, and it is typically found in expository texts that outline procedures or cause–effect chains.

Another simple thematic pattern is the ***constant theme***. In this pattern, each sentence begins with the same subject and theme, although the wording usually changes (e.g., through the use of pronouns, close synonyms, etc.). A constant theme pattern is useful when you don't want to switch topics, and is typically found in sections of text that focus on describing one topic in detail, such as in the following example:

> (i) Dogs are domestic animals.
>
> (ii) They have four legs, a tail, and sharp teeth.
>
> (iii) Some dogs are very large and strong.

You can use the passive to your advantage in certain situations, such as manipulating what you give thematic prominence to, but this depends on your ability to accurately switch from active voice to passive voice when appropriate. Exercise 1.1 will give you practice in using passive and active voice to control the flow of information between clauses.

Exercise 1.1. Using passive/active voice to control information flow

For each of the items below, write the corresponding passive/active voice sentence for sentence (a) on the dotted line. Then choose which sentence, (a) or (b), achieves the desired thematic progression. The first item has been done for you.

1. If you experience a panic attack, it is important to control your breathing. (LT☝)
a) ~~Inhaling slowly and deeply through your nose can slow down breathing.~~
b) Breathing can be slowed down by inhaling slowly and deeply through your nose.
   These actions are followed by breathing out slowly and deeply through the mouth.

2. The symptoms of a panic attack are not dangerous but can be frightening. (CT☝)
a) A fast heartbeat, shaking, and nausea are included as common symptoms.

b) You may also experience dry mouth, breathlessness, sweating and dizziness.

3. The citizens of Thailand are served by the members of a coalition government. (LT☝)
a) A coalition government is formed by several political parties working together.

b) In working together, these parties form a unified majority.

4. Particulate matter (PM) is a mix of liquids and solids suspended in the air. (CT☝)
a) Some types of PM can be observed without special equipment.

b) However, the most dangerous types are the ones we cannot see: PM10 and PM2.5.

5. Constitutions define the rights of an individual at the state or national level. (CT☝)
a) The powers of government are limited by a carefully designed constitution.

b) In other words, a good constitution protects the people.

16   ESSENTIAL KNOWLEDGE AND SKILLS FOR ESSAY WRITING

6. The internet is basically a worldwide system of computer networks. (LT↗)
a) These networks are connected by devices called routers.

b) Routers ensure that signals from one computer get to another computer.

7. The introduction to an essay typically ends with a thesis statement. (LT↗)
a) The overall topic and main idea(s) of the essay are presented through this statement.

b) Thus, it differs from a topic sentence in that it functions at the level of the essay and not the paragraph.

8. Filter bubbles are a type of intellectual isolation. (CT⇩)
a) A distorted view of reality with negative consequence can be created by them.

b) Fortunately, filter bubbles can be burst once you know what to look out for.

9. Scientists have discovered several layers of dry ice on Mars. (LT↗)
a) These layers cover the north and south poles.

b) If both these poles melted, the planet would be covered in about 35 meters of water.

10. Increased CO_2 in our atmosphere has led to climate change. (LT↗)
a) Climate change is defined by scientists as globally shifting weather patterns and seasons.

b) It also refers to the warming of seas and melting of ice, leading to rising sea levels.

The following sections explore dependent clauses, complex sentences, and punctuation. Along the way, I introduce some of the difficulties that many students encounter early on in writing classes, particularly at the sentence level.

ESSAY WRITING BASICS   17

1.1.2. Dependent Clauses

In English, a ***dependent clause*** is a group of words or phrases that contains a subject and verb but does not express a complete thought. In other words, it *depends* on another clause to complete its meaning and so it cannot stand on its own. For example, if a connector such as a conjunctive adjunct (e.g., *because*) or coordinating conjunction (e.g., *so*) is added to a clause, then it becomes dependent on something else. Consider the following sentences:

✓ 1.	Neil is thirsty = complete thought/sentence
✗ 2.	When Neil is thirsty = incomplete thought (When Neil is thirsty, then what?)

In order for (2) to be complete, the dependent clause must be joined to an independent clause functioning as the main clause within a sentence. If the dependent clause comes before the independent/main clause, separate it with a comma. If it comes after the independent/main clause, do not use a comma. This is illustrated below.

DEPENDENT CLAUSE BEFORE INDEPENDENT CLAUSE = COMMA

✓ As soon as he drank the water, Neil was happy.

DEPENDENT CLAUSE AFTER INDEPENDENT CLAUSE = NO COMMA

✓ Neil was happy as soon as he drank the water.

The comma signifies that what starts the sentence is not the main clause but something tacked on ahead of it—in this case, a dependent clause.

If you present a dependent clause on its own (i.e., not attached to an independent clause), it cannot count as a sentence because it is an incomplete thought. Even if you punctuate it like a sentence, a dependent clause is actually a *sentence fragment*. This can be fixed by attaching it to an independent clause to complete the thought or by removing the dependent connector.

18   ESSENTIAL KNOWLEDGE AND SKILLS FOR ESSAY WRITING

Exercise 1.2. Identifying sentence fragments

Put an *X* in the box next to any of the examples 1–10 below that are fragments. Fix any fragments by completing the thought or removing the connector.

1. Until I can learn to be on time, I will lose attendance marks. ☐

2. Whether I complete this course and get a good grade. ☐

3. If I do not take my iPhone and I need to contact you. ☐

4. While I was driving to class and there was a traffic jam. ☐

5. When I took the test, I was very anxious. ☐

6. Because it was raining and windy. ☐

7. She was disappointed since she missed the movie. ☐

8. I like many types of fruit such as. ☐

9. She showed no improvement in her work. ☐

10. Discovered the cure for cancer. ☐

1.1.3. Complex Sentences

Connectors are one way that you can ensure *cohesion* in your writing. For instance, you can use *coordinating conjunctions* or *conjunctive adjuncts* to connect independent clauses.

Coordinating conjunctions are *FANBOYS*: *for, and, nor, but, or, yet, so.* When you use a coordinating conjunction to join two independent clauses, you need a comma before the conjunction, as shown below.

✓ The student studied hard for the exam, *but* she was still worried about it.

Conjunctive adjuncts are connectors that construct semantic ties between ideas, propositions, reasons, things, or people, and they can be used to begin a sentence that stands alone. If the second independent clause in a sentence has a conjunctive adjunct, then you can use a semicolon to join the two clauses:

> ✓ The student studied hard for the exam; *however*, she was still worried about it.

Table 1.1 is from Halliday and Matthiessen (2014, pp. 613–614). The table gives a good overview of the most common English words/phrases that serve as conjunctive adjuncts. It is a valuable resource that you will want to refer to as you go through this book. You may also want to continue using this table to help you select appropriate adjuncts in your future written work. Note that the elements marked with an asterisk* in the table are typically used between two clauses. Technically, they are coordinating conjunctions, so it is advisable in academic writing to avoid using them to start a sentence. The underlined items are ones I have added to Halliday and Matthiessen's list; items with an asterix (*) are coordinating conjunctions.

Table 1.1. Examples of items serving as conjunctive adjuncts

Type	Subtypes		Items
elaborating	apposition	expository	*in other words, that is (to say), I mean (to say), to put it another way*
		exemplifying	*for example, for instance, thus, to illustrate, such as*
	clarification	corrective	*or rather, at least, to be more precise*
		distractive	*by the way, incidentally*
		dismissive	*in any case, anyway, leaving that aside*
		particularizing	*in particular, more especially*
		resumptive	*as I was saying, to resume, to get back to the point*
		summative	*in short, to sum up, in conclusion, briefly*
		verifactive	*actually, as a matter of fact, indeed, in fact*

20 ESSENTIAL KNOWLEDGE AND SKILLS FOR ESSAY WRITING

extending	addition	positive		*and, also, moreover, in addition*
		negative		*nor*
		adversative		*but, yet, on the other hand, however*
	variation	replacive		*on the contrary, instead*
		subtractive		*apart from that, except for that*
		alternative		*or, alternatively, whether ... or*
enhancing	spatio-temporal; temporal	simple	following	*then, next, afterwards*
			simultaneous	*as, just then, at the same time,*
			preceding	*before that, hitherto, previously*
			conclusive	*in the end, finally*
		complex	immediate	*at once, thereupon, straightaway*
			interrupted	*soon, after a while*
			repetitive	*next time, on another occasion*
			specific	*next day, an hour later, that morning*
			durative	*meanwhile, all that time*
			terminal	*until then, up to that point*
			punctiliar	*at this moment*
		simple internal	following	*next, secondly ("my next point is...")*
			simultaneous	*at this point, here, now*
			preceding	*hitherto, up to now*
			conclusive	*lastly, last of all, finally*
	manner	comparing	positive	*likewise, similarly*
			negative	*in a different way*
		means		*thus, thereby, by such means*
	causal-conditional	general		*so, then, therefore, consequently, hence; for*
		specific	result	*in consequence, as a result*
			reason	*because, *as, on account of this, for that reason*
			purpose	*for that purpose, with this in view*
			conditional: positive	*then, in that case, in that event, under the circumstance*
			conditional: negative	*otherwise, if not*
			concessive	*yet, still, though, despite this, however, even so, all the same, nevertheless, although*
	matter	positive		*here, there, as to that, in that respect*
		negative		*in other respects, elsewhere*

Copyright © 2014. Adapted from *Introduction to Functional Grammar* by Halliday, M. A. K., & Matthiessen, C. M. I. M. Reproduced by permission of Taylor and Francis Group, LLC, a division of Informa plc.

The following exercise will give you practice in using Table 1.1.

Exercise 1.3. Choosing the correct conjunction

The example below is an agree/disagree paragraph. Your task is to insert an appropriate coordinating conjunction or conjunctive adjunct into each of the spaces. The square brackets tell you what type of conjunction from Table 1.1 is required.

I agree with the idea that only rich people are successful, [1] [extending: addition: adversative] only if the definition of "successful" is to live with convenience, comfort, [2] [extending: addition: positive] happiness, without worrying about burdens. First, money is a key enabler in life. [3] [elaborating: apposition], if you live with poverty, you rarely have enough money to get food. [4] [extending: addition: positive], many poor people need to work very hard for just a little reward. This does not seem like a successful life. [5] [extending: addition: adversative], rich people are born with a lot more opportunities. [6] [elaborating: apposition: exemplifying] the son or daughter of rich parents can attend famous schools, [7] [extending: addition: positive] they are able to improve through expensive lessons. [8] [enhancing: causal-conditional: specific], they are often highly "educated" and [9] [enhancing: causal-conditional: specific] have a lot more chances to get better work. [10] [enhancing: spatio-temporal: simple internal], when rich people have done something illegal, they will usually be acquitted because of the power of money in Thailand. [11] [enhancing: spatio-temporal: simple], if we define success as an easy life, then I agree that only rich people are successful.

From *Yes, Rich People can be Called Successful*
by Thanawat Chayangkul

You will have noticed that most of the conjunctions that you just inserted into the student's paragraph were preceded by commas or some other form of punctuation. Without these punctuation marks and appropriate conjunctions, many of the sentences would have been ***fused sentences*** (or *run-ons*).

A fused sentence is putting two independent clauses next to each other with no form of punctuation or conjunction between them. This problem can be fixed by adding a period, a semicolon, or a conjunction between the two sentences, as shown below.

> ✗ I do not like using commas they are tricky.
> ✓ I do not like using commas *[insert . or ; or **because**]* T/they are tricky.

Exercise 1.4. Identifying fused sentences

This exercise will help you identify and fix fused sentences. Put an *X* next to each example of a fused sentence below. Fix the sentence by using correct punctuation or inserting a connector.

1. She told me to write every day I am regretting not listening to her. ☐
2. My friend was upset yesterday she did not pass her exam. ☐
3. Because Tommy was late for class, he missed some important information. ☐
4. The student fell asleep in class everyone laughed at him. ☐
5. I received an A from my writing teacher I am very happy. ☐

1.1.4. Advanced Punctuation

A *comma* is a very versatile punctuation mark and can be used to separate all kinds of grammatical units. Although it may seem simple to use, because of all its different functions, it can often be tricky to use it properly. Rather than give an extensive presentation of all the different ways in which commas can be used, I will forgo most of the basics and focus on errors that confuse readers or break up the flow of information in illogical ways.

- Do not separate the subject from its verb with a single comma.
- Do not separate two verbs or verb phrases in a compound predicate where the same subject is carrying out both actions/states at the same time.
- Do not separate the two parts of a compound subject or compound object.

- Do not separate two independent clauses with just a comma—this is called a *comma splice*.

Fortunately, the first three of these errors can be fixed by simply removing the comma. The last error—the comma splice—can be remedied by replacing the comma with a period or semicolon, by inserting a coordinating conjunction before the comma, or by inserting a subordinating conjunction without the comma, as show below.

- ✗ I do not like using commas, they are tricky.
- ✓ I do not like using commas. They are tricky.
- ✓ I do not like using commas; they are tricky.
- ✓ I do not like using commas, for they are tricky.
- ✓ I do not like using commas because they are tricky.

Exercise 1.5. Identifying comma splices

This exercise will help you identify and correct comma splices. Put an *X* next to each example of a comma splice 1–5 below. Correct the punctuation or add a conjunction to fix the sentence.

1. Lee is always late for class, nobody seems to care. ☐
2. Hot weather is not nice, high temperatures can harm some people. ☐
3. Amber broke her arm on Friday; now she is in the hospital. ☐
4. Travelling on the bus is quicker, riding a bicycle is healthier. ☐
5. Because I am very busy this week, I do not have time to relax. ☐

At a more advanced level of study, it also helps if you know the difference between a hyphen (-), an en dash (–), and an em dash (—).

Hyphens (-) are the shortest of the three marks, and are used to create compound nouns and hyphenated adjectives:

- ✓ father-in-law, wife-to-be, six-pack, well-being (nouns);
- ✓ cold-blooded animals, part-time worker, up-to-date information (adjectives).

An *en dash (–)* is slightly longer than a hyphen, but not as long as an em dash. It is called en dash because the dash is approximately the width of the letter *n*. Essentially, the en dash means "through." For example, below, I have used en dashes to indicate inclusive dates and numbers:

> ✓ July 9–August 17;
> ✓ Pages 37–59;
> ✗ Pages 37-59 (this is incorrect because it is a hyphen).

The *em dash (—)* is significantly longer than the hyphen. It is called an em dash because the dash is approximately the width of the letter *m*. It can be used to create a strong break in a sentence, or to set off extra information such as descriptions, examples, or elaborating clauses from the main sentence. If the extra information follows the main information of the sentence, then an em dash is placed before that extra information. Typically, the em dash attaches information that explains or expands upon the main clause, as shown in the next two examples.

> ✓ The teacher is never late for class—or never has been so far.
> ✓ Cats are generally much quieter than dogs—though there are exceptions.

The em dash acts like a break or a pause that draws attention to the information placed after it; it can also give added information, such as a quality or an afterthought, which the writer wants to bring to the attention of the reader. It is also possible to insert extra information in the middle of a sentence using a pair of em dashes to set off the added information from the rest of the sentence, as in the next pair of examples.

> ✓ The teacher is never—or, to be precise, never has been—late for class.
> ✓ Cats are generally—though there are exceptions—much quieter than dogs.

In this type of case, the em dashes function somewhat similarly to parentheses—though using parentheses (as I have done here to insert author commentary) tends to background rather than foreground the information that is added.

ESSAY WRITING BASICS   25

If your keyboard does not have an en dash or em dash, you can insert them via your word processor's menu options. In MS Word, go to Insert → Symbol. In Google Docs, go to Insert → Special Characters. On a Mac, you simply press Option + hyphen (-) for an en dash, and Shift + Option + Hyphen (-) for an em dash. You can also copy and paste the appropriate character from https://en.wikipedia.org/wiki/Help:CharInsert

A *semicolon (;)* is another tricky punctuation device. It is most commonly used to link two independent clauses that are closely related in thought. When a semicolon is used, those ideas are then given equal importance and grammatical rank.

> ✓ Some people write with a word processor; others write with a pen or pencil.

You can also use a semicolon between two independent clauses that are connected by a conjunctive adjunct.

> ✓ However they choose to write, people are allowed to make their own decisions; as a result, many people swear by their writing methods.

You should also use a semicolon between items in a list or series, if any of the listed items contain commas.

> ✓ Students can write essays in three ways: with a pen and paper, which is inexpensive and easily accessible but produces text that can be hard to read; by computer and printer, which is more expensive but produces neat and readable text; or by a combination of pen-and-paper and computer-and-printer, which is often the choice of students these days.

Finally, use a semicolon between independent clauses joined by a coordinating conjunction, if the clauses are already punctuated with commas, or if they are quite long.

> ✓ Some people write with a word processor, tablet, or even a phone; but others, for different reasons, choose to write with a pen or pencil.

Like the comma and the semicolon, the *colon (:)* has a number of uses. Its main use is to announce, introduce, or direct attention to a list, word, phrase, quotation, example, or explanation that completes a sentence or larger unit such as a set of instructions or a quoted block of text.

26 ESSENTIAL KNOWLEDGE AND SKILLS FOR ESSAY WRITING

TO INTRODUCE A LIST OR SERIES

> ✓ We covered many of the fundamentals in our writing class: grammar, punctuation, style, and voice.
> ✓ There are six steps to making a plain omelet for one:
> 1. Put a tablespoon of vegetable oil in a small skillet on low heat;
> 2. Place two large eggs in a small bowl;
> 3. Add a tablespoon of milk or cream and a pinch of salt to the eggs;
> 4. Whip the egg mixture with a fork till frothy;
> 5. Pour egg mixture into the skillet, cover, and cook until puffy and dry on top;
> 6. Use a spatula to lift the omelet onto a plate, and enjoy it while still hot.

To call attention to information by placing it at the end of a sentence (similar to the use of a dash):

> ✓ My roommate gave me the things I needed most: companionship and quiet.

TO INTRODUCE A QUOTATION OR BLOCK QUOTATION

> ✓ Shakespeare said it best: "To thine own self be true."
> ✓ Bowen et al. (2022) challenged students to reflect on how they revise/edit their written work in three ways:
>> (a) encouraging students to see revision as a continual process rather than just something you do to a final draft; (b) advising students to focus on macro-level revisions that attend to rubric items rather than surface-level revision of grammar and spelling; and (c) encouraging students to reflect on what they revise and why. (p. 6)

You can also use a colon to connect two sentences when the second sentence summarizes, sharpens, or explains the first. However, both sentences should be complete, and their content should be very closely related.

> ✓ Life is like a puzzle: half the fun is in trying to work it out.

In the latter case, an em dash is sometimes used instead of a colon, but the colon is more common in academic writing.

Colons are also used when expressing time, ratios, and two-part titles, as shown below.

ESSAY WRITING BASICS

> ✓ 4:45:00 = four hours, forty-five minutes, and zero seconds;
> ✓ 5:1 = five to one;
> ✓ Everest: The Last Frontier (book title with subtitle).

Some common mistakes when using colons include using a colon between a verb and its object or complement:

> ✗ The very best peaches are: those that are grown in the great state of Georgia.

Using a colon between a preposition and its object:

> ✗ My favorite cake is made of: carrots, flour, butter, eggs, and cream cheese.

Using a colon after *such as, including, especially*, and similar phrases:

> ✗ There are many different types of paper, including: college ruled, wide ruled, and plain copy paper.

Exercise 1.6. Identifying advanced punctuation errors

Mark each of the examples 1–10 below as either correct (✓) or incorrect (✗). Underline any incorrectly used punctuation marks. Give the correct punctuation, where appropriate.

1. We can make a list using: colons, semicolons, and commas. ☐
2. Mastering punctuation is important; it helps us with clarity. ☐
3. Classes finish at 4.45 PM. ☐
4. I really love kimchi—especially for lunch. ☐
5. The worst kinds of friend are: ones who ignore you, ones who lie to you, and ones who always turn up late. ☐
6. There are only two ways to live your life: one is as though nothing is a miracle, which means everything is ordinary, and one is as though everything is a miracle, which means everything is extraordinary. ☐
7. June 15th-18th is a holiday. ☐
8. It was a well known problem. ☐
9. Space—The Final Frontier. ☐
10. All three desserts—cake, ice cream, and chocolate mousse—were delicious. ☐

28 ESSENTIAL KNOWLEDGE AND SKILLS FOR ESSAY WRITING

1.2. COMMON PROBLEMS AT THE SENTENCE LEVEL

1.2.1. Tense Consistency

One of the most frequent mistakes in student writing is an inconsistent use of tense. Students often start writing in one tense and then have switched to another tense for no reason (as I have done in this sentence). Tense consistency refers to the ability to choose a primary tense and stick with it unless you need to shift to indicate changes in timeframe. For instance, you need to decide if an event happened, is happening, or will happen, and then not suddenly change your mind or alter the timeframe mid-sentence or mid-essay for no reason. In the first example below, I have chosen to represent a collection of actions initiated by Adam (grammatical subject / actor) as finished (*simple past tense verbs*), but in the last clause I have shifted to the *simple present tense*—a shift in tense there makes the tense inconsistent. In the second (revised) example, the tenses remain consistent through all three actions.

> ✕ Adam *finished* (past tense) his homework, *turned off* (past tense) his computer, and then *plays* (present tense) video games.
> ✓ Adam *finished* his homework, *turned off* his computer, and then *played* video games.

However, there are occasions when a writer needs to switch tenses, such as when showing cause and effect over time and when moving from direct to indirect (reported) speech. For instance, in the example below I cannot eat the cheeseburger until after I have bought it. Hence, in the second clause, I need to shift to the simple past tense to signal that I bought the cheeseburger before I started eating it:

> ✕ I *am eating* (present progressive) a cheeseburger that I *am buying* (present progressive) at McDonalds.
> ✓ I *am eating* (present progressive) a cheeseburger that I *bought* (past tense) at McDonalds.

A writer also needs to shift tense when using indirect (reported speech). Put simply, the tense in indirect speech is one step further back in time from the tense in direct speech. Consider the following example, where the content is the same, but there is a tense shift when switching from direct (quoted) speech to indirect (reported) speech:

→ She said, "I am hungry." (Direct speech)
→ She said that she was hungry. (Indirect speech)

In the above example, also note how the first-person pronoun *I* in the direct speech sentence has changed into the second person pronoun *she* in the indirect speech sentence. This is because the person is no longer being directly quoted—what she said is being reported (indirectly) by someone else. Since someone else is reporting what was said, the event represented in the speech must now be in the past, because it is not possible to report what someone said unless they have already said it. Hence, the verb shifts from simple present tense (*am*) to simple past tense (*was*). Notice how the verb form has also changed to agree with the shift in grammatical person. The change in pronouns from *I* (first-person singular) to *she* (second-person singular) has necessitated a corresponding change in the verb, from *am* (first-person singular form of *be*) to *was* (second-person singular form of *be*). This is known as *verb agreement* and is another area of grammar that you should have a firm grasp on at this level. However, the next section gives a quick overview for those of you who might need a quick refresher.

1.2.2. Verb Agreement

The basic premise of verb agreement is relatively simple: All elements of your sentence that are required by the verb should agree (or match) in number (singular or plural), and in person (first, second, third). This is commonly referred to as ***subject–verb agreement***.

One way to determine if a verb is singular or plural is to put *it* (singular pronoun) or *they* (plural pronoun) before it. However, this does not work in all cases, and rather than getting into a long list of rules and exceptions to subject–verb agreement, which is a topic for a grammar book and not a writing book, I suggest that you consult a good online resource or published book. For instance, *Purdue University's Online Writing Lab* (https://owl.purdue.edu/owl/english_as_a_second_language/esl_students/) has a good section for ESL students, while a good reference book on English grammar is the *Longman Student Grammar of Spoken and Written English* (Biber et al., 1999). For the time being, you can complete Exercise 1.7 to see how comfortable you are with subject–verb agreement and tense agreement. If you get more than three wrong, perhaps you should review these areas of grammar.

Exercise 1.7. Identifying subject-verb agreement errors

Choose the best answer for each of the sentences 1–8 below. If you are unsure, ask a friend or your teacher, or perform a quick internet search. There is only one correct answer for each.

1. Anyone _____ to join the team please stand up.
A. who want   B. who wants   C. that want   D. that wanted

2. Each boy and each girl _____ to take the antigen text before school.
A. are ask   B. are asked   C. is ask   D. is asked

3. The shape and the size of the room _____ both perfect for what we wanted.
A. is   B. are   C. was   D. were

4. The World Taekwondo championships _____ every four years.
A. is hold   B. is held   C. are hold   D. are held

5. Everybody _____ asked to have two COVID jabs and every jab _____ free.
A. is, is   B. is, are   C. are, are   D. are, is

6. If you fly to Koh Samui, then ten kilos _____ the baggage allowance.
A. are   B. is   C. has   D. have

7. A donation of five thousand baht _____ to the student group as a gift.
A. is offered   B. has offered   C. are offered   D. have offered

8. Late to rise and late to bed _____ a bad habit.
A. is   B. are   C. has   D. have

1.2.3. Subject–Verb Separation

In more complicated sentence structures, it is a good idea to use commas when placing syntactic units inside other syntactic units. For example, when inserting dependent clauses in the middle of independent clauses—commonly known as interrupting clauses—you should separate the two units with commas, as shown below.

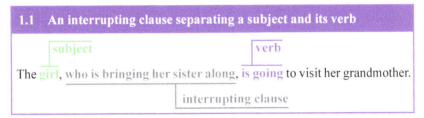

1.1 An interrupting clause separating a subject and its verb

In Example 1.1, the writer has inserted an interrupting clause (6 words) between the subject and its verb. Without the commas in place, this sentence might be confusing to a reader the first time they read it.

As a rule, try to keep subjects close to their verbs. If you need to separate a subject and verb with a long interrupting clause, then mark the end and start of the interrupting clause with commas. This will help your reader to see when one syntactic unit (the independent clause in the above example) is being interrupted by another syntactic unit (the interrupting clause in the above example).

1.2.4. Avoiding Wordiness and Conflicting Ideas

By the time students enter university, many have developed a (bad) habit of being verbose or, to put it more simply, they try to impress readers by throwing as many words as possible into a sentence, with little regard to how this affects the readability of their work. For instance, consider the following sentence. Is it good, bad, or OK?

> → She lay in the early morning light listening softly to the roar of traffic gently rising like mist in the streets when it was only just four AM and still dark.

32 ESSENTIAL KNOWLEDGE AND SKILLS FOR ESSAY WRITING

The above sentence is clearly not well constructed. Not only is it 31 words long with no internal punctuation, but how can you listen *softly* to *roaring traffic*? Do sounds rise like *mist*? Is there traffic at *four AM*? Is four AM *early morning*? Moreover, is it *light* or *dark* outside? In the space below, rewrite the example above to remove any conflicting ideas or unnecessary words, and to make it clearer and more concise. Break it into multiple clauses if needed.

Reducing wordiness and conflicting ideas are two principles of **plain language**. Other principles include using active voice wherever possible, keeping most of your sentences under 20–25 words, avoiding unnecessary jargon, and minimizing the use of hidden verbs—hidden verbs are nouns that started out life as verbs but through derivational processes became nouns, such as *consumption*, *evolution*, *growth*, and *learning*.

There are numerous other principles of plain language, such as using lists, sequencing information appropriately, and limiting each paragraph to one idea. In fact, there are whole organizations and websites devoted to promoting plain language usage, so I invite you to investigate further on your own. A good place to start is https://www.plainlanguage.gov or https://centerforplainlanguage. org. For now, Exercise 1.8 will give you practice in using plain language principles for revising text. Specifically, it will give you further practice in revising for the active voice, as well as introducing techniques to reduce wordiness, sentence length, and the number of hidden verbs in a sentence. *The idea for this exercise came from Stephen Wilbers' *Make Every Word Count*, which can be found at http://www.wilbers.com/Keys1Exercises.htm.

Exercise 1.8. Make every word count!

The seven techniques described below will help you eliminate wordiness. Each technique is accompanied by three sentences for you to revise and target word counts in brackets. When revising, use the active voice.

1. Delete redundant modifiers and other words that serve no purpose, rearranging the sentence if needed to make it more compact.

a. *Nowadays, in today's modern world, a fun, enjoyable, and pleasurable life is wanted by each and every man, woman, and child.* (Reduce to 6 words)

b. *The suggested proposal for a future plan was, to some degree, a little bit silly.* (7)

c. *Free, complimentary advice is given at no extra charge to any prospective clients who purchase any one of our several assorted collections or bundles of items.* (10)

2. Replace redundant word pairs and phrases with single words.

a. *Automobiles and cars are increasingly becoming more and more technologically advanced and high tech.* (6)

b. *My dog and my other dog love and adore me unconditionally and without question.* (6)

c. *The table on the left and the table on the right were prepared by the waiters for the upcoming and impending wedding party.* (10)

3. Replace wordy expressions with single words.

a. *If it so happens that you are not on time, you will not be allowed to come inside the classroom.* (9)

b. *In the period following Nadia's withdrawal from the team, the team that Nadia was in lost nine out of a total of ten of their games.* (12)

c. *Due to the fact that learning to write takes practice, it should be noted that students should write as much as humanly possible.* (11)

34   ESSENTIAL KNOWLEDGE AND SKILLS FOR ESSAY WRITING

4. <u>Delete needless repetition of words, statements, and ideas.</u>
a. *At around 6.30 PM in the evening, I stood on the shoreline and personally watched the evening sunset.* (12)

b. *I could hear the frozen ice cracking with my own ears. In my opinion, I thought the sound of the frozen ice cracking was scary.* (8)

c. *Students took turns presenting short summaries, one after another, because presenting short summaries was a necessary requirement for passing the course.* (10)

5. <u>Avoid long, pointless introductions to clauses (unless you are purposely trying to invoke an ironic or questionable tone in your writing).</u>
a. *At the end of the day, the fact of the matter is that bananas are yellow.* (3)

b. *To be honest with you, the bottom line is that we are losing money, and with all due respect, this is not acceptable.* (9)

c. *As a matter of fact, the reality is that writing is difficult, and if you really think about it, it takes a lot of practice.* (9)

6. <u>Trim sentence endings or reorganize the content for closing emphasis.</u>
a. *The results from the study were not significant for any of the datasets.* (8)

b. *You must eliminate the wordiness in your writing when you come across it.* (5)

c. *The argument made by Jack was not persuasive in the way that he expressed it.* (5)

7. <u>Prefer action verbs to hidden verbs (aka nominalizations [nouns formed from verbs]). Rewrite sentences a–c to remove the nominalizations and put the verbs back in.</u>
a. *I came to the conclusion that I could provide assistance.* (6)

b. *We should carry out an analysis of their needs and undertake an assessment of their weaknesses.* (9)

c. *The removal of the errors in the student's essay resulted in an increase in their score.* (13; two clauses)

1.3. THE STRUCTURE OF A PARAGRAPH

A paragraph is a group of sentences that share one main idea, topic, or focus. Paragraphs are generally six to seven lines long, but the length is dependent on the type of writing and purpose of the paragraph.

Paragraphs can be indented on the first line (like this one), where the indentation tells the reader that a new paragraph has begun; or paragraphs can be separated with an empty line or noticeable gap—the empty line or gap tells the reader that a new paragraph has begun. You may choose to indent paragraphs or insert a new line or gap between them—choose one or the other option, not both. In many cases, this choice will be made for you, according to the type of style guide your teacher or profession requires.

In terms of function, or purpose, an effective paragraph is one that is *unified*, *cohesive*, and *fully developed*.

A paragraph is **unified** when all the sentences within it have one singular goal, which is to build upon the topic sentence (thus the one topic, one paragraph rule). Exercise 1.9 illustrates the concept of unity and helps you to recognize off-topic sentences.

Exercise 1.9. Ensuring unity

In each of the paragraphs 1–3 below, one sentence does not tie into the main idea of the paragraph. Cross out the unnecessary sentence and create a unified paragraph in each case.

1. Australia is a very interesting and mysterious continent. My favorite animal is the Kangaroo. It is truly a wonderful creature and it can jump over 6 feet in the air! I have always wanted to visit Australia to see Kangaroos up close. I think it will be a wonderful experience to get close to a Kangaroo.

2. I think learning English is important. There are approximately two thousand languages in the world. When you can speak English, you have more job opportunities. If you can speak English, you can watch Western movies and read Western literature. Overall, it can change your life in a positive way.

3. Jane is a very old woman who is about 100 years old and is very kind. She has a lot of money but not many friends. Some people have no money problems. She lives in a villa near the beach and likes to watch the sunset from her balcony. She does not fear death and is already planning to leave her money to charity.

An effective paragraph is also ***cohesive***, which means that all the elements are tied to one another through transitions, connectors, and reference chains (e.g., appropriate use of repetition/synonyms, pronouns, and ellipsis). Exercise 1.10 will help illustrate some key aspects of lexical cohesion.

> **Exercise 1.10. Establishing lexical cohesion**
>
> In the paragraph below, fill in the missing pronouns (on the red solid lines) and connectors (on the gray dotted lines). For a reminder about connectors, see Section 1.1.3.

Many students think that learning to write is a pointless, time-consuming task, [1]_____ that [2]_____ has nothing to do with "real life" problems. [3]_____ [4]_____ think that [5]_____ has nothing to do with [6]_____ future occupations. [6]_____ may be true if [7]_____ plan to become car mechanics, waiters, [8]_____ waitresses, [9]_____ it is certainly not true if [10]_____ plan to have a white-collar job. No matter what profession [11]_____ choose—business, sales, government—[12]_____ will have to write.

Finally, an effective paragraph is one that is ***fully developed***; specifically, it has all three of the elements listed below:
- Topic sentence (topic + *main idea*).
- Support for your topic sentence.
- Conclusion related to your topic sentence.

In Example 1.2, the general topic (*India's economy*) is given thematic prominence at the start of the paragraph. The author then uses the remainder of the first sentence to introduce the *main idea* (i.e., "This is what I will be telling you about my topic"). Three supporting sentences follow, each of which ties into the topic and provides information in support of the main idea. The paragraph concludes by reminding the reader what the topic was and links back to the main idea.

1.2   Example of a cohesive, unified, and fully developed paragraph

India's economy *is predicted to be the third-largest economy within two years because of a number of factors*. Firstly, India's trade deficit continues to shrink due to low the cost of fossil fuels in the area. Secondly, consumer-spending power is on the rise as inflation remains at its lowest level in ten years. Thirdly, the global trend of low commodity prices puts India in pole position to capitalize on its status as a net importer and consumer. It is understandable why the World Bank sees India's economy as maintaining its status as the world's fastest growing economy, and how it may well be the third largest economy by 2022.

1.3.1. Topic Sentences

As you saw above, a topic sentence gives the overall topic and states the main idea of a paragraph. When first writing a paragraph, it is usually better to write the topic sentence first. Writing the topic sentence first can help establish unity for the rest of the paragraph.

- TOPIC. Put simply, this is the topic of the upcoming paragraph. It answers the question: What is this paragraph about?
- MAIN POINT. What you will say about the topic. It answers the question: What interesting thing about the topic will I be elaborating upon or trying to persuade the reader of?

Topic sentences introduce the paragraph topic and limit what should be written in a single paragraph. They are the most important sentence in a paragraph. They contain controlling ideas—that is, ideas that will be explained, defined, clarified, or illustrated in sentences that follow the topic sentence.

BASIC GUIDELINES FOR TOPIC SENTENCES
- Topic sentences are never just a fact. For example, *I came to Hong Kong in 2021* is a simple fact.

38 ESSENTIAL KNOWLEDGE AND SKILLS FOR ESSAY WRITING

- Topic sentences consisting of only your own opinion are weak. Avoid the use of *I like* and *I think*. For example, avoid a topic sentence that says, *I like dogs more than cats* or *I think dogs make better pets than cats*.
- Good topic sentences should reflect the purpose of a paragraph.

For instance, a topic sentence for an opinion paragraph should contain a provable or arguable opinion that can be supported by relevant and reliable evidence, as well as an indication that you are making a claim supported by reasons:

> → Cats make better indoor pets than dogs for a number of reasons.

Similarly, a topic sentence for an instructional paragraph should announce/suggest the structure and content of the upcoming essay:

> → The seven steps to making a good spaghetti sauce, one with a fantastic aroma, will be explained in detail here.
> → The seven steps to making a good spaghetti sauce can be learned by anyone.

The topic sentence should identify the main idea *and* purpose of a paragraph. To write an appropriate topic sentence, think about how the paragraph's main idea and purpose is linked to the topic and make this clear for your reader. For instance, consider the topic sentences presented in Example 1.3.

1.3   Examples of weak topic sentences versus effective topic sentences

ESSAY QUESTION 1: *Where is India's economy heading?*
- ✗ This essay will cover India's economy.
- ✓ India's economy is predicted to be the third-largest economy within two years because of a number of factors.

ESSAY QUESTION 2: *How is air pollution affecting Asian cities?*
- ✗ I am going to talk about air pollution.
- ✓ Air pollution is a growing concern in many Asian cities for good reason.

Problems with the weak topic sentences above:
- Neither of them has a main point.
- Both of them just announce a topic; use the topic sentence instead as a point of departure to introduce what the paragraph will cover.

ESSAY WRITING BASICS 39

- The second one uses *talk about*. It is a piece of writing, so how can you be talking?
- Neither of them gives the reader any clues as to what the paragraph will be covering, nor what kind of paragraph the reader can expect (e.g., a paragraph that describes, explains, or defines something or that argues a point of view).

When writing a topic sentence, remember the following guidelines and refer back to them throughout the book whenever you are writing a topic sentence.

BASIC GUIDELINES FOR WRITING A TOPIC SENTENCE
- Be general enough to show the paragraph's main idea instead of just one detail.
- Be specific enough that the reader will have an idea of the structure and content of the paragraph to come.
- Be brief. Avoid long, rambling sentences. The rest of the paragraph adds details.
- Be clear. State the topic and the main point clearly.

Exercise 1.11. Evaluating topic sentences

This exercise will help you to recognize good topic sentences. What is wrong with topic sentences 1 and 2 below? Make suggestions for better ones in the spaces provided.

1. I am going to talk about Thaksin's time in office.

2. Thaksin Shinawatra was a Thai Prime Minister born in 1949.

NUMBER 1 IS A WEAK TOPIC SENTENCE FOR THE FOLLOWING REASONS:
- It is too broad.
- There is no main point of discussion, opinion, or thing to be expanded upon.

40 ESSENTIAL KNOWLEDGE AND SKILLS FOR ESSAY WRITING

- You should not use phrases such as *I am going to talk about…* when writing.

A better topic sentence is shown below.

> ✓ Thaksin, the prime minister of Thailand from 2001–2006, initiated many effective policies during his time in office.

The topic sentence written above is stronger for the following reasons:

- It clarifies the topic by making clear exactly who—Thaksin, *the prime minister of Thailand from 2001–2006*—and what—Thaksin's policies—the essay will be about.
- It makes a strong main point—*Thaksin … initiated many effective policies during his time in office*—that reflects the writer's point of view (i.e., that many of Thaksin's policies were effective).
- It tells the reader (implicitly) what the paragraph will cover—what effective policies did Thaksin initiate?

NUMBER 2 IS A WEAK TOPIC SENTENCE FOR THE FOLLOWING REASONS:

- ✓ It just gives some basic facts.
- ✓ There is no main point of discussion, opinion, or idea to expand upon.

A better topic sentence would be one like the following:

> ✓ Thaksin Shinawatra, born in 1949, was one of the most controversial prime ministers in Thailand's recent history.

This topic sentence is stronger for two reasons:

- It makes a strong main point about the topic—that *Thaksin Shinawatra* was controversial—which the writer will ideally back up with plenty of facts and good information.
- It tells the reader what to expect. Namely, that this paragraph will introduce, list, and/or discuss some of the controversies surrounding Thaksin.

Exercise 1.12. Identifying topic sentences

While a topic sentence is usually found at the beginning of a paragraph, it can be placed in the middle or at the end. In each paragraph below, underline the topic sentence.

1. It took us two days to get there. I did not think the trip would be worth such a long journey, but I was wrong. We saw the Mekong River, rode an elephant in the Jungle, and visited a temple where the monks had taken a vow of silence. I liked the street food best of all, especially the spicy Thai salad called SomTum. My trip to the northern most part of Thailand was the best trip I ever took.

(This is an example of a *Recount paragraph*.)

2. It is important to sterilize medical utensils before and after using them. Clean equipment does not transmit germs and bacteria. Unclean utensils may cause infections and lead to conditions that are more serious. No medical professional wants to be responsible for giving a patient an infection. Clean your equipment before and after use.

(This is an example of a *Conditional explanation paragraph*.)

3. Growing a flower garden can be fun and it can provide good exercise; it can also be a source of beautiful gifts for your loved ones. It is interesting to watch the flowers blossom over time, and it is often hard to believe that such a little seed can produce something so majestic and beautiful. Digging up the soil for planting and pulling out the unwanted weeds are good forms of light exercise.

(This is an example of an *Informational process paragraph*.)

4. Many people think poetry is old-fashioned and boring. They do not realize that poetry can be found in song lyrics. Many popular song lyrics use rhythm, rhyme, and figurative language to appeal to the listener. Poetry is not old-fashioned; it is simply the grandmother of the latest hit song!

(This is an example of an *Observational paragraph*.)

Now that you can recognize and evaluate a topic sentence, Exercise 1.13 will give you practice in creating appropriate topic sentences for a number of writing prompts.

Exercise 1.13. Writing topic sentences

This task will give you practice in writing topic sentences. For each of the prompts, write a corresponding topic sentence in the space provided. Remember to include topic + main point.

1. Do fat burning pills work? (Calls for *an argument/opinion paragraph.*)

2. Why are we required by law to wear motorbike helmets? (Calls for *explanatory paragraph.*)

3. What techniques can we use to write an effective essay? (Calls for *an informational [descriptive] paragraph.*)

4. Firstly, Butterflies lay eggs on leaves. After a while, the eggs hatch into small larvae. Then, the larvae grow and grow, and they eventually turn into caterpillars. When they reach maturity, the caterpillars spin a chrysalis or cocoon, and the process starts over again. (Calls for a topic sentence that introduces the topic + main point, and hints that what follows is *an informational [descriptive] process paragraph.*)

5. One of the most important things is to eat a "clean" diet of whole-foods and vegetables. Daily exercise also helps, as does drinking lots of water. Somewhat paradoxically, eating "good" fats also helps. Finally, limiting calories consumed may also help control weight. (Calls for *an informational [factorial] process topic sentence.*)

6. Falling asleep can be difficult,

First, try counting sheep, or just counting, which will keep your mind from drifting into complex thoughts. Alternatively, listen to soft music or focus on rhythmic sounds, like rain. Second, tell yourself a story, which may distract your mind enough that you will be asleep in no time. (Calls for *an instructional [factorial] process* topic sentence.)

1.3.2. Supporting Sentences

Supporting sentences give support to your topic sentence. They form the ***body of the paragraph*** and contain details, facts, examples, definitions, reasons, or other information that helps develop the main idea found in the topic sentence.

Look at the sentences below about crocodiles and alligators. What kind of paragraph would you expect to see developed from these supporting details? What might the topic sentence look like?

→ Crocodiles are a grayish green color.
→ Crocodiles have a triangular snout.
→ Alligators prefer fresh water.
→ Alligators have a rounded snout.
→ The fourth tooth is exposed on a crocodile when their mouth is closed.

Here there seem to be two clear topics: crocodiles and alligators. You may have guessed that the job of this paragraph will probably be to compare and contrast crocodiles and alligators.

With a clear idea of what kind of paragraph is needed, I can now write an appropriate topic sentence using my topic and my purpose (main idea):

- TOPIC. Crocodiles and alligators
- MAIN POINT. Compare and contrast the differences between them

→ Topic sentence: While crocodiles and alligators have much in common, they also have some distinctive notable differences.

Using the supporting sentences listed above, and the topic sentence I have created, I can now connect all of these elements together into a paragraph as per Example 1.4.

1.4 Example of a topic sentence plus its supporting sentences
While crocodiles and alligators have much in common, they also have some distinctive notable differences. For instance, Crocodiles are a brownish grey color, and have a triangular snout. Alligators, on the other hand, are a darker grey, and have a rounded snout. Additionally, the fourth tooth is exposed on a crocodile when their mouth is closed.

44 ESSENTIAL KNOWLEDGE AND SKILLS FOR ESSAY WRITING

You may notice that all I have done is add connectors (the underlined words) to join up the supporting details so that they flow into each other. These connectors, and others, can be found in Table 1.1 at the start of this unit. You may also notice that the final paragraph was indeed a compare/contrast one. Compare/contrast is a type of *expository writing*—a superordinate category of writing termed a *genre*. In this book, I use the term *Exposition* with a capital *E* to denote that it is a class (or grouping) of text types that share several functional features—comparison/contrast being just one text type. Expository writing will be the topic of Unit 4.

1.3.3. Concluding Sentences

The concluding sentence finishes off a paragraph. Its function is to tie the supporting sentences back to the topic sentence in some way. For example, it may do one or more of the following:
- Rephrase the main idea by summarizing the supporting sentences.
- Give a final thought, opinion, or observation.
- Set up a transition to the next paragraph.

In Example 1.5, note how each concluding sentence is clearly linked to its corresponding topic sentence (topics in red).

1.5	Comparing topic sentences to concluding sentences
→	Topic sentence: Bees are important for a balanced ecosystem.
	Conclusion: In conclusion, without bees there would not be no life on this planet.
→	Topic sentence: A good teacher should be more than just an educator.
	Conclusion: In summary, the best teachers go above and beyond their job description.
→	Topic sentence: People prefer living in the countryside for a number of reasons.
	Conclusion: It easy to see why many people favor life in the countryside.

The following exercise is designed to help you recognize the elements of a paragraph.

> **Exercise 1.14. Analyzing a paragraph**
>
> Read the following student paragraph and answer the questions that follow. As you read the paragraph, try to identify the main elements of a paragraph that we have just covered.

As far as I am concerned, after I graduate from university, I would like to get a government job as it offers several benefits. First, I would be working to a set schedule and get more vacation time. I will also have more free time outside of work because there is no overtime. Contrast this with working in the private sector, such as being a freelancer, which does not sound good for my mental and physical health. Office syndrome, for example, happens to many private office workers. Personally, I need rest days to refresh my mind and body. Second, a government job will provide me with increased job security in comparison to the private sector, where workers are at a higher risk of being laid off. Specifically, a government job has a checking system, which means it takes a long time to render a decision, and even then, a committee has to be formed from within another department before a final decision can be made. Consequently, they hardly ever fire anyone unless they make a serious mistake. Last of all, the government guarantees retirement benefits. During my working life, they would take a bit of my salary and they will hand it back to me as pensionable options: each month or a whole sum. This ensures I will not end up starving. In conclusion, after graduation, I would rather take a government job than a private sector one for the benefits related to time off, personal health, job security, and financial support after retirement.

The Benefits of a Government Job by Waritsaraporn Chittakarnnateekit

1. What is the topic? What is the main idea?

2. How has the writer structured her paragraph to promote the benefits of a government job over a private sector one? (i.e., what type of paragraph is it?)

3. In the paragraph, the writer offers three points of comparison in favor of choosing a government job. These three points are listed below. In the spaces provided, list the number of words given to each point and the supporting details that the writer uses to elaborate on each point.

i) <u>WORKING HOURS.</u> No. of words =

Support

ii) <u>JOB SECURITY.</u> No. of words =

Support

iii) <u>PENSION BENEFITS.</u> No. of words =

Support

4. Underline all the connectors. Can you see any from Table 1.1?

5. Is the concluding sentence effective? Explain your answer.

6. How might this paragraph be improved? Discuss this with your peer(s).

1.4. THE STRUCTURE OF AN ESSAY

On the surface, an essay is just a collection of paragraphs. The overall structure of many essays is also much like the structure of individual paragraphs: Most essays have an introduction, a body, and a conclusion, meaning that most essays have, at a minimum, three paragraphs. This book, for pragmatic reasons, focuses mainly on five-paragraph essays. It focuses on five paragraphs because this allows you to practice writing longer texts while still maintaining a balance between the four types of knowledge introduced in the book's introduction: namely, formal, rhetorical, subject, and process knowledge. In other courses, especially if you go on to postgraduate level, you may be asked to write much longer essays that are more complex in their overall rhetorical structure or draw significantly on subject knowledge for their construction. In those situations, it is easy for a writer's cognitive resources to become overloaded, and if they do not have a good level of formal and process knowledge to lighten their mental load, then writing can be doubly difficult. For these reasons, the basic organizational pattern of a five-paragraph essay is a good starting point for you to develop all four knowledge types. Moreover, the knowledge and skills developed from five-paragraph writing can often be transferred to other types of writing.

The basic structure of a three-paragraph essay is often called "hamburger writing"—modeled as a hamburger patty, representing the "meat" or body of the essay, sandwiched between top and bottom buns, representing the introduction and the conclusion. You may also hear this kind of writing being referred to as a "rhetorical sandwich" or even "Oreo writing" (after the cookie). A five-paragraph essay can be considered to have the structure of a triple burger, as shown in the image. Using this analogy, the three body paragraphs (meat patties) are sandwiched between the introduction and the conclusion (top and bottom buns). The same analogy can be applied at the paragraph level, where the topic sentence is the top bun, supporting sentences are burger patties, and the conclusion is the bottom bun.

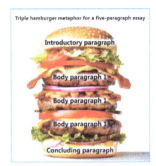

Triple hamburger metaphor for a five-paragraph essay

1.4.1. Introductory Paragraph

An introductory paragraph is like any other paragraph. It is made up of a collection of sentences, each of which has a job to do. In terms of rhetorical structuring, an introductory paragraph typically moves through three stages, which can be represented by means of an inverted triangle, as shown on the right. These three stages reflect the three main elements that are typically found in an introductory paragraph.

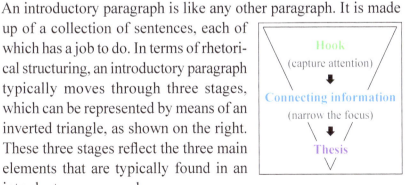

The "Hook" – Hooks are used to catch fish. In writing, hooks catch a reader's attention. A hook gives the reader a reason to continue reading. It can be a sentence (or sentences) containing a relevant quotation, anecdote, question, fact, definition, or anything interesting that will attract the reader's attention.

Connecting information – After the hook, the writer usually provides one or two sentences with connecting information that takes the reader "off the hook" and puts them on to a topic.

Thesis Statement – At the paragraph level, there is a topic sentence. At the essay level, there is a thesis statement. A thesis statement tells the reader what to expect. It may include your chosen points of development, the basis of an upcoming argument, and/or how the essay will be structured. It is usually the last sentence (or two) in an introductory paragraph, but it can sometimes occur earlier on.

BASIC GUIDELINES FOR WRITING THESIS STATEMENTS

- Must be a complete sentence.
- Should not be a question.
- Should be something that can be argued for or expanded upon (not a fact).
- Should not be an example or supporting sentence.
- Generally contains a single topic.
- Is not too general or too broad—can be answered in one essay.
- Is clear and concise.

Exercise 1.15. Analyzing an introductory paragraph

Read the introductory paragraph below and answer the questions that follow. Then underline the hook, connecting information, and thesis statement.

Have you ever wondered what kind of a person you would be if you had different parents? The documentary "Three Identical Strangers" (Wardle, 2018) explores such a case: Bobbie, Eddie, and David are triplets who were separated at birth and raised in different families. During childhood, they were observed and tested as part of a psychological experiment. Even though the study was never published, and deemed unethical, it did raise a very interesting question. What influences our development the most: nature or nurture? In attempting to answer this question, it seems that both have a role to play in an individual's development, only in different ways.

Reference

Wardle, T. (2018). *Three Identical Strangers* [Film]. CNN Films; Raw TV.

Opening paragraph from ***Nature versus Nurture*** by Noppanun Sookping

1. What do you think the main idea/content of this essay will be?

2. What type of essay will it be? (Descriptive, Narrative, Argument, etc.)

1.4.2. Body Paragraphs

We have already covered the three basic elements for a body paragraph in the sections above. In each body paragraph, there is a *topic sentence* followed by *supporting sentences* and a *concluding sentence*. As a quick reminder, the supporting sentences in a body paragraph provide details, facts, examples, definitions, reasons, or other information that help develop the main idea found in your topic sentence. In moving from single paragraphs to essays, the supporting and concluding sentences remain pretty much the same, as they are generated based on the topic sentence contained in their own respective paragraphs. However, at the essay level, some topic sentences and concluding sentences take on a dual function. More specifically, at the essay level, topic sentences and concluding sentences may also be used to achieve the following functions: (1) tie the topic and the main point back to the overall thesis statement found in the introduction; (2) link the current paragraph to the previous or next paragraph. If you can create well-crafted topic sentences and concluding sentences, then maintaining a unified and cohesive piece of writing as you move from single paragraphs to multiple paragraphs becomes a little easier for you and for the reader.

At the paragraph level, unity is essentially making sure that each of your sentences is connected to a central topic or focal point stated in the topic sentence. This is also somewhat true at the essay level. At the essay level, unity is achieved when each of your topic sentences is tightly tied to your thesis statement. If you do not have a solid thesis statement to tie subsequent topic sentences to, then it will be difficult for you to create unity in your essay.

Think of your thesis statement as a pier or jetty, and your body paragraphs as boats attached to it. Your topic sentences are the ropes (or links) which tie the two together. Without a solid pier (solid thesis statement) and ropes (topic sentences), your boats (paragraphs) will drift off and get lost. Tie your body paragraphs to your thesis through sound topic sentences and do not let them drift away from you!

You also need to consider cohesion at the level of the essay. At the paragraph level, cohesion means that all the elements are clearly linked and logically tied to one another through transitions, connectors, and reference chains (e.g., appropriate use of pronouns and ellipsis). The same is true at the essay level: You arrange all the elements in your essay so that they are connected in clear, logical ways.

At the essay level, as well as cohesion within paragraphs, you need to consider cohesion across paragraphs. This can be achieved through ***rhetorical structuring***, which organizes your essay's contents according to its overall purpose. This purpose can be a staged, goal-oriented one in which each paragraph has a particular function that contributes to an overall function, such as constructing a narrative, making a comparison/contrast, or building an argument. In the upcoming units, I will show you how to recognize and produce these functions in terms of the main organizing patterns that help realize them, as shown below:

Type of writing	Central organizing pattern
Description (of things, people, places, etc.)	*Spatial arrangement* (of shapes, sizes, colors)
Chronological (narrative and description of a process)	*Temporal arrangement* (of events, stages, or steps)
Exposition (of compare/contrast, classification, cause–effect)	*Relational arrangement* (of ideas, things, people, places)
Argument (opinion)	*Logical arrangement* (of evidence, warrants, backing, and claims)

Cohesive devices are elements that explicitly, or implicitly, set up these organizational patterns. For example, in writing a description, writers predominantly use cohesive constructions that signal spatial arrangements, such as *Next to the lake is an amusement park* or *The dog is lying under the chair*. A narrative would typically have more temporal cohesive devices, such as *The next day, he joined the army.* or *Following lunch, she was going to start packing*. In an exposition, it is likely there would be more devices that set up connections between elements in terms of relationships such as comparison (*In general, Hong Kong is hotter than Taiwan.*), cause and effect (*Heavy rain often causes flooding, especially near bodies of water.*), or classification (*A hatchback is a popular type of car.*). As these examples illustrate, cohesion can be realized through any unit of language. In the previous examples, cohesive ties are formed by the grammatical categories of prepositional phrase (*next to the lake*, *under the chair*), adverbial phrase (*the next day*, *following lunch*), noun phrase (*a popular type of car*), comparative adjective (*hotter*), and verb (*causes*, *is*).

The best time to ensure unity and cohesion is during the planning stage of writing. Accordingly, in subsequent units, I introduce several different outlining techniques. These can be used to ensure that all the elements in your essay relate to the thesis statement, and thus help to create unity. These outlining techniques can also be used to create explicit links between elements by outlining the relationships between them. This outlining can help you achieve cohesion. However, you also need to check for unity and cohesion during the editing stage of writing. Exercise 1.6 will help you recognize and evaluate elements that contribute to unity and cohesiveness.

> **Exercise 1.16. Creating unity and cohesion in an essay**
>
>
>
> Read the essay and pay attention to how it creates unity and cohesion. Then complete the activities in the "Questions of unity" and "Questions of cohesion" exercises that follow.

1. You may have seen great travel documentary shows, with action-packed adventures, mind-blowing locations, and hosted by famous personalities with great charisma and indisputable charm and humor. Now imagine that the host is an attractive man in slippers, who constantly complains using foul language. Despite this unusual formula, the show, *An Idiot Abroad*, is successful because of its unusual host, his reluctance to partake in any form of activity, and the relatability of its locations.

2. The host of the show, Karl Pilkington, stands out physically. He is bald with an egg-shaped head, and a piglet like belly, which seems to indicate a hatred of the gym and a penchant for junk food and beer. His only redeeming physical quality is his height, which unfortunately, is hidden by a hunchback that belongs on a 90-year-old man. Moreover, the locations he visits are just as unappealing. However, what he lacks on the outside, he more than makes up for with an unpretentious, genuine, and truehearted naivety. For example, in one interaction with an elderly Thai lady, from whom he is learning how to make a spicy Thai salad, he unwittingly repeats the Thai word "fok, fok, fok" until he realizes it has a different meaning in English. Thus, his comedic genius does not come from perfect timing or planned punchlines. Instead, it flows naturally from his authentic and friendly nature. This is just one trait that makes people love him.

3. In *An Idiot Abroad*, our homunculus host takes us around the world with a heart full of reluctance and a mind full of ignorance. Whether it is swimming with sharks in Australia, bungee jumping in New Zealand, or blindfolded boxing in Thailand, he always begins with a doubtful frown and a discontented look. Yet, there are moments when you see his lips curve, and you smile back as he finally starts enjoying himself. Such moments come through activities he is forced to do, such as his visit to a village in rural Thailand. Thailand has a very hot and humid climate. Here, he reluctantly harvests an ant's nest, is bitten, cooks with foreign implements, and eats with the locals. At first, he hates it, but after spending time with the villagers, they become friends and we see a marked change in Karl's outlook. These authentic moments add a much-needed layer to Karl and the show, which go from a one-dimensional slapstick character and mundane television program to a real person and a relatable reality.

4. The places the show takes us to are also relatable. Although the countries it visits have many beautiful landmarks and amazing wonders, the show mostly takes us to normal, everyday places, and shows us local life and hidden places. It essentially digs out new angles and makes us realize that such places hold many wonders on a par with other well-known landmarks. Even though we are occasionally taken somewhere famous, Karl still manages to make it seem like a normal place that everybody, no matter rich or poor, can visit. Through his honesty and authenticity, he forms friendships that reach beyond the confines of the screen, and into the audience at home.

5. To sum up, *An Idiot Abroad* uses the formula of great travel shows backwards: It may be hosted by an oddball, doing ordinary, silly things, in seemingly mundane places, but it still manages to hold its own and offer something unique and entertaining. This makes the show a great travel documentary with perhaps the most authentic host of all time. Watch it or don't watch. I don't think Karl is bothered either way.

An Idiot Abroad by Pitcha Dangprasith

Questions of Unity

1. Underline the thesis statement in the introduction with a double line (==).
2. What is the topic of this essay?
3. What are the three main ideas that will be expanded upon in the body paragraphs?

(i)   (ii)   (iii)

4. Underline each of the topic sentences in the body paragraphs.
5. List the key phrases in each topic sentence that link back to the thesis statement.

Key phrase in paragraph 2:

Key phrase in paragraph 3:

Key phrase in Paragraph 4:

6. With reference to the metaphor of piers, boats, and ropes in the discussion of body paragraphs earlier in this section, what are these three key phrases effectively doing?

7. One supporting sentence in each body paragraph is not linked to its topic sentence. Cross out each of these sentences.

54   ESSENTIAL KNOWLEDGE AND SKILLS FOR ESSAY WRITING

Questions of Cohesion

1. Underline all the pronouns in the above essay. Note how they contribute to cohesion by creating reference chains that span across sentences. What they do they tell you about the central topic of each paragraph?

2. In the spaces below, write down all the coordinating conjunctions and conjunctive adjuncts found in each paragraph of the essay above. Using Table 1.1 (pp. 13–14), label each adjunct as to its type (elaborating, extending, or enhancing) and subtype. For example, *instead* = extending: variation: replacive.

Adjuncts in Paragraph 1 (7 examples; 4 different conjunctions/adjuncts):

Adjuncts in paragraph 2 (11 examples; 7 different conjunctions/adjuncts):

Adjuncts in paragraph 3 (15 examples; 7 different conjunctions/adjuncts):

Adjuncts in paragraph 4 (9 examples; 4 different conjunctions/adjuncts):

Adjuncts in paragraph 5 (4 examples; 3 different conjunctions/adjuncts):

3. Using your answers to the previous question, what is the main organizational pattern in this essay?

4. What type of essay do you think it is? Descriptive, narrative, exposition, argument, or something else? Discuss your answer with your peer(s).

1.4.3. Concluding Paragraphs

The conclusion is found in the last paragraph of an essay. In terms of rhetorical structuring, a conclusion paragraph, like an introductory paragraph, typically moves through three stages, which can be represented by means of a triangle, as shown on the right. These three stages (or elements) are *restating the thesis*, *restating or summarizing the main ideas* covered in the paragraphs, and making a *final memorable point*.

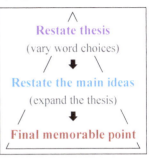

When *restating the thesis*, be sure to vary your word choices from those in the introductory paragraph.

When *restating (or summarizing) the main ideas*, aim for one to three sentences and, again, vary your word choice so that you are not simply repeating what you have already written; review the main ideas in the order that they appeared in your essay; finally, this is NOT the time to introduce new ideas.

The *final memorable point* leaves the reader with something to think about and makes the essay feel finished. In making this final point, you need to stay true to the type of essay you are writing. If you have been writing a descriptive essay, do not end with a recommendation; end with a striking observation. If you have been writing a persuasive essay, do not end with a factual statement; end with an especially convincing point or example.

Note that while the final memorable point may contain a new insight or piece of information, if a concluding paragraph contains largely new information or ideas, then it can lose the sense of connection with the rest of the essay and its thesis. In that case, the essay will appear disorganized and lacking in unity. Thus, if new ideas come to you as you are writing your final memorable point, which often happens when writing, then you cannot just stick them in your conclusion as afterthoughts. If they are good ideas that you want to include in your essay, you will need to figure out how those ideas relate to your existing introduction and body paragraphs, and then make revisions so the additional ideas fit in well with your other ideas.

Exercise 1.17 gives you practice in critically evaluating a concluding paragraph. It includes a concluding paragraph from a five-paragraph student essay (the corresponding introductory paragraph was presented in Exercise 1.15).

Exercise 1.17. Analyzing a concluding paragraph

Read the following concluding paragraph and underline those parts which express each of the three elements of a conclusion that were outlined above. Then answer the questions that follow.

In conclusion, a person's behavior is not developed purely by nature or nurture. It requires both to create behavioral foundations and trait expressions in a person. Ultimately, a person behaves based on the genes he/she inherits from his/her family, and the environment in which he/she was growing up. Apart from its informative presentation of nature versus nurture, "Three Identical Strangers" (Wardle, 2018) also questions the moral standards of scientists when they conduct experiments on other human beings. As shown in the triplets' case, it is ironic that to discover the secrets of human development, the scientists were willing to conduct and hide such a malicious experiment from the world.

Reference
Wardle, T. (2018). *Three Identical Strangers* [Film]. CNN Films; Raw TV.

Concluding paragraph from *Nature versus Nurture* by Noppanun Sookping

1. How has the writer reflected upon the thesis statement? (The thesis statement for this essay can be found in Exercise 1.15.)

2. How many main points of the argument has the writer revisited?

3. Has the writer restated why the topic is important? If so, how?

4. Is there a final memorable point or not? If there is, what kind of statement is it?

1.5. UNDERSTANDING THE WRITING PROCESS

Except for a few incredibly outstanding writers, no one writes an essay from start to finish without making edits or changes. Moreover, writing is not like learning a subject. It is a skill, and as such, it requires practice. Some good writers, like great musicians, have an inherent talent; but for the rest of us, we must treat it as a continual learning process. Many students also have to deal with the additional factor of learning to write in a second language, which makes their task even more difficult.

Fortunately, we can break down the process of writing longer texts into three broad activities: writing the first draft, writing the second draft, and submitting your draft. Within these three broad activities, we can break down the writing process into seven stages. By using this 7-stage approach, you can sequence your activities to free up time and cognitive resources for more important things, like developing content. Moreover, by paying attention to these activities at key stages in your writing process, you can improve *what* you write and *how* you write. For instance, before you begin writing each draft, you should set yourself clear and achievable goals that relate to what your writing is going to achieve (Graham & Harris, 2018). If your writing is going to be assessed, for example, then you should set goals related to the task rubric or assignment sheet and the higher scoring elements outlined in that rubric or assignment sheet. Once you have set those goals, then you turn your attention to generating ideas and planning (Bennet et al., 2020).

Efficient time management makes an important contribution to the quality of your writing (Rosário et al., 2017). Time management can be something simple, like putting aside time each day to write—preferably a time when you are free of distractions—or it can relate to when you decide to engage in certain activities. For instance, you may find it more beneficial to delay revising until you have a substantial proportion of your essay completed. Moreover, when you do start revising, it may be more beneficial to make

58 ESSENTIAL KNOWLEDGE AND SKILLS FOR ESSAY WRITING

macro-level (global) revisions first, as you may delete sentences and paragraphs that contain many small errors. Thus, you would have wasted time by revising micro-level features that ended up being deleted in your pursuit of macro-level goals such as rhetorical structuring or cohesion. For the most part, unless it is hindering your ability to read your own text, you should probably leave the small stuff until the end of the writing process, when most of your content is organized logically and clearly.

1.5.1. Writing the First Draft

Although the stages I present below are set out in a linear sequence, they are in fact cyclical, meaning that you can move backward to a previous stage and repeat each stage if need be. Moreover, I recognize that there are additional activities related to writing that I do not mention. Specifically, I do not cover some of those activities that reside in the mind of a writer, such as time spent thinking about an appropriate word, or translating ideas into language. I have not introduced such activities below because they are primarily internalized, and so it is difficult to incorporate them in feedback loops or collaborative activities without significantly disrupting the writing process. For these reasons, throughout this book, I have purposefully chosen activities that will help you engage with the writing process, as well as with your peers and teacher.

Stage 1. Choose a Topic

In many instances, your teacher might choose the topic for you. However, if you are asked to choose your own topic, then consider the following suggestions:

CHOOSE A FAMILIAR TOPIC. Research shows that one of the biggest impacting factors on essay quality is how well a writer knows their subject matter. This is even more so for students writing in a second language. Therefore, if possible, choose a subject that you already know a lot about.

CHOOSE A TOPIC THAT INTERESTS YOU. If you have ever wanted to learn more about something, use your writing task as an excuse to do some research on the topic. You will be more motivated to write, which is another factor that usually affects the quality of a finished essay.

Stage 2. Brainstorm Ideas for Your Topic

Make a list. Write down your thoughts on the topic and on anything you can research about it. Use *bullet points* and do not worry at this stage about the spelling and grammar. However, try to write your notes in English. That way, you become familiar with the vocabulary associated with the topic.

On the other hand, you could make a *cluster diagram* or *mind map.* Write down your main idea in the middle of a page. Put a circle around it. Write down related ideas and thoughts and put circles around them. Connect your circles to the main idea and to each other where relevant.

Alternatively, you could just start writing. This technique is called *freewriting*. The idea is that you get your ideas down on paper without stopping to make edits or revisions. However, set yourself a time limit so you do not end up going too far off course or down a rabbit hole (a long, winding journey where you get stuck and lost in the dark).

Stage 3. Decide on a Purpose and Create an Outline

This stage is where an awareness of genre comes into play. What will the purpose of your essay be: to describe something, show advantages and disadvantages, or tell a story? Are you going to argue something controversial, classify something, compare two or more things, show cause and effect, or present a problem and solution? Look at your brainstorming notes. What are the relationships and connections between your ideas? This can help you imagine what type of essay you need. Then try writing a draft thesis statement for it.

After you decide what type of essay you need, choose an appropriate outlining technique. Underline the best ideas in your brainstorming notes. Group these ideas into main categories or themes. For a five-paragraph essay, aim for three groups. The contents of these three groups will be the supporting details for your three body paragraphs.

In Units 2–5, you will be introduced to several different outline templates, but they all serve a similar purpose, which is to populate your five-paragraph essay with content that is sequenced in the right order. A general outline for a five-paragraph essay is shown below. Modified versions of this will be used in each unit.

Introduction	Paragraph 1	CONTENT: INTRODUCE YOUR TOPIC **Hook**. Grab your reader's attention with something memorable. **Background information**. Introduce general topic. **Background information**. Introduce specific topic. **Present thesis**. Offers a concise summary of the main idea or claim of your essay, usually in one sentence. It can also give the reader an indication of what type of essay it will be (descriptive, expository, argument/opinion, etc.).
Body paragraphs	Paragraph 2	CONTENT: THIS WILL DEPEND ON THE TYPE OF ESSAY YOU ARE WRITING **Topic sentence 1**. **Supporting sentences** (usually 2 to 4). These provide details, explanations, examples, evidence, statistics, or other kinds of data that support the idea contained in this paragraph's topic sentence. **Concluding sentence** (*can also be used as a link to the next paragraph).
	Paragraph 3	CONTENT: THIS WILL DEPEND ON THE TYPE OF ESSAY YOU ARE WRITING **Topic sentence 2**. **Supporting sentences** (usually 2 to 4). These provide details, explanations, examples, evidence, statistics, or other kinds of data that support the idea contained in this paragraph's topic sentence. **Concluding sentence** (*can also be used as a link to the next paragraph).
	Paragraph 4	CONTENT: THIS WILL DEPEND ON THE TYPE OF ESSAY YOU ARE WRITING **Topic sentence 3**. **Supporting sentences** (usually 2 to 4). These provide details, explanations, examples, evidence, statistics, or other kinds of data that support the idea contained in this paragraph's topic sentence. **Concluding sentence** (*can also be used as a link to the next paragraph).

		CONTENT: CONCLUDE YOUR ESSAY
Conclusion	Paragraph 5	**Restate thesis**. Remind the reader what your central purpose for writing this essay was (i.e., reiterate why the topic is important). **Summarize**. Review the main points you compared/contrasted. **Final memorable point**. Address or reflect upon your essay in a memorable and thoughtful way that gives the reader something to think about.

Stage 4. Write the First Draft

Some writers start at the beginning, with an introduction. Others jump right into writing body paragraphs and only later construct an introduction. There is no right or wrong way. Choose the order for your writing that works best for you. Nevertheless, generally speaking, it is wise to have a well-written thesis statement (for reasons mentioned above) as a starting point.

Another point to remember is to give your essays imaginative titles that capture the essence of what you have written. Use a larger font for the title and center it near the top of the first page. On the assumption that you are using a word processing program, set the line spacing to double, the page size to A4 or letter size, and the margins to normal, and use Times New Roman size 12 font for the essay itself—unless your instructor, course book, or style guide has different formatting requirements.

1.5.2. Writing the Second Draft

Stage 5. Get Feedback (e.g., through Collaborative Peer Review)

Having someone else review your work is one of the best ways to improve your writing. Give the person a list of questions to answer, or better still, provide them with a scoring rubric or grading guideline—preferably, the same one your teacher will use to grade your finished essay. If you do not have anyone to review your work, then do not panic. Leave your draft alone for a few days so you forget about what you wrote. Come back to it as a new reader with a fresh perspective and leave comments for yourself as you read it. Ignore the temptation to fix spelling mistakes or grammatical errors. Simply highlight them and fix them after you have finished writing comments. You should focus on the content and organization first. Attend to the smaller stuff, such as improving spelling, grammar, and word choice as a final step.

Stage 6. Reread, Rethink, and Rewrite

It is hard to write a perfect paragraph or essay on the first try. It is therefore important that you get into the habit of editing and revising. As you revise your first draft and any subsequent drafts, incorporate the feedback received from your peers or other readers and add any new ideas or changes where relevant. If you are using word processing software, make use of its reviewing function to leave yourself notes and comments in the margin or off the page. Try to establish a dialogue with yourself—you will be surprised at how previous notes or comments can stimulate new ideas or ways of looking at things, especially once you have had some time away from your draft.

Stage 7. Let Your Revised Draft Sit a While and Then Proofread It Carefully

Do not forget to proofread the revised draft before you submit it, and try to finish well before any established deadlines so you do not need to rush through last minute. It is also a good idea to give yourself a few days break from your revised draft before proofreading it and doing any necessary editing. That way, you approach it as an unfamiliar reader would.

1.5.3. The Stages of the Writing Process

As the last section highlighted, the writing process can be broken down into a number of phases, stages, and activities, each of which can be realized in a number of ways. For example, when generating ideas, your thoughts can be written down as bullet points or put into a cluster diagram or mind map. Alternatively, you can start writing and hope that ideas will come to you through the activity of writing itself. Some activities can be realized verbally, through spoken interaction with others, such as when discussing an outline with your teacher or asking questions of a peer's draft.

You partake in these activities and others because they open up a dialogic space—an area where you, and others, can reflect and engage with the writing process and the evolving text. For example, I often use MS Word's comment function to leave messages for my future self. These can be reminders to do something later when I have more time, or they can be questions for which I do not have answers to at that moment. In other words, you should see these activities as opportunities for collaboration—with others and yourself—as well as windows into the writing process, and not just simply something your teacher asks you to do.

Throughout the writing process, you should be questioning what you are doing and why, as well as figuring out what works best for you in different situations. This kind of self-regulating behavior will ultimately help you to streamline your writing process, meet deadlines, and finish essays in exam situations.

To help you remember and better understand some of the key activities and thought processes introduced so far, complete the flow chart below (Figure 1.1). First, label each of the stages. Then, list some key activities that are useful during each stage. Once you have done these two tasks, summarize each of the activities you have listed in one sentence. Last, compare your finished chart with that of a peer. Make sure both of you have labeled each stage correctly and included clear summaries of at least one activity per stage.

64 ESSENTIAL KNOWLEDGE AND SKILLS FOR ESSAY WRITING

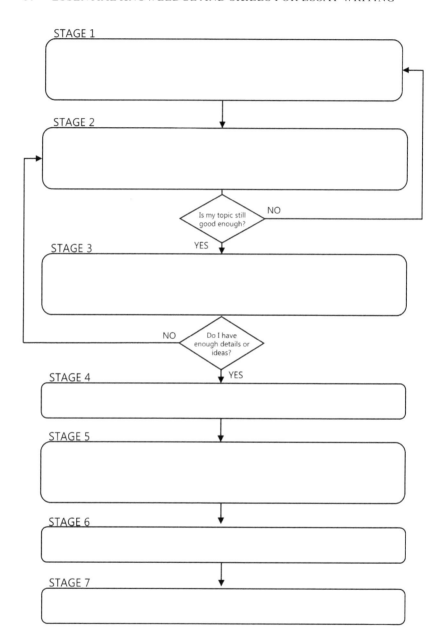

Figure 1.1. Flowchart for the writing process

ESSAY WRITING BASICS   65

APPENDIX 1A. UNIT 1 ANSWER KEY

Exercise 1.1 (answers may vary; these are suggestions only)

1b. *Breathing can be slowed down by inhaling slowly and deeply through your nose.*

In this instance, the linear theme (LT) is achieved through sentence (b), the **passive voice**—the object from the first clause is rephrased and used as the subject for the second clause.

2b. *Common symptoms include fast and irregular heartbeats, shaking, and nausea.*

This constant theme (CT) is achieved through sentence (b), the **active voice**—the subject from the first clause is reused as the subject for the second clause.

3b. *Several parties working together form a coalition government.*

This LT is achieved through sentence (a), the **passive voice**—the object from the first clause is repurposed as the subject of this clause.

4b. *We can observe some types of PM without special equipment.*

This CT is achieved though sentence (a), the **passive voice**—part of the subject from the first clause [head noun] is reused, but it is also pre-modified so that the writer can now write about subtypes of "PM."

5b. *A carefully designed constitution limits the powers of government.*

This CT is made possible through sentence (b), the **active voice**—the subject from the first clause is reused (it is pre-modified with the adjectives *carefully* and *designed*)

6b. *Devices called routers connect this network.*

This LT is achieved through sentence (a), the **passive voice**—part of the object from the first clause, together with a determiner ("these"), is used to form the subject of this clause.

7b. *This statement outlines the topic and main idea(s) of the upcoming essay.*

This LT is made possible through sentence (b), the **active voice**—part of the object from the previous clause, together with a determiner (*This*), is repurposed as the subject of this clause.

66 ESSENTIAL KNOWLEDGE AND SKILLS FOR ESSAY WRITING

8b. *They often create a distorted view of reality with negative consequences.*

This CT is achieved through sentence (b), the **active voice**—the subject from the first clause is reused ("Filter bubbles" is substituted for a pronoun to avoid repetition).

9b. *The north and south poles are covered by these layers.*

This LT is achieved through sentence (a), the **active voice**—part of the object from the previous clause (head noun) is reused with a determiner (*These*) to form the subject of this clause.

10b. *Scientists define climate change as globally shifting weather patterns and seasons.*

This LT is achieved through sentence (a), the passive voice—part of the object from the previous clause is used as the subject of this clause.

Exercise 1.2
Fragments are sentences 2, 3, 4, 6, 8, and 10.

Exercise 1.3
Answers will vary so consult with your peers or teacher.

Exercise 1.4
Fused sentences are 1, 2, 4, and 5.

Exercise 1.5
Comma splices can be found in sentences 1, 2, and 4.

Exercise 1.6
1. ✗ We can make a listing using: colons, semicolons, and commas. *(No colon is needed since the sentence continues after using.)*
2. ✓ Mastering punctuations is important; it helps us with clarity.
3. ✗ Classes finish at 4.45. *(A colon is needed.)*
4. ✓ I really love kimchi—especially for lunch.
5. ✗ The worst kinds of friend are: ones who ignore you, ones who lie to you, and ones who always turn up late. *(No colon is needed since the sentence continues after are.)*

ESSAY WRITING BASICS   67

6. × There are only two ways to live your life: one is though nothing is miracle, which means everything is boring, or one is though everything is a miracle, which means everything is exciting. *(A semicolon is needed.)*
7. × June 15th-18th is a holiday. *(An en dash is needed.)*
8. × It was a well known problem. *(A hyphen is needed.)*
9. × Space—the final frontier. *(A colon is needed.)*
10. ✓ All three desserts—cake, ice cream, and chocolate mousse—were delicious.

Exercise 1.7
1 = B, **2** = D; **3** = D; **4** = D; **5** = A; **6** = B; **7** = A; **8** = A

Exercise 1.8 (answers may vary; these are suggestions only)
1a. Nowadays, everyone wants a fun life. – This needed rewriting in the active voice.
1b. The proposal was a little bit silly.
1c. We give free advice to clients who purchase a collection. *(This needed rewriting in the active voice, which also meant that the subject needed to be re-inserted into the sentence.)*
2a. Cars are becoming more high tech.
2b. My two dogs love me unconditionally.
2c. The waiters prepared both tables for the upcoming wedding party. – This needed rewriting in the active voice.
3a. If you come late, you cannot enter the classroom.
3b. After Nadia left the team, they lost 90% of their games.
3c. Because learning to write takes practice, students should write as much as possible.
4a. At around 6.30 PM, I stood on the shoreline and watched the sunset.
4b. The sound of the ice cracking scared me.
4c. Students took turns presenting summaries, because it was a requirement for passing the course.
5a. Bananas are yellow.
5b. We are losing money, and this is not acceptable.
5c. Writing is difficult and takes a lot of practice.

68   ESSENTIAL KNOWLEDGE AND SKILLS FOR ESSAY WRITING

6a. The results from the study were not significant. – You want to highlight *not significant*, because this is the most important point after the main verb,

6b. Eliminate wordiness in your writing. – You can drop the subject as this is an imperative.

6c. Jack's argument was not persuasive.

7a. I concluded that I could help.

7b. We should analyze their needs and assess their weaknesses.

7c. The errors in the student's essay were removed, and this increased their score.

Exercise 1.9

Lines to be crossed out:

1. Australia is a very interesting continent.

2. There are approximately 2000 languages in the world.

3. Some people have no money problems.

Exercise 1.10

1 = *and*; **2** = *it*; **3** = *Moreover/Furthermore/In addition*; **4** = *they*; **5** = *it*;

6 = *their*; **7** = This; **8** = *or*; **9** = *but*; **10** = *they*; **11** = *they*; **12** = *they*

Exercise 1.11

Answers will vary so consult with your peers or teacher.

Exercise 1.12

1. The final sentence is the topic sentence.

2. The first sentence is the topic sentence. The final sentence concludes the paragraph by recapping the topic sentence.

3. The first sentence is the topic sentence.

4. The final sentence is the topic sentence.

Exercise 1.13

Answers will vary so consult with your peers or teacher.

Exercise 1.14

1. Topic = jobs after graduating; main idea = advantages of a government job

ESSAY WRITING BASICS   69

2. The paragraph is structured to compare and contrast three main points. These points mainly highlight advantages of working for the government. Disadvantages of working in the private sector are somewhat vague and general; there does not appear to be any advantages to private sector work in the mind of this author.

3. i) Working hours (79 words): set schedule; more vacation time; no overtime
ii) Job security (72 words): checking system
iii) Retirement benefits (42 words): monthly pension or lump sum.

4. The connectors in this text are as follows (the underlined ones can be found in Table 1.1): *after*, *as*, *First*, *also*, *because*, *such as*, *for example*, *Second*, *Specifically*, *and even then*, *before*, *Consequently*, *unless*, *Last of all*, *In conclusion; after*, *and* occurs six times.

5. Yes, it is an effective concluding sentence because she restates the topic sentence and summarizes the three main points.

6. The first way this paragraph could be improved is to include some more benefits of private sector work. As it stands, the paragraph is one-sided, and the author has left out some important evidence that readers would need to make up their own mind. Second, although the first two points are given a balanced amount of space (79 words versus 72 words), the first point is quite implicit and has three supporting details while the second point has only one supporting detail—a rather long-winded and wordy explanation. The third point, on the other hand, is noticeably shorter (42 words) and not well thought out—it kind of states the obvious and ends in a somewhat questionable reason: *I will not end up starving*. Third, the paragraph is a little list-like, which is mainly the result of the topic sentence setting it up this way as it ends with *it offers a number of benefits*. Overall, the paragraph is somewhat unbalanced, lacks coherence and clarity of thought in several places (notably the comment about "office syndrome"), and

70 ESSENTIAL KNOWLEDGE AND SKILLS FOR ESSAY WRITING

the author has mixed general statements about the positive features of government jobs, negative features of private sector jobs, and points about her own needs (physical and mental).

Exercise 1.15

1. The essay will probably be about the effects of nature and nurture on a child's development
2. The introduction seems to be leading up to an expository essay: a mixture of comparison/contrast and cause–effect.

Exercise 1.16

Questions of unity

1. _An Idiot Abroad_ is successful because of its unusual host, his reluctance to partake in any form of activity, and the relatability of its locations.
2. Topic = the TV show, "An Idiot Abroad."
3. Main ideas = (i) unusual host; (ii) unusual activities; (iii) relatable places.
4. The topic sentences are the first sentences in body paragraphs 2 and 4, and second sentence in paragraph 3.
5. The key phrases are as follows:

   PARAGRAPH 2 _the host of the show._

   PARAGRAPH 3 _swimming with sharks in Australia, bungee jumping in New Zealand, or blindfolded boxing in Thailand._

   PARAGRAPH 4 _The places the show takes us to are also relatable._

6. Look at the answers to number 3 above. Now compare those answers to the answers for number 5. If you think back to the metaphor of the pier, boats, and ropes on page 38, then these _key phrases_ are effectively the **ropes** that tie the **boats** (_body paragraphs_) to the **pier** (_thesis statement_).
7. Sentences to be crossed out in each body paragraph are as follows:

   PARAGRAPH 2 _Moreover, the locations he visits are just as unappealing._

ESSAY WRITING BASICS   71

PARAGRAPH 3 *Thailand has a very hot and humid climate.*
PARAGRAPH 4 *Through his honesty and authenticity, he forms friendships that reach beyond the confines of the screen, and into the audience at home.*

Questions of cohesion

1. These are the pronouns in each paragraph and their referents (in order):
    PARAGRAPH 1 *Who* = the host, *its* = the show's, *his* = the host's, *its* = the show's.
    PARAGRAPH 2 *He* = Karl Pilkington, *His* = Karl Pilkington's, *his* = Karl Pilkington's, *he* = Karl Pilkington, *he* =Karl Pilkington, *he* = Karl Pilkington, *he* = Karl Pilkington, *his* = Karl Pilkington's, *it* = comedic genius, *his* = Karl Pilkington, *This* = authentic and friendly nature, *him* = Karl Pilkington.
    PARAGRAPH 3 *he* = Karl Pilkington, *his* = Karl Pilkington's, *he* = Karl Pilkington, *he* = Karl Pilkington, *his* = Karl Pilkington's, *he* = Karl Pilkington, *he* = Karl Pilkington, *they* = villagers + Karl Pilkington.
    PARAGRAPH 4 *it* = the show, *It* = the show, *it* = somewhere famous, *his* = Karl Pilkington's, *he* = Karl Pilkington.
    PARAGRAPH 5 *It* = the show, *it* = the show, *its* = the show's, *This* = something unique and entertaining.

2. These are the coordinating conjunctions and conjunctive adjuncts in each paragraph:
    PARAGRAPH 1 **and* (extending: addition: positive), *Now* (enhancing: simple internal: simultaneous), *Despite this* (enhancing: causal-conditional: concessive), *because* (enhancing: causal conditional: specific) – **and* occurs four times.
    PARAGRAPH 2 **and* (extending: addition: positive), *Moreover* (extending: addition: positive), *However* (extending: addition: adversative), *For example* (elaborating: apposition: exemplifying), *until* (enhancing: temporal: complex: terminal), *Thus* (enhancing: manner: means), *Instead* (extending: variation: replacive) – **and* occurs five times.

72 ESSENTIAL KNOWLEDGE AND SKILLS FOR ESSAY WRITING

PARAGRAPH 3 *and (extending: addition: positive), **Whether ... or (extending: variation: alternative), Yet (extending: addition: adversative), as (enhancing: temporal: simple, following), such as (elaborating: apposition: exemplifying), Here (enhancing: spatio-temporal: simple internal), but (extending: addition: adversative), *and occurs 9 times; **Whether .. or is a two-part phrasal conjunction.

PARAGRAPH 4 Although (enhancing: causal-conditional: specific: concessive), *and (extending: addition: positive), **Even though (enhancing: causal-conditional: specific: concessive), or (extending: variation: alternative) – *and occurs six times. **Even though is a phrasal conjunction meaning "despite the fact that…"

PARAGRAPH 5 To sum up (elaborating: clarification: summative), but (extending: addition: adversative) – *and (extending: addition: positive), – *and occurs twice.

3. There are mostly extending (addition) and enhancing (causal) relations. The extending relations are used to increase the descriptive power of the text—new elements are added in a sequence. The enhancing relations typically give reasons or concessions that link the added elements together.

4. There are very few temporal relations or cause–effect chains. This signifies it is probably not a narrative. There are also quite a lot of comment adjuncts and other words that add evaluative meanings, which rules out exposition. This combined with the number of concessive adjuncts tells me that this is an argument essay or opinion essay. The thesis statement confirms this—the author is arguing that the show is successful because of A (contents of body paragraph 1), B (contents of body paragraph 2), and C (contents of body paragraph 3).

Exercise 1.17

1. In the first two sentences, the author directly answers the question raised in his two-part thesis statement: What influences our development the most: nature or nurture?

2. The author appears to mention three main points:
   - The contribution of genes (*nature*) to human development.
   - The contribution of the environment (*nurture*) to human development.
   - The importance of *moral standards* in research involving human participants.
3. The author has not restated why the topic is important. The first two sentences are used to link back to the thesis statement. The third sentence is a paraphrase of the first two sentences but with the addition of *genes* and *environment*—two words that reflect the topics of body paragraphs one and two. The fourth sentence is also a summary sentence—it refers to the contents of body paragraph 3.
4. The concluding sentence is not very memorable because it seems like another summary sentence, thus I am left feeling somewhat uninspired by it.

To highlight why you should restate the importance of the topic and include a memorable statement in a conclusion, I have made two additions to this student's paragraph (the underlined sentences below).

In conclusion, a person's behavior is not developed purely by nature or nurture. It requires both to create behavioral foundations and trait expressions in a person. (1) Yet it is important to understand what nurture can contribute, because this can help us develop better ways to help children become well-rounded adults. Ultimately, a person behaves based on the genes he/she inherits from his/her family, and the environment in which he/she was growing up. Apart from its informative presentation of nature versus nurture, "Three Identical Strangers" also questions the moral standards of scientists when they conduct experiments on other human beings. As shown in the triplets' case, it is ironic that in order to discover the secrets of human development, the scientists were willing to conduct and hide such a malicious experiment from the world. (2) Tragically, if the love and care they had given to their research were given to Eddie instead, perhaps he would still be alive today. Conclusion from *Nature versus Nurture* by N. Sookping (additions made by me)

In the revised paragraph above, sentence (1) highlights why it is important to discuss the nature versus nurture topic—it can make a difference in people's lives. Sentence (2) is a final memorable point. This concluding sentence is more memorable than the original final sentence because it invokes an emotional response from the reader. It would also make the majority of readers think about the negative effects of unethical research and the importance of nurturing children.

Unit 2
DESCRIPTIVE WRITING

Unit Goals

Upon completing this unit, you should be able to demonstrate the following knowledge and skills:

- Recognize the most common types of descriptive writing.
- Use figurative language, vivid words, and "show, don't tell."
- Organize and sequence information via spatial (locative) and temporal (time) connectors, as well as by order of importance.
- Write three major types of descriptions.

Definition

A *descriptive text* describes a thing, person, place, or process. It includes detailed information that helps readers form an image in their mind. The better the description, the clearer the image.

Good writers often draw on their own experiences to write descriptions. This does not mean that you can only describe things that you have experienced. It means that you can also draw on memorable, real-life experiences to fuel imagined descriptions.

> **Description** *To enhance, elaborate, or extend upon existing meanings so you are doing more than just listing more details; to bring some person, place, process, or thing to life in detail.*

76 ESSENTIAL KNOWLEDGE AND SKILLS FOR ESSAY WRITING

General guidelines for descriptions include precise vocabulary, appeals to the five senses of touch, smell, sight, sound, and taste, and "show, don't tell." Descriptions can also be artistic and may deviate occasionally from grammatical norms.

Although there are no hard and fast rules for how descriptions should be written, this unit will provide practical suggestions and techniques that can help you write an effective and appealing descriptive paragraph, section, or essay.

Before we begin, let us look at a short example of description from a student's essay. Example 2.1 consists of three paragraphs that describe a place.

2.1   Example of three paragraphs from a description of a place

I finally reached the market's entrance. Towering above me was a deep-green, gigantic billboard, on which some very large off-white Thai letters said "ตลาดไท." Below the billboard was a colossal golden Buddha statue: Cross-legged and glittering gleefully in the midday sun, it somehow calmed me. I would later learn that these two assuming, yet contrastive, synthetic structures would come to typify the contradiction that is Talad Thai—the land of the wholesale merchant.

Zapped by the midday heat, I slowly shuffled inside. Filled with a diversity of sensual aromatic scents and innumerable shades of colors, my first stop—the flower market—seemed quite alluring. Fascinated by the intriguing fragrances and colorful blooms, I glided through this covered oasis in a trance.

I first noticed a row of giant plastic iceboxes, and I imagined what it would be like to climb inside one of them and be transported to some far off place, perhaps to where they grew the flowers. The boxes were very old and had accumulated a number of ingrained stains. They were primarily pale red and blue and looked like sun-bleached American flags. One of their heavy-looking lids was broken at its corner, disclosing a moldy sponge-like material inside with some moss around it. Despite their decadence and obvious neglect, they were somewhat familiar and reassuring, and reminded me of my childhood and the fish market in my hometown.

Extract from The Blooming Bliss of Talad Thai By Apiwhat Wichai

---

The student who wrote this piece was asked to travel to a nearby market—one of the largest wholesalers in South East Asia—and describe what he encountered. The resulting essay was full of vivid imagery and metaphor that helped immerse the reader in this place and experience the visit along with the author. In addition, the student made good use of placing dependent clauses at the beginning of some sentences as a way to vary the rhythm of his writing, and as a way to build up to the introduction of a new descriptive element. Imagine, for instance, how flat the second paragraph would be if you removed the three dependent clauses (two past-participle phrases and an adjective phrase).

2.1. KEY SKILLS

2.1.1. Using All Five Senses

As the above example illustrates, good descriptive writing immerses a reader in the writer's world. An effective way to do this is to include details that appeal to the five senses: sight, smell, sound, taste, and touch. In your own descriptions, you should try to include as many of these senses as you can (where appropriate). As regards appropriateness, if you are describing your dog, you may not want to include taste or smell unless you are trying to create a negative or weird tone with your writing.

Some questions to ask when you describe senses:

Touch	What do you feel on your skin? Is it hot or cold? Is it wet or dry? Is it smooth or rough?
Smell	Are the smells good or bad? What do they remind you of? Is there food involved?
Sound	What do you hear? Is it quiet or noisy? Is there traffic? Are people talking? What about the sounds of nature? Are they present? *(Even a soft wind makes a sound.)*
Taste	What taste or sensation do you have in your mouth or your memory? Sweet, sour, dry, bitter, or the taste of some specific thing? *(This is a difficult sense to describe, and the degree to which you pay this any attention depends on the subject matter.)*
Sight	What do you see? Colors, size, depth, height, width, shape, some specific items, or people?

78 ESSENTIAL KNOWLEDGE AND SKILLS FOR ESSAY WRITING

Before writing a description, make five columns: one for each of the senses. Then, list words or ideas for your description based on your answers to the above questions. Sight (what we can see) is the easiest sense to make a list for, so fill in this column last.

For example, suppose I have decided to write a paragraph that describes a beach. I start by making a list of what I can sense at a beach, drawing on experiences where relevant. I try to make my list as evenly balanced as possible, but I am careful not to overstretch my imagination and start listing things that would be very unlikely (e.g., there are no seagulls in Thailand where this beach is located, so I would not hear them here).

Touch	Smell	Sound	Taste	Sight
water	salt in the air	breaking waves	lotion	sun, surf, sand
sand	smoke from	laughing	smoke	people
seashells	barbecue	splashing	cold drink	tables & chairs
heat	specific food	music	salt water	boats
	sunblock	jet skis	specific food	specific colors

Next, I choose the most interesting details from my list to put into my description paragraph. My goal is to give the reader a good sense of what it is like to be at this beach. As you read the resultant paragraph in Example 2.2, underline any senses that you encounter.

2.2 Describing a place through the five senses

Chaweng beach is a great place to swim and relax. In the heat of the day, the sweet scent of sunblock wafts through the air. If you need to cool off, the water is a refreshing and tempting sight and is perfect for swimming. The beach is also large enough to accommodate tourists and locals seeking fun in the sun. Children laugh and splash in the water and nearby volleyball games stir passionate shouts in the heat of competition. In the distance, sailboats catch the soft breezes, while closer to the shore, canoeists glide quietly past. This is a beach vacation to remember!

Extract from *Chaweng Beach* by Neil Bowen

Now go back and look at the things/people/places (nouns) that I described and make a note of how these were modified with adjectives.

DESCRIPTIVE WRITING   79

Exercise 2.1. Choosing what to describe

Now it is your turn. Describe the place pictured in the two images below in terms of what you might feel (on your skin), smell, hear, taste, and see. Put five words in each column given below the picture and remember not to overstretch your imagination.

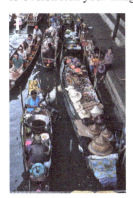

Touch	Smell	Sound	Taste	Sight
1.	1.	1.	1.	1.
2.	2.	2.	2.	2.
3.	3.	3.	3.	3.
4.	4.	4.	4.	4.
5.	5.	5.	5.	5.

2.1.2. Figurative Language

Figurative language is using words and phrases in a non-literal way. In other words, you take words/phrases that typically refer to one thing but you use them in a "deviant" or "non-conventional" way to mean something else. For example, *she cried a river of tears*—a person cannot literally cry a river, but we have taken the concept of a river and used it in a non-literal sense to mean she is crying a lot. Compare *She cried a river of tears* to *She cried a lot*. It is obvious which one has more flavor, color, and memorability.

There are many types of figurative language. Here, I introduce five of the most frequently used types in descriptive writing.

Onomatopoeia

Onomatopoeia is using words to recreate sound(s). For example, in the *Pied Piper of Hamelin*, Robert Browning (1842) uses the words in bold to represent sounds.

> → And ere three **shrill** notes the pipe uttered,
> You heard as if an army **muttered**;
> And the **muttering** grew to a **grumbling**;
> And the **grumbling** grew to a mighty **rumbling**;
> And out of the houses the rats came tumbling. (Browning, 1842, p. 14)

Hyperbole

Hyperbole is exaggerated language. It is used to create a strong impression or emphasize a point as in the following examples:

> → The queue for the sushi buffet was a mile long.
> → The teacher told his students a million times what hyperbole was.

Simile

A simile compares two things through a connecting word, usually *like* or *as*.

> → "My chest bumps like a dryer with shoes in it." (Foster Wallace, 1996, p. 5)
> → Wayne being late was as certain as death and taxes.

In the first example above, from *Infinite Jest* by David Foster Wallace (1996), the protagonist of the story is describing how his anxiety is manifesting itself physically. His heart is beating so hard and fast that is resembles the violent motion of a clothes dryer spinning with shoes inside it.

In the second example, the author is using the simile *as certain as death and taxes* to describe how *Wayne* is always late with no exception.

DESCRIPTIVE WRITING   81

Exercise 2.2. Writing similes

In the spaces below, write down a simile that describes each of the trees labeled 1, 2, and 3. Provide examples of similes using both as and like.

IMAGE 1

IMAGE 2

IMAGE 3

Metaphor

A metaphor, like a simile, also establishes a relationship or similarity between two separate things, but it does so by stating that one thing is the other (i.e., it does not use *like* or *as*). Metaphors usually get their meaning from the connotation of words (associated sense experiences or societal/cultural meanings). For example, consider the following metaphor.

→ This coffee shop is a sauna!

In this example, the word *sauna* has connotations of something very hot, humid, and uncomfortable. Thus, these connotative meanings are being used to tell us that the air inside the coffee shop is too hot, sticky, and perhaps not very pleasant.

In the next example, from *As you Like it* by William Shakespeare (1623/1994), the literal meaning is that we are all actors performing life on the biggest stage of all:

> → "All the world's a stage. And all the men and women merely players."
> (Shakespeare, 1623/1994, Jaques, Act II, scene vii)

We can also realize metaphors through our choice of **verbs** as in the following example:

> → He **barked** commands at the recruits.

Here, the way the man is giving orders is being compared to the way a dog barks. The connotation is that he is very angry, loud, and possibly scary.

Alliteration

Alliteration is repeating the same sound from the beginning or end of a syllable. Technically, it is a sound device rather than figurative language, but it is an easy way to inject some creativity into writing. It is often found in poetry, where it is used to help create a certain tone or rhythm as in the sentence below, which is taken from the *The Raven* by Edgar Allen Poe (1854):

> → "While I **n**odded, **n**early **n**ap**ping**, sudde**n**ly, there came a tap**ping**." (Poe, 1854, p. 1)

Personification

Personification is giving human characteristics or qualities to non-human objects, entities, or ideas. *Beclouded* by Emily Dickinson (1890/2004), for instance, contains several examples of personification—four are shown below in bold:

> → The sky is low, the clouds are **mean**
> A **travelling** flake of snow
> Across a barn or through a rut
> **Debates** if it will go.
> A narrow wind **complains** all day. (Dickinson, 1890/2004, p. 103)

Exercise 2.3. Identifying personification

In sentences 1–5 below, an object or entity is personified. Identify what is being personified and then state which human action or trait has been assigned to the object or entity.

1. The wind whispered lightly in his ear as the moon gazed down upon him.
   Personified object/idea:
   Human action(s) or trait(s):

2. He wiped his brow in frustration but the sun continued beating down on him.
   Personified object/idea:
   Human action(s) or trait(s):

3. The flowers danced happily in the breeze.
   Personified object/idea:
   Human action(s) or trait(s):

4. The deadline had slowly crept up to him.
   Personified object/idea:
   Human action(s) or trait(s):

5. The car's engine coughed and spluttered to life. Then it died an agonizing death.
   Personified object/idea:
   Human action(s) or trait(s):

*A WORD OF WARNING. While figurative language can help your writing come alive, some instances have been used so much that they have become old and tired. These are called ***clichés***. For example, *as quiet as a mouse*, *straight as an arrow*, or *flat as a pancake*. The comparisons being made in these similes have been heard/read so many times that people no longer engage with them emotionally. It is therefore advisable to avoid using clichés like this *at all costs*, as it were.

Also, avoid "overstretching," which is when someone tries to get creative but fails because of stretching too far for a comparative image. In other words, they have created a metaphor or simile that is too difficult or even impossible to imagine. For example, look at the following attempts to be creative. What is wrong with each one?

> × His legs looked like square cut carrots (*simile*).
> × His sapphire orbs dribbled out juicy tears (*metaphor*).
> × The dog looked like a cupcake crossed with a cowboy (*simile*).

Exercise 2.4. Vivid language and figurative language

For each of the examples below identify if it is a simile or a metaphor. Then, discuss with a peer the meaning of the simile or metaphor and write the literal meaning in the spaces.

1. The man was like an octopus, snatching up the plates.   Simile ☐   Metaphor ☐

2. This class is like the monkey cage at the zoo.   Simile ☐   Metaphor ☐

3. My bed was a tomb made of clouds.   Simile ☐   Metaphor ☐

4. His arms looked like wet noodles.   Simile ☐   Metaphor ☐

5. Those girls are like two peas in a pod.   Simile ☐   Metaphor ☐

6. I tried to tell her but she was a brick wall.   Simile ☐   Metaphor ☐

7. Today was a roller coaster.   Simile ☐   Metaphor ☐

8. He moved nervously like a gecko being watched.   Simile ☐   Metaphor ☐

The next exercise contains an extract from a *recount* (description of an event). It describes the first time I went scuba diving. I later went on to become a scuba diving instructor and complete thousands of dives, but I will never forget my first time under the water. As you read the extract, note how my description of this event includes examples of vivid word choices, five types of figurative language (seven examples in total), and how the description evokes more than just the sense of sight. Also make note of how the paragraphs are divided. What signals the start of a new paragraph?

Exercise 2.5. Vivid language and figurative language

Read the following extract and underline all the examples of figurative language (seven in total). When you have found all seven, answer the questions that follow.

"Ssssssss" goes the air as it escapes the tube above my head. I descend slowly, like a teabag in a very large pot. The sounds of the waves and speedboat crew fade away, and my shortness of breath becomes ever more noticeable, "usshh ..., usshh ... usshh." I slow down my breathing, relax, and continue sinking toward the ocean floor.

As I reach the 15-meter mark, the temperature suddenly changes: I am passing through a thermocline. I now understand why they made me wear a wetsuit that could double as a yoga mat. We reach the ocean floor seconds later, and my guide makes an ok sign with his hand. I respond in kind and we move off toward the reef.

Like a camera focusing in on its subject, the reef becomes clearer, and I can now make out the skeletal remains of the once vibrant coral metropolis. Although the reef itself is now a sun-bleached homunculus, the life around it is awash with color: radiant reds, peaceful purples, and gentle greens break up the barren blue backdrop. I kick once and I float forward. It has me in its tractor beam...

Extract from *Journey to the Ocean Floor* by Neil Bowen

1. What are the five types of figurative language used in the above extract? Give one example of each type taken from the text.
   a)
   b)
   c)
   d)
   e)

2. Write down what kind of tone, feeling, or "atmosphere" is generated in this description? Give examples to support your answer.

2.1.3. Enhancing, Elaborating, and Extending Details

One way we can add to our level of description is through circumstantial elements. These elements are optional to the grammar of a clause, but nonetheless add meanings that *enhance*, *elaborate*, or *extend* existing ones.

In functional grammars, these elements are often called circumstances. They can function as *circumstantial elements* (adjuncts at the clause level) or *qualifiers* (post-modifiers at the phrase level). For instance, in Example 2.3, the sentence contains four circumstantial elements: two adjuncts and two qualifiers:

2.3 Example of a clause incorporating circumstantial elements
Adjunct: manner: quality (how?)   **Qualifier:** extent: duration (how long?)
In the morning, the girl carefully brushed her teeth for two minutes at the sink
Adjunct: location: time (when?)   **Qualifier:** location: place (where?)

The core content of the above sentence is "the girl brushed her teeth" (subject^ verb^ object). The rest of the information is optional: It adds more precise details that are secondary to the core description (hence the use of the term *circumstantial*).

Many circumstantial elements consist of adverbs or prepositional phrases. We will look at adverbs in detail in Unit 5; here we will focus on prepositional phrases.

In English, prepositional phrases are composed of [preposition + noun phrase], such as *in the bag*, where *in* is a preposition and *the bag* is a noun phrase.

Noun phrases, on the other hand, can be made up of four key structural elements: *(determiner)^(modifier)^person/place/thing^*(qualifier). The *( ) denotes that these elements are optional—the person/place/thing (head noun) is the only element we really need to create a noun phrase. For instance, we could have multiple elements that surround the head noun in a noun phrase, such as in, *those three fantastic young university students at the back*, where *students* is the head noun and all the other elements modify or add to its meaning in some way. We could even break

DESCRIPTIVE WRITING   87

this noun phrase down to see each of the structural elements in more detail as follows:

Word	those	three	fantastic	young	university	students	at the back
Function	Deictic	Num.	Epithet	Epithet	Classifier	Person	Qualifier
	det.	numeral	adjective	adjective	noun	noun	prep. phrase

At an intermediate level, most students are good at choosing words that go before the head noun (pre-modifiers), thus we will focus on qualifiers (post-modifiers).

Most qualifying elements in English consist of prepositional phrases. Prepositional phrases functioning as qualifiers are useful when writing descriptions as they allow us to attach more (non-essential) information on to the end of noun phrases. Moreover, the words acting as head nouns typically function as the grammatical subjects and objects in our sentences, so qualifiers can help us to add more detail to or further specify the main focal points of our clauses. For example, consider how the following *prepositional phrases* (pp)—which are functioning as qualifiers—allow us to add more information to the thing (head noun = table) we have placed in subject position:

→ The table [1][*in the corner*]pp [2][*of the dark room*]pp was odd and out of place.

In the above example, we have ***enhanced*** our description of the grammatical subject of the clause by adding two details about the location of *the table*. We have done this by post-modifying the Thing (head noun = table) with two prepositional phrases: 1 = Qualifier: location: place (*in the corner* answers the question: Where?); 2 = Qualifier: location: place (*of the dark room* also answers the question: Where?).

Now, consider the next example.

→ The boy [1][*with broken glasses*]pp and [2][**a crooked nose*]pp sulked in the corner.

In this example, we have ***extended*** our description of *the boy* by adding two details. We have done this by post-modifying the head noun (boy) with two prepositional phrases (*note that the second phrase is technically, *with a crooked nose*, but there is no need to

88 ESSENTIAL KNOWLEDGE AND SKILLS FOR ESSAY WRITING

repeat the preposition). There are thus two qualifiers (prepositional phrases) that function as extending circumstantial elements (accompaniment: comitative (both answering the question: What with?).

In the final example, we will *elaborate, extend,* **and** *enhance* upon the details in a clause through *prepositional phrases*. However, this time, the first one is functioning as a circumstance (adjunct at the clausal level), while the other three are functioning as qualifiers (post-modifying the phrase preceding it).

> → [1][*As a young woman*]$_{pp}$, Natalie would cut her hair [2][*with a knife*]$_{pp}$ [3][*as a protest*]$_{pp}$ [4][*against her mother*]$_{pp}$.

These four elements have the following functions:
1. Elaborating circumstance: role: guise (*as what?*).
2. Extending qualifier: accompaniment: comitative (*what with?*).
3. Elaborating qualifier: role: guise (*as what?*).
4. Enhancing qualifier: cause: behalf (*who for?*).

*A NOTE OF CAUTION. While adding details via circumstantial elements is a way to increase description, a writer can overdo this. Therefore, as a rule of thumb, it is usually best to limit the number of prepositional phrases in a clause to three (i.e., include no more than three prepositional phrases between punctuation marks). This is important because you do not want to overload your reader with too much information in one sentence, nor do you want to deviate from principles of plain language use (see Unit 1). Always put your reader first, and never make them read a sentence more than once.

To help you choose appropriate circumstantial elements, Table 2.1 should prove helpful. It is adapted from Halliday and Matthiessen (2014, pp. 313–314). The table offers a list of circumstance types and examples that a writer can use to enhance, elaborate, or extend the existing information in a phrase or clause, resulting in a lengthier but more descriptive and specific unit of language. You will see that many of the examples make use of prepositions to introduce the circumstance, while others make use of adverbs or some of the conjunctions from Table 1.1 (see Unit 1).

DESCRIPTIVE WRITING   89

Table 2.1. Types of circumstantial elements

	Type		Wh- Item	Examples of realization
enhancing	extent	distance	*how far?*	*for; throughout;* 'measured' noun phrase
		duration	*how long?*	*for; throughout;* 'measured' noun phrase
		frequency	how many times?	'measured' noun phrase
	location	place	*where? [there, here]*	PREPOSITIONS: *at, in, on, by, near; to, towards, into, onto, (away) from, out of, off; behind, in front of, above, below, under, alongside ...* ADVERBS OF PLACE: *abroad, overseas, home, upstairs, downstairs, inside, outside; out, up, down, behind; left, right, straight ...; there, here*
		time	*when? [then, now]*	PREPOSITIONS: *at, in, on; to, until, till, towards, into, from, since, during, before, after* ADVERBS OF TIME: *today, tomorrow; now, then*
	manner	means	*how? [thus]*	*by, through, with, by means of, out of* [+ material verb], *from*
		quality	*how? [thus]*	PREPOSITIONS: *in a* + quality (e.g., *dignified*)+ *manner/way, with* +abstraction (e.g. <u>*dignity*</u>); *according to* ADVERBS IN: *-ly, -wise; fast, well; together, jointly, separately, respectively*
		comparison	*how? what like?*	*like, unlike; in* + *the manner of ...* ADVERBS OF COMPARISON: *differently*
		degree	*how much?*	*to* + *a high/low/... degree/extent;* ADVERBS OF DEGREE: *much, greatly, considerably, deeply* [often collocated with a lexical verb, e.g. *love* + *deeply,* understand + *completely*]
	cause	reason	*why?*	*because of, as a result of, thanks to, due to, for want of, for, of, out of, through*
		purpose	*why? what for?*	*for, for the purpose/sake of, in the hope of*
		behalf	*who for?*	*for, for the sake of, in favour of, against* [i.e., 'not in favour of'], *on behalf of*
	contingency	condition	*why?*	*in case of, in the event of*
		default		*in default of, in the absence of, short of, without*
		concession		*despite, in spite of*

extending	accom- paniment	comitative	*who/what with?*	with; without
		additive	*and who/what else?*	as well as, besides; instead of
elaborating	role	guise	*what as?*	as, by way of, in the role/shape/guise/ form of
		product	*what into?*	Into

Copyright © 2014. Adapted from *Introduction to Functional Grammar* by Halliday, M. A. K., & Matthiessen, C. M. I. M. Reproduced by permission of Taylor and Francis Group, LLC, a division of Informa plc.

To use the table, think carefully about what you need to include in a description. For example, if you need to add information about where something is located in space (physical position) or time (temporal order), look through Table 2.1 until you find "location," and then scroll across to "place" and "time" options.

Exercise 2.6. Choosing circumstantial elements

Using the information from Table 2.1, identify the types of qualifiers (*green*) and circumstances (blue) used in the phrases numbered 1–15 below. Do they enhance, elaborate, or extend upon the existing description?

*As you read, pay attention to how the adjectives also augment the description by modifying the noun phrases they are attached to.

Széchenyi Thermal Bath [1][*in Budapest*] is an unmissable tourist attraction. It is [2][heavenly] for those who adore a luxury lifestyle. The first impression starts [3][*in front of the hall*]. You can see an elegant white building, which has Roman pillars and wonderful sculptures. The aroma of flowers covers the welcoming hall. Customers queue [4][*at the ticket office*], which is located on the right of the door. [5][Next to the office], there is a service shop. They sell and rent every necessary amenity [6][*for the bath*]. Moreover, you can keep your personal belongings [7][*in a locker*] near the pool. [8][Behind the shop], there is an entrance to an enormous outdoor bath. [9][On the left], there is a chilling bath, which has a splendid fountain [10][at the back]. Beside that is another huge pool, which is for swimming only. The steam rising from the pool spreads [11][like a magical mist]. The smell of cold fresh air is refreshing, but when you step on the freezing ground, it convinces you to run [12][swiftly] into the warm water. [13][After you get into the pool], you will be [14][pleasantly] surprised at the difference in temperature between the hot water surrounding your body and the cold air [15][*over your head*]. For me, the Bath is completely worth the price of entry.

Extract from *Széchenyi Thermal Bath* by Bandhita Srinualnad

Write your answers down using the format shown here for number one from above, which has been done for you.

1. Enhancing qualifier (prepositional phrase): location: place (*where?*)

You should have noticed that there are many circumstances of place in this paragraph. This is because the writer is describing a place. This means the writer is working hard to locate things in terms of spatial arrangement. When we look at describing processes later on in this unit, you will see a different pattern of circumstantial elements. Namely, there will be more circumstances of time or sequence, as this type of writing calls for things to be located in time (temporal relationships with one another). Moreover, when we come to look at narrative writing in the next unit, you will see another pattern of circumstantial elements. Specifically, circumstances of place, time, cause, and others, will be more varied. This is because narration calls for descriptions of things and events to be located in terms of time, space, and cause–effect (or action–reaction).

2.2. DESCRIBING THINGS AND PLACES

A description of a place gives us sensory details (touch, smell, sound, taste, and sight), but it should also tell the reader how the writer feels about the place and why. Example 2.4 is an extract from *The Great Gatsby*, a novel by F. Scott Fitzgerald (1925/2021). As you read the extract, underline all the words that describe something. When you have finished, think about what feelings this description evoked. Is it a place you would want to go to? Is it a quiet/noisy place? A slow/fast-paced place?

92   ESSENTIAL KNOWLEDGE AND SKILLS FOR ESSAY WRITING

> **2.4   Description of a place example**
>
> The lights grow brighter as the earth lurches away from the sun, and now the orchestra is playing yellow cocktail music, and the opera of voices pitches a key higher. Laughter is easier minute by minute, spilled with prodigality, tipped out at a cheerful word. The groups change more swiftly, swell with new arrivals, dissolve and form in the same breath; already there are wanderers, confident girls who weave here and there among the stouter and more stable, become from a sharp, joyous moment the center of a group, and then, excited with triumph, glide on through the sea-change of faces and voices and color under the constantly changing light.
>
> Extract from *The Great Gatsby* by F. Scott Fitzgerald (Fitzgerald, 1925/2021, p. 34)

In this paragraph you can hear, see, and feel the setting in which the story takes place. When I read this paragraph, I get the impression that it is a vibrant party taking place outdoors and during the summer. It seems to be a large and happy event, with lots of guests coming and going, mingling and meeting briefly, then moving on.

When you write a description of a place, in addition to addressing all the aspects of the physical world, you should also aim to evoke some kind of emotional response from your reader as per the extract above. One way to do this is by carefully choosing your words to be descriptive and evocative—that is, *vivid*.

2.2.1. Using Vivid Words

The image below shows the entrance hallway to a house. If you wanted to describe this scene to someone, what might you say? What might you describe first? What might make a reader feel some emotional connection to what you sense? How could you create a tone that reflects how this hallway looks, smells, and feels when you are in it?

Exercise 2.7. Choosing descriptive words

Make a list of ten things in the image that can be used to write a description of this hallway using more than one sense. Put you answers in the spaces below.

1.   6.
2.   7.
3.   8.
4.   9.
5.   10.

You have probably listed mostly nouns and some adjectives. These words name or describe things. If you want your writing to be interesting, you should choose specific, vivid phrases rather than vague, general ones. For instance, the word *car* does not create much of a mental image for the reader. A more specific noun phrase like *luxurious limo*, *family-friendly sedan*, or *scrappy little hatchback* would be better.

Typically, as you may already have worked out, when describing things, places, people, or processes, writers focus on what they put in noun phrases or adjectival phrases. Using the car example from above, for instance, would it not be more interesting (and beneficial) to the reader if the writer had written, *a scrappy little hatchback with a patchwork paint-job*? In terms of structure, several descriptive items have been added to the head noun, as shown below:

Word	a	scrappy	little	hatchback	with a patchwork paint job
Function	Deictic det.	Epithet adjective	Epithet adjective	Thing noun	Qualifier prepositional phrase

*<u>A WORD OF WARNING.</u> Do not needlessly fill your writing with complex descriptive phrases. Use such phrases sparingly and construct them purposefully. Also vary the length of elements—words, phrases, sentences, and paragraphs—to create rhythm and to give the reader a chance to absorb information of different kinds and in different amounts. Bombarding the reader with three or four long phrases, sentences, or paragraphs in a row can bog down the reading process and overload their cognitive resources, especially their short-term memory. Therefore, in order not to risk losing the reader's attention and interest, be careful to vary the level of complexity and length of your grammatical units, such as by preceding and following each complex unit with a simple one. If you make a complex unit, be sure that it is purposeful and understandable—in other words, that it helps to create a vivid image and does not overstretch in trying to be original.

Exercise 2.8. Choosing vivid nouns and noun phrases

This exercise will give you practice in creating phrases that add to your descriptions. In sentences 1–8 below, replace the underlined word or phrase with a more specific, vivid choice.

1. For my birthday, he bought me <u>a watch</u>.
2. We ate at <u>a restaurant</u>.
3. I have <u>a cute dog</u>.
4. Sonny bought <u>a used car that was not very good.</u>
5. My place has a view of <u>the river.</u>
6. The food was <u>delicious.</u>
7. The <u>sky</u> was a wondrous sight at night.
8. We went on an awful trip around the island on <u>a boat</u>.

DESCRIPTIVE WRITING   95

Now go back and look at the list of ten words you chose to describe the hallway in Exercise 2.7. Can you improve upon any of these words by making them more specific and/or vivid? Would it be beneficial to post-modify any of them with a qualifier (e.g., a prepositional phrase) to enhance, extend, or elaborate their description? Choose six of them that would benefit from more vivid word choice, or from having their descriptions enhanced, extended, or elaborated through additions to their phrase structure. Write down your new word choices and/or modifications in the spaces below:

1.   2.

3.   4.

5.   6.

2.2.2. Sequencing Descriptions of Things

To describe how things are located in space, we can use prepositions and prepositional phrases of place or direction (such as those introduced in the previous section, when we made use of Table 2.1). The table below provides further examples of words or phrases that you can use to transition between things in terms of spatial arrangements. These can be used for any kind of description when / in which you need to set up relationships between things or features in terms of their relative locations in the physical world, including when you go on to describe a person's appearance in section 2.3.

Table 2.2: Spatial transitions

in front of	across from	above/over	between	beside	near to
in back of	opposite to	under/below	around	on the left of	toward
behind	next to	underneath	in parallel	close to	along
inside	adjacent to	beneath	at the bottom	far from	atop
outside	on top of	midway	in the middle	in the center	

In writing a description, things are often placed in a spatial arrangement to each other. When setting up this arrangement, it is usually best to start from one position and then move in a clear

96　ESSENTIAL KNOWLEDGE AND SKILLS FOR ESSAY WRITING

direction. For example, you can move from left to right, bottom to top, or even clockwise/anti-clockwise. Since readers cannot see the scene and the things in it, you need to organize everything for them so that a coherent picture can emerge in their mind's eye. It is therefore important that you do not randomly jump around.

Exercise 2.9. Sequencing descriptions of things

Using prepositional phrases of location: place (qualifiers for phrases; circumstances at the clause level), write a description that moves between the ten things you chose in Exercise 2.7.

*Organize your description such as moving left to right, near-to-far, or in some other obvious or understandable pattern that is easy for your reader to follow.

The following exercise will also help you to sequence a description of a place. The extract it uses is from a student essay. The essay describes a hospital waiting room from the first-person perspective. I have provided you with the three body paragraphs that make up the bulk of this five-paragraph essay.

Exercise 2.10. Sequencing descriptions of things

Correctly sequence the information (sentences) in each of the paragraphs below. The resulting text should flow logically from start to finish. (The first two have been done for you.)

BODY PARAGRAPH 1

- [1] a. As I shuffled into the entrance of the hospital's after-hour clinic, I knew a depressing experience was awaiting me.
- [ ] b. The smell of sweat, antiseptic, food, and cheap coffee lingered in the air; it invaded my nose like an army of disorganized, disgusting, deviants.
- [ ] c. Although it was frigidly cold in the air-conditioned area, my hands and feet sweated excessively. The waiting area was a melancholy sight: Rows of tandem and beam seating were all occupied by similarly confused and anxious individuals.
- [ ] d. Like many hospital waiting rooms, this one was not particularly pleasant.

DESCRIPTIVE WRITING   97

2 **e.** The air seemed languid and lethargic as everyone seemed to be pathetically suffocated by anxiety and depression.

☐ **f.** There was a symphony of "Ahem," "Hack," "Choo" combined with distressed breathing, whispering, whimpering, crying, groaning, and shouting.

BODY PARAGRAPH 2

☐ **g.** With its low volume, a lonely wall-mounted television in front of the seats desperately whispered to people to glance at it. Above it, and contrasting with the patients' extinguishing hopes, the lights on the ceiling were shining brightly, as if they were trying to inject hope into the room.

☐ **h.** The first thing I saw was the enquiry counter manned by an awkward smiling nurse. In front of the counter were hopeless bodies, slouching in tandem, wilting like dying daisies in a flowerbed.

☐ **i.** The waiting room sure looked neat and tidy. Yet I had to squint in an attempt to sharpen my increasingly blurred vision.

☐ **j.** Overall, the area seemed both functional and dysfunctional.

☐ **k.** Around me, each examination room had its own seat next to its door for patients who had been called to go into the room.

BODY PARAGRAPH 3

☐ **l.** Still, it seemed like we were bonded with the same tensions and fears.

☐ **m.** Much later, it felt like nothing had happened for an eternity. All these imprisoned souls and I seemed destined for a purgatory of inaction, where our hopes were slowly suffocated by the abeyance of it all.

☐ **n.** Patients ranged from babies, kids, teenagers, middle-aged to old-timers. There were Thai, Lao, Burmese, Indian, and more.

☐ **o.** Apart from patients, there were doctors, nurses, nurse assistants, medical record officers, patient transport personnel, and security guards.

☐ **p.** Some took a nap. Many complained.

☐ **q.** The nurse called name after name, yet no one seemed to move.

Body paragraphs from *Waiting* by Benjamin Yu

Discuss with your peer(s) or teacher how the writer created an overall feeling or tone. What was this feeling?

2.2.3. Describing a Place Paragraph

Stage 1. Choosing the Topic

For this task, you will write a description of one of your favorite places. This place could be one you visit regularly or one that has happy memories. Be sure to choose somewhere interesting and/or unique so that it will appeal to a reader. For example, no one wants to read about a Starbucks since they are all the same, and people probably do not want to read about your bedroom since they are never going to go there. In other words, choose a place your reader could potentially visit after reading your description.

Stage 2. Pre-Writing Activity: Using a Spatial Sketch to Generate Ideas

Before you begin writing, sketch a rough drawing of the place, the things in it, and label it with words related to the five senses. Think about the best position to describe it from; or perhaps your reader needs to be taken on a tour, in which you move them from inside to outside. Sketching it out will help you to (a) list the items that are essential to your description, and (b) focus on the more interesting aspects that can be described best through vivid or figurative language.

Stage 3. Outlining

Look at the items you have chosen to describe. How will you move between them? How will your writing flow seamlessly from one sentence to the next? Make an outline of bullet points, or draw a mind map to help you organize your notes. Remove anything that does not contribute to the overall tone or feeling you are trying to create.

Stage 4. Drafting

Use your outline and write a draft paragraph of 150–200 words. Make sure you have a brief topic sentence or thesis statement at the beginning and concluding remark at the end. Give it a title that is imaginative and captures the essence of what you have written.

On the assumption that you are writing with a word processing program, make sure to set the line spacing to double and the page size to fit the printer paper (letter or A4 size), with normal margins all around and Times New Roman size 12 font—unless your teacher or a required style guide specifies other settings. Do not forget to put your name (or student ID number) as a running header.

--------------------- **SUBMIT FIRST DRAFT** ----------------------

Stage 5. Post-Writing Activity: Collaborative Peer Review

Now it is time to check your draft through peer review. Swap drafts with one of your peers. Ask them to check what you have written. Check their draft in return. For added feedback (and fun), use the scoring rubric at the end of the unit to grade each other's essays. At a minimum, the feedback should answer the following questions:

1. Does the draft include a topic sentence or thesis statement?

2. Do the sentences flow logically and smoothly in terms of locating things? If not, where does the text break down and why?

3. Is there evidence of strong, vivid word choices? List two examples below:

4. Is there at least one example of figurative language? Is it a good example?

5. Is there more than one sense being invoked in the description?

6. Is there an overall tone to the piece? Does it evoke any emotions in the reader?

Stage 6. Edit and Revise Your Draft

When your classmate returns your draft, edit and revise it according to their feedback. Check your edits against the general scoring rubric for descriptive writing at the end of this unit. See if you can identify your strong and weak points.

-------------------- **WRITE SECOND DRAFT** --------------------

Stage 7. Let Your Revised Draft Sit a While and Then Proofread It Carefully

It is a good idea to give yourself a break from your revised draft before proofreading it. That way, you approach it as an unfamiliar reader would. Also, before proofreading, it is usually a good idea to reread the instructions for the assignment or task rubric and/or to look at the grading criteria or scoring rubric again. This will help to ensure that you have not gone off task or missed something important during the revision process.

-------------------- **SUBMIT FINAL DRAFT** --------------------

2.3. DESCRIBING PEOPLE

A description of a person gives us details about who the person is, what they look like, and any good or bad qualities they have. It should also describe some important aspect(s) about their personality, and how they make others feel. Consider Example 2.5 from *The Dependents*, a short story by Anton Chekhov (1886/2004). Rather than directly *tell* us that Mihail Zotov is a lonely, grumpy old man with diminishing mental capacities, Chekhov *shows* us these aspects.

DESCRIPTIVE WRITING   101

> **2.5   Description of a person**
>
> MIHAIL PETROVITCH ZOTOV, a decrepit and solitary old man of seventy, belonging to the artisan class, was awakened by the cold and the aching in his old limbs …
>
> Zotov cleared his throat, coughed, and shrinking from the cold, got out of bed. In accordance with years of habit, he stood for a long time before the ikon, saying his prayers. He repeated "Our Father," "Hail Mary," the Creed, and mentioned a long string of names. To whom those names belonged he had forgotten years ago, and he only repeated them from habit. From habit, too, he swept his room and entry, and set his fat little four-legged copper samovar. If Zotov had not had these habits he would not have known how to occupy his old age.
>
> Extract from *The Dependents* by Anton Chekov (Chekhov, 1886/2004, para. 1)

In this extract, we have a great example of "show, don't tell." Read the text again and then ask yourself: What impression of the man do I get? What would he look like? What does this description show you about the old man's state of mind and/or feelings? More about "show, don't tell" later on in the unit.

2.3.1. Describing Faces, Body Shapes, and Clothes

Describing Faces

One of the focal points when describing a person is their face. As the novelist, George Orwell famously once said, "At 50, everyone has the face he [*sic*] deserves" (Orwell, 1949/1968, p. 515). In other words, someone's face can tell us a lot about his or her lifestyle choices and life experiences.

At a minimum, ask yourself the following questions when describing someone's face:

- What is the shape of their face?
- What shape and size are their lips, mouth, and nose?
- What kind of skin/complexion do they have?
- What are their eyes like? (Eyes can often tell us a lot about a person.)

- What kind of hair do they have? How is it cut and styled? What about facial hair?

> **Exercise 2.11. Guess who?**
>
> Choose one of the faces below and write a paragraph describing that person's face in 150–200 words. *Do not describe any colors of hair, skin, or clothing until your last few sentences.

When you are finished, read out your description to the class. As you read out your description, your peers will guess whom you have written about as soon as they think they know. If you have done a good enough job, someone will guess correctly before you have finished reading your whole paragraph. The first person to guess correctly chooses the next person to read out their paragraph.

Describing Body Shapes and Clothes

When describing someone's body shape, you can make comparisons to shapes that are easy for the reader to picture. For instance, if someone's hips are much wider than their shoulders, then you can say they have a *triangle body shape* (aka "pear shaped").

Conversely, if a person has broad shoulders and a narrow lower body, then you can describe them as having an *inverted triangle body shape*. Other vocabulary that is commonly used to describe body types include *oval*, *rectangle*, *round* (aka "apple"), *hourglass*, *diamond*, *trapezoid*, and other shape-related words. You can also make comparisons of your own, such as *he looked like a gorilla in a suit* or *she was shapely like a bottle of cola*.

In addition to overall shape and size, you may also want to describe posture and clothing, as these can give clues about a person's personality or current emotional state. For instance, if a person is sitting in a slouched position, shoulders forward and head down, that body position can suggest a tired, shy, depressed, or even guilty individual. If a person is wearing an expensive, neatly pressed and perfectly fitting outfit, that clothing can portray a very disciplined or proud individual.

The extract in Example 2.6 is a great example of a description of a person. It is from Chapter 28 of *Moby Dick*, a novel by Herman Melville (1851/2001). It describes the first appearance of Captain Ahab—the mysterious captain of a whaling ship, who is obsessed with chasing (and killing) the giant white whale, Moby Dick. Up until this point in the novel, Captain Ahab has not been seen by Ishmael (the narrator), and the only description the reader has of him is when Captain Peleg remarks, "He's a grand, ungodly, god-like man, Captain Ahab; doesn't speak much; but, when he does speak, then you may well listen. Mark ye, be forewarned" (Melville, 1851/2001, p. 93). As you read the extract, note how Melville builds a description of Ahab as an imposing, frightening, larger than life figure, who is seemingly madness personified (and part whale through his prosthetic leg).

> ### 2.6 A vivid description of a person
>
> He looked like a man cut away from the stake, when the fire has overrunningly wasted all the limbs without consuming them, or taking away one particle from their compacted aged robustness. His whole high, broad form, seemed made of solid bronze, and shaped in an unalterable mould, like Cellini's cast Perseus. Threading its way out from among his grey hairs, and continuing right down one side of his tawny scorched face and neck, till it disappeared in his clothing, you saw a slender rod-like mark, lividly whitish. It resembled that perpendicular seam sometimes made in the straight, lofty trunk of a great tree, when the upper lightning tearingly darts down it …
>
> So powerfully did the whole grim aspect of Ahab affect me, and the livid brand which streaked it, that for the first few moments I hardly noted that not a little of this overbearing grimness was owing to the barbaric white leg upon which he partly stood. It had previously come to me that this ivory leg had at sea been fashioned from the polished bone of the sperm whale's jaw …
>
> Extract from *Moby Dick* by Herman Melville (Melville, 1851/2001, pp. 135–136)

The following exercise will help you to develop the kind of vocabulary you need to describe a person's appearance. Feel free to use an internet search engine to find suitable words or phrases you need—it may be a good idea to look at some clothing retailers, fashion blogs, or social media pages for inspirational word choices.

Exercise 2.12. Vocabulary for describing people

Write down five to six vivid and/or specific words for each of the prompts below. If you struggle for ideas, then you could also search for images related to these prompts on the internet.

Posture (e.g., *slouching*):

Fabric (e.g., *cotton*):

Bottoms (e.g., *trousers*):

Tops (e.g., *t-shirt*):

Other items (e.g., *dress*):

Footwear (e.g., *sandals*):

Accessories (e.g., *scarf*):

Fabric (e.g., *tartan*):

Clothing style (e.g., *chic*):

When you are making notes to describe a person's appearance, it is a good idea if you start in one place and then move in a pattern—much as you did for describing a place.

2.3.2. Describing Personality or Character

A person's personality or character can often be seen in how they speak to others, how they look, and in how they act. Therefore, this aspect of your description is calling out for "show, don't tell." Do not tell us *He was an angry man*, but show us: *He smashed his hands into the table and stared straight into my soul with murderous intent*.

The "show, don't tell" approach has long been promoted by famous novelists and playwrights from Ernest Hemingway to Chuck Palahniuk. The first attributable source of its use in popular culture stems from the Russian playwright and master of short stories, Anton Chekhov. In his oft-quoted letter to his brother, Chekov (Yarmolinsky, 1954) writes, "In descriptions of Nature one must seize on small details, grouping them so that when the reader closes his eyes he gets a picture" (p. 14). He goes on to write that you do not simply tell the reader the moon is shining, you show them "a piece of glass from a broken bottle glittered like a bright little star" (p. 14). Look at the following two examples. Which one is better?

> → He was disappointed that he missed the bus.
> → He raced down the road, wildly thrashing his arms in the air and yelling, "Stop! Stop!", but the bus turned the corner. It was gone. He sat down on the curb; his head slumped forward and he sighed loudly.

Remember that "show, don't tell" means giving readers actions, sounds, senses, and feelings rather than simple descriptions. In the following example, from *Hills like White Elephants*, Ernest Hemingway (1927/2016) uses the character's dialogue to show or imply two things: (a) "the man" and "Jig"/"the girl" are in some kind of romantic/sexual relationship, wherein the man is clearly dominant; (b) they seem to be discussing the girl getting an abortion, although it is never mentioned.

2.7 Showing personality through dialogue

"It's really an awfully simple operation, Jig," the man said. "It's not really an operation at all."

The girl looked at the ground the table legs rested on.

"I know you wouldn't mind it, Jig. It's really not anything. It's just to let the air in."

The girl did not say anything.

"I'll go with you and I'll stay with you all the time. They just let the air in and then it's all perfectly natural."

"Then what will we do afterward?"

"We'll be fine afterward. Just like we were before."

"What makes you think so?"

"That's the only thing that bothers us. It's the only thing that's made us unhappy."

The girl looked at the bead curtain, put her hand out and took hold of two of the strings of beads.

"And you think then we'll be all right and be happy."

"I know we will. You don't have to be afraid …"

Extract from *Hills like White Elephants* by Ernest Hemingway

(Hemingway, 1927/2016, para. 41)

Although it is generally a good thing, too much showing can become monotonous and tiring for the reader. So you may want to consider alternating between showing and telling to vary the pace of your writing—taking the time to highlight some aspects by showing them, and then skimming quickly over some other aspects by telling them. In *The Old Man and the Sea*, also by Ernest Hemingway (1952), for instance, the entire story takes place over just five days, and Hemingway frequently skims/skirts through hours of time by simply telling the reader what has transpired. He then slows down the pace of the story and uses showing to illustrate how the passage of time has affected the old man's physical and emotional state.

In certain instances, telling is also simply more natural and thus appropriate. The following example will highlight what I mean. Example 2.8 is an extract from the beginning of Chapter II, *Great Expectations* by Charles Dickens (1867/1998). Here, the reader is introduced to Joe and Mrs. Joe through the past memories of Pip, who is now an adult and is looking back on his childhood. It would be quite odd for Pip, who is recounting a memory, to describe his sister's and Joe's appearance and personality solely through their actions. It is far more natural for him to tell the reader what they looked like or what personality traits they possessed. Read the extract carefully and see if you can identify where Pip is simply telling the reader about his sister and Joe.

2.8   Telling the reader things when it is more natural to do so

She was not a good-looking woman, my sister; and I had a general impression that she must have made Joe Gargery marry her by hand. Joe was a fair man, with curls of flaxen hair on each side of his smooth face, and with eyes of such a very undecided blue that they seemed to have somehow got mixed with their own whites. He was a mild, good-natured, sweet-tempered, easy-going, foolish, dear fellow,—a sort of Hercules in strength, and also in weakness.

Extract from *Great Expectations* by Charles Dickens
(Dickens, 1867/1998, Chapter II, para. 2)

108 ESSENTIAL KNOWLEDGE AND SKILLS FOR ESSAY WRITING

As you read this example, you probably noticed how most of the telling is done through relatively simple grammatical structures that state, "A is/has B," where A and B are adjective/noun phrases that nonetheless provide the reader with vivid descriptions. Specifically, in Example 2.8, Dickens uses a series of telling statements—*She was…, …, Joe was …, he was…* —to tell the reader what his sister and joe look like and to list the personality traits of Joe as attributes he possesses. If Dickens had chosen to show the reader instead of tell them, then he may have rewritten some of the description as follows (my transformed "showing" sentences are in italics):

→ "She was not a good-looking woman, my sister" (Dickens telling) becomes
  Men would pass my sister in the street and not give her a second look (me showing).
→ "Joe was a fair man" (Dickens telling) becomes
  Joe never ventured much into the sun (me showing).
→ "Joe was a good natured, sweet tempered … dear fellow" (Dickens telling) becomes
  Joe always held my sister's hand in public and kissed her cheek before saying goodbye (me showing).

As you have probably surmised at this point, showing is not inherently better than telling. It is simply a matter of choosing when it is better to show and when it is better to tell. Indeed, in many forms of writing, showing is not appropriate or conventional, and seems quite odd. If you were writing up the results of an experiment, for instance, it would be a bit strange if you started showing what happened through vivid, dynamic actions. It is far more conventional (and effective) simply to tell (report) the results. Exercise 2.13 gives you practice in mixing telling and showing.

Exercise 2.13. "Show, don't tell!"

Transform the description below using "show, don't tell" where appropriate and vivid language and figurative language where needed. Aim to write a paragraph of 150–200 words.

It was their first date. They did not laugh at anything. They did not seem to have any facial expressions. When they talked, it was always in full sentences and there was no intonation or stress added to their words. They had a bad attitude.

2.3.3. Sequencing Descriptions of People

When describing a person, it is usually easiest to start with a *physical description* and then move on to mainly showing (not telling) the reader about that *person's personality*. For example, start with the shape of their head/face, describe the key features of their face and link some feature to an aspect of their personality, then move to the neck, torso, arms, legs, and finish with the feet. As you move from top to bottom, also describe their clothing and accessories and, once again, link some physical element(s) to their personality if it is appropiate. Alternatively, you can start from the bottom and work your way up. The important thing is that you sequence the information in a way that is easy for the reader to follow, and bring in personality traits through your description. Consider the following example:

> → The mass of limp, orange hair piled loosely atop her head resembled a dried out pumpkin, but she seldom paid any attention to it.

In this example, I have linked a notable feature of the woman's appearance—her hair—to something quite different in an attempt to create a vivid image in a reader's mind. You can enjoy trying to make similarly creative connections in your own descriptions where appropriate.

Exercise 2.14 will give you practice in building up a description of a person and correctly sequencing it (if you are unsure about

110 ESSENTIAL KNOWLEDGE AND SKILLS FOR ESSAY WRITING

what transitions to use, then go back and look at Table 2.1, which occured earlier in the unit).

Exercise 2.14. Sequencing a description of a person

For the image below, fill in the boxes with suitable words/phrases (descriptors). Using these descriptors, the spatial transitions given in Table 2.2, and the checklist under the image, write a paragraph of 150–200 words.

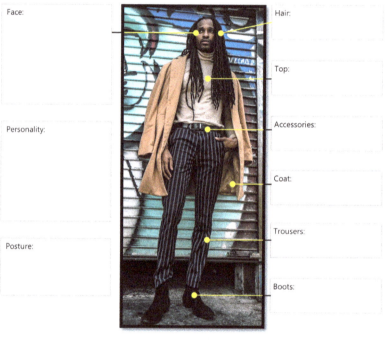

1. Have you described both appearance and personality? ☐
2. Have you used circumstantial elements to enhance, extend, or elaborate? ☐
3. Have you sequenced your description appropriately and in a recognizable way? ☐
4. Have you used a variety of short and long sentences? ☐
5. Have you included a least one example of figurative language? ☐
6. Have you established a clear tone? ☐

2.3.4. Describing a Person Paragraph

Stage 1. Choosing the Topic

For this writing assignment, you are to describe a person who lives in one of the houses shown in Figure 2.1. How do they look? Are they poor, rich, eccentric, fun, scary, or something else? Describe both their appearance and their personality. Start by thinking about interesting details and how many details you can cover within the word limit. Be imaginative but be realistic—if you were to read your paragraph out loud to the class, they should be able to guess which house you have chosen.

Figure 2.1. Who lives in a house like this?

Stage 2. Pre-Writing Activity: Brainstorming to Generate Ideas

A good way to generate ideas for a description is to use a concept map (Figure 2.2). To create a concept map, you draw a circle for <u>appearance</u> and a circle for <u>personality traits</u>. Add a box in the middle that states the <u>tone</u> (emotional mood) you will be aiming for in your description. Enter descriptive details into the nodes and join them to other nodes. Think about how certain aspects of someone's appearance can help you represent their personality. For example, colorful, unkempt clothes with holes in them might suggest a carefree attitude; deep laugh lines around the eyes might suggest a convivial personality.

Figure 2.2. Sample concept map for describing a person

Create a concept map to describe your chosen house's owner/resident and populate it with items that contribute to your overall tone.

Stage 3. Using Bullet Points for Outlining

This writing task is a short one, so outlining will be minimal. However, I recommend that you write down your topic sentence. Then, write down three to four supporting details that relate to it. Be sure that you are creating a strong and clear personality, and feed into this with your description of their appearance. Do not forget about the overall tone of the piece, and make sure that this is reflected in the topic sentence somehow.

Stage 4. Drafting

Write a draft paragraph of 150–200 words. Make sure you have a topic sentence at the beginning and a concluding remark at the end. Give your paragraph a title that is imaginative and captures the essence of what you have written. Remember to use vivid language and figurative language, and to "show, don't tell" where appropriate. Put your name (or student ID) at the top of the page as a running header.

--------------------- SUBMIT FIRST DRAFT ---------------------

Stage 5. Post-Writing Activity: Collaborative Peer Review

Now it is time to check your draft through peer review. Swap drafts with one of your peers. Ask them to check your draft. Check theirs in return and either make notes directly on their draft or in a separate document. For added feedback (and fun), use the general scoring rubric at the end of the unit to grade each other's essays. At the very minimum, the feedback should answer the following questions:

1. Have they included a hook? If not, suggest one.

2. Is there a good balance between describing the person's appearance and describing their personality? What could be improved?

3. Underline at least one example of figurative language. Is it a good example?
4. How many senses are evoked in each body paragraph? Make suggestions for improvements.

5. What is the overall tone of the piece (if any)? What emotions does it evoke in the reader? Note how you felt after reading it.

Stage 6. Edit and Revise Your Draft

When your peer returns your draft (and possible score), read their feedback. Then reread, rethink, and rewrite your own draft. It is hard to write a perfect paragraph on the first try. It is therefore important that you get into the habit of editing and revising to

114   ESSENTIAL KNOWLEDGE AND SKILLS FOR ESSAY WRITING

improve your work, and to improve the way you approach writing. As you revise your first draft, incorporate the feedback from your peers and add any new ideas that may have come to you as you read their draft.

-------------------- **WRITE SECOND DRAFT** --------------------

Stage 7. Let Your Revised Draft Sit a While and Then Proofread It Carefully

It is a good idea to give yourself a break from your revised draft before proofreading it. That way, you approach it as an unfamiliar reader would. Also, before proofreading, it is usually a good idea to reread the instructions for the assignment or task rubric and/or to look at the grading criteria and scoring rubric again. This will help to ensure that you have not gone off task or missed something important during the revision process.

-------------------- **SUBMIT FINAL DRAFT** --------------------

2.4. DESCRIBING PROCESSES

Process descriptions describe the key stages, steps, events, or actions needed to reach a specific outcome. They are ordered sequentially (chronologically or numerically), where subsequent steps are often contingent upon the successful completion of previous steps. Thus, appropriate transitions and clarity of thought are very important. There are two types of process descriptions, which basically reflect the difference between description (explanation) and prescription (instruction):

- AN INFORMATIONAL TEXT explains what happens/happened during a process or sequence of steps/stages. It answers questions such as *What happens when I flush the toilet? Eat food? Take my driving test?*

- A DIRECTIONAL TEXT instructs <u>how</u> to do, make, or operate something through a process or sequence of steps/stages. It answers questions such as *How do I get to X? Make Y? Operate Z?*

2.4.1. Informational (Explanatory or Analytical) Writing

Informational (or explanatory) texts use first person or third person, depending on whether the writer (first person) or someone else (third person) carried out the process. They can also be in the past or present tense, depending on whether the description is of something that happened once (past) or something that is habitual and ongoing (present). For instance, the following paragraph is written in third person, present tense. It gives detailed information about how food moves from our mouths to our stomachs. It is informational (explanatory), which means only objective facts are given.

2.4   Description of an informational process
Food begins its journey at the mouth. Mechanical breakdown starts when chunks of food are chewed into bits and pieces. While chewing, the food is mixed with saliva, which helps break down starch. This process indicates the beginning of chemical breakdown. The two processes create a moist lump called bolus. When sufficiently malleable, the bolus is swallowed, and it travels through the esophagus to the stomach.
Extract from *The Digestive System* by Iwarin Suprapas

2.4.2. Sequencing Explanations

The following task is to give you practice in sequencing informational texts. It will also give you an idea of the kind of information contained in a five-paragraph explanatory essay. Exercise 2.15 includes a complete introduction, three body paragraphs, and a conclusion from a student's essay. The essay explains how the Thai political system has changed over an eighteen-year period from 2001 to 2019.

Exercise 2.15. Sequencing explanatory information

Each of the sentences marked with a letter is out of order. Put the sentences into their correct order by placing the relevant number next to each letter. (Numbers 1 and 2 are done for you.)

Governments often blame external factors for a state's decline and ignore internal ones. This happens in Thailand too. For two decades, Thai politics has been stuck in a vicious circle because of numerous military coups and political struggles between the Yellow Shirts and Red Shirts. The sequence of Thai contemporary politics can be divided into two periods, the Thaksin period, and the post-Thaksin period.

BODY PARAGRAPH 1

- [2] a. His policies gave more access to welfare, benefitting the lower class.
- [ ] b. In 2006, Yellow Shirts held a protest against Thaksin based on allegations of corruption and a lack of loyalty to the monarchy.
- [ ] c. Thus, Thaksin was favorable to Thai laborers. Then, the opponents— conservatives and middle-class people— formed the Yellow Shirts (the yellow color represented the Thai King).
- [1] d. Back in 2001, Thaksin Shinawatra became prime minister.
- [ ] e. From the chaos, the military mounted a coup to maintain social order.
- [ ] f. Thaksin sought political asylum in Britain.

BODY PARAGRAPH 2

- [ ] g. Essentially, the Red Shirts or Yellow Shirts would protest if the current prime minister was not the person they supported.
- [ ] h. This political instability frequently ousted prime ministers.
- [ ] i. After Thaksin left, his supporters established themselves as the Red Shirts.
- [ ] j. From 2008 to 2014, Thailand had four prime ministers: Samak Sundravej, Somchai Wongsawat, Abhisit Vejjajiva, and Yingluck Shinawatra.
- [ ] k. Because of the different beliefs between Yellow Shirts and Red Shirts, Thai politics has been a two-polar system since then.

BODY PARAGRAPH 3

- ☐ **l.** The junta limited public opinions and imposed a ban on political activities.
- ☐ **m.** Thai democratic development came to a halt when Yingluck's rice subsidy scheme was judged negatively by the court, and in 2014 Thai coup leader Prayuth Chan-Ocha became prime minister.
- ☐ **n.** Furthermore, Prayuth's government tried to delay an election date during the long mourning period after the death of King Bhumibol.

From *Military, Monarchy and Colored Shirts: Thailand's Political Power Players* by Panisara Tantikitti

2.4.3. Writing an Explanatory Essay

Because of the complexity and length of this task, I recommend that you work with two of your peers. If this is not possible, you may want to choose to write only one or two of the body paragraphs (stages of the process).

Stage 1. Choose Your Topic

The topic for your essay will be the process of getting fuel from food—in other words, how we take nutrients into our body and how the body then turns this into energy to keep us alive. This is an exercise in selecting important details, sequencing them correctly, and using appropriate vocabulary.

Stage 2. Pre-Writing Activity: Planning and Researching

Use your time wisely before writing. When writing an explanatory text, you should spend about 20% of your total time researching and making notes about your topic. Otherwise, you may miss some important detail that is crucial to understanding the overall process. Consider the following questions:

1. What is your central topic or point of focus? What are you explaining? Are you explaining how something happens or how to do something?
2. What are the key stages/steps/activities you want (or need) to explain?
3. How will you describe these stages/steps/activities in terms of their component parts? Which parts need to be described in detail and which ones do not?
4. How does the process you are describing work? What happens first, second, third, etc.? Are there any conditions that need to be met before the process can move to the next stage/step/ activity? Are there are any hazardous or dangerous stages/ steps/activities that need be explained very carefully?
5. What else might you need to include? For example, is there any specialized vocabulary that you need to define in simpler terms for the reader?

Do some research and find out how the human body gets fuel from food. You will see that there are three major steps involved: ingestion, digestion, and absorption. Make notes on what you feel are the most important parts of the process that a reader needs to know.

Stage 3. Using a Template for Outlining

For a topic as complex as the human digestive system, you would usually need to write more than one paragraph. The outline below will help you organize your notes into a five-paragraph essay that will cover each of the stages in detail. As in Stage 2, expect to spend about 20% of your total time on the outlining stage for this type of text. The writing part will then be relatively easy as your ideas and structure are already in place.

Fill in the following outline from your research. Write an appropriate hook, thesis, and concluding sentence to frame your body paragraphs as part of a unified essay.

Introduction	Paragraph 1	**Hook**. Grab your reader's attention with something memorable. **Background information**. Introduce general topic. **Background information**. Introduce specific topic. **Present thesis**. Name the process you will describe, label the major stages/steps, and give a reason why the reader should care about this process.
Body paragraphs	Paragraph 2	CONTENT: HOW FOOD IS INGESTED **Topic sentence for Stage 1**. → Stage 1A → Stage 1B → Stage 1C → Stage 1D… until you have described all the necessary sub-stages. **Concluding sentence** (*can also be used as a link to the next paragraph).
	Paragraph 3	CONTENT: HOW FOOD IS DIGESTED **Topic sentence for Stage 2**. → Stage 2A → Stage 2B → Stage 2C → Stage 2D…until you have described all the necessary sub-stages. **Concluding sentence** (*can also be used as a link to the next paragraph).
	Paragraph 4	CONTENT: HOW FOOD IS ABSORBED **Topic sentence for Stage 3**. → Stage 3A → Stage 3B → Stage 3C → Stage 3D… until you have described all the necessary sub-stages. **Concluding sentence** (*can also be used as a link to the next paragraph).
Conclusion	Paragraph 5	**Restate thesis**. Remind the reader what your central purpose for writing this essay was (i.e., reiterate why the topic is important). **Summarize**. Review the main points you compared/contrasted. **Final memorable point**. Address or reflect upon your essay in a memorable and thoughtful way that gives the reader something to think about.

Stage 4. Drafting

Use your outline and write a draft of 500–650 words. Make sure you have (1) included all the elements required in each paragraph, (2) transitioned smoothly between sentences and paragraphs, and (3) used clear and concise language. Give your essay a title that is imaginative and captures the essence of what you have written. Set the line spacing, paper size, margins, and font type and size according to the instructions given by your teacher or as specified in the course book or another style guide.

--------------------- **SUBMIT FIRST DRAFT** ------------------------

Stage 5. Post-Writing Activity: Collaborative Peer Review

Now it is time to check your draft through peer review. Swap drafts with one of the other groups in class. Ask them to check what you have written is accurate and detailed enough. They have written about the same topic, so they should have some valuable feedback to give you. Check their draft in return. For added feedback (and fun), use the general scoring rubric at the end of the unit to grade each other's essays.

Stage 6. Edit and Revise Your Draft

When your peers return your draft (and possible score), read their feedback. Then reread, rethink, and rewrite your own draft. It is hard to write a perfect essay on the first try. It is therefore important that you get into the habit of editing and revising to improve your work, as well as the way you approach writing. As you revise your first draft, incorporate the feedback from your peers and add any new ideas that may have come to you as you read their draft.

-------------------- WRITE SECOND DRAFT --------------------

Stage 7. Let Your Revised Draft Sit a While and Then Proofread It Carefully

It is a good idea to give yourself a break from your revised draft before proofreading it. That way, you approach it as an unfamiliar reader would. Moreover, before proofreading, it is a good idea to reread the assignment's instructions or task rubric and/or to look at the grading criteria or scoring rubric again. This will help to ensure that you have not gone off task or missed something important during the revision process.

-------------------- SUBMIT FINAL DRAFT --------------------

2.4.4. Instructional (Directional) Writing

Instructional (or directional) texts use mainly the imperative mood where the subject of the sentence (*you*) is usually omitted, as per the following examples:

Pass the soy sauce.	Move out of the way!	Clean your room.
Please be quiet.	Wait for me.	Take it down.

An instructional text is an informational piece of writing whose goal is for readers to be able to follow steps or a procedure to produce a result. It must therefore be characterized by clarity and directness, and thus it would not include much figurative language. In writing an instructional text, stick to simple, active sentences and easy-to-understand words as much as possible. Include simple descriptive elements such as shape, size, color, and quantity when they will enhance the meanings you are conveying to the reader. Use adverbs when actions need to be carried out in a specific way. For example, _carefully_ place X on top of Y. The following is an example instructional text I wrote about cooking rice.

2.5   Description of an instructional process

1. Rinse the rice with clean water.
2. **Add water.** Add 1 part rice and 2 parts water to a large pot. If you want slightly firmer rice, use 2/3 rice to 1 part water.
3. **Bring the water and rice to the boiling point.** Cover your pot with a tight-fitting lid and place on the stove.
4. **Reduce to a simmer.** Once the water has started bubbling (boiling point), reduce heat to low and maintain a gentle simmer.
5. **Leave to cook.** Cook until the water is absorbed, about 15–18 minutes, depending on the amount of rice and the temperature of the stove. Do not peek too early or too often, as too much steam (thus necessary moisture) will escape. Do not stir the rice while it is cooking, as this will lead to soggy rice.
6. **Let the rice settle.** Turn off the stove and let the pot sit for 10 minutes with its lid on. This ensures that the rice will become fluffy.
7. **Separate the rice with a fork and serve.**

A Guide to Cooking Plain Rice by Neil Bowen

Now, reread the above instructional text and think about how you might change it, based on your own or your family's method of cooking rice. Are there any details you would add (e.g., about the type of rice, the cooking device, the cooking process, or the serving of the rice)? Revise the example text to represent your own

2.4.5. Sequencing Instructions

Moving between instructions is relatively easy. We mainly use transitions of time or cause, as shown in Table 2.3:

Table 2.3. Sequential and causal connectors			
Sequential			
First, second,	Next	Before	Then
At the outset	Following this	Prior to	The last step
To start	Subsequently	After	Finally
Causal			
Consequently	Hence	Thus	Subsequently
As a result	Because	Since	For the purpose of

You can also use some of the circumstance types introduced in Table 2.1, especially the ones that represent the following functions:
- **Contingency**: condition (Why will they do X?): *in case of..., in the event of...*
- Accompaniment: **comitative** (With what will they do X?): *with*; *without*
- Accompaniment: **additive** (What else will they do?): *as well as, besides; instead of...*
- **Manner**: means (How will they do X?): *by, through, with, by means of...*

Exercise 2.16 will help you choose appropriate connecters for sequencing an instructional text. It includes a student essay by Kornravee Sailamul, who chose to write about cooking instant noodles in a rice cooker. As you complete the exercise, pay attention to the language choices she makes, especially the variations in sentence structure. Also, note how she modifies verbs with adverbs in important steps, and how most of the noun phrases are relatively simple.

DESCRIPTIVE WRITING 123

Exercise 2.16. Sequencing instructional information

Fill in the blanks with appropriate connectors or connecting phrases. The blanks can be filled with adverbs, prepositional phrases, or a combination of conjunction + adverb + phrase.

(INTRO.) What can you cook in a rice cooker besides rice? Many things is the answer! One of the most delicious, and easiest, dishes is stir-fry instant noodles. There are only three simple steps: preparing the ingredients, boiling the noodles, and stir-frying the noodles.

(PARA. 2) [1] _____ is to prepare the rice cooker and the ingredients, which are two packages of instant noodles with any flavor, four cups of water, garlic, two eggs, sausages, bacon and any kinds of vegetables that you like. [2] _____ scramble two eggs and then chop garlic, bacon, sausages and vegetables into small pieces. These ingredients will be used in the last step. [3] _____ is to boil the instant noodles in the rice cooker. [4] _____ four cups of water into the rice cooker and close the lid. [5] _____ plug in the rice cooker and turn it on to boil the water. This step might take approximately 10 to 15 minutes. [6] _____ take the dried noodles and seasoning powders out of their packages. [7] _____ the water is boiled, break the noodles into quarters and gently place them into the rice cooker and leave them there for about 3 minutes. [8] _____ the noodles are loosened up from the block, [9] _____ from the rice cooker and drain in a bowl.

(PARA. 3) [10] _____ is to stir-fry the cooked noodles in the rice cooker. Add the chopped garlic and small pieces of bacon into the rice cooker and slowly stir them. Please be careful during this step [11] _____ the grease in the bacon might splash on your face or hands. [12] _____ push the bacon to the side of the rice cooker and add the scrambled eggs in the empty space nearby. [13] _____ the bacon and eggs are well cooked, add the drained noodles and the seasoning powders into the rice cooker and stir them together. [14] _____ add the rest of the cut up ingredients, such as sausages and vegetables, into the rice cooker and [15] _____ tossing everything together for about 3 minutes. [16] _____ everything is coated with seasoning, remove the stir-fry instant noodles from the rice cooker and place it on a serving plate.

(CONCLUSION) Stir-fry instant noodles are an easy and quick dish that can be done by practically anyone. There are only three steps: preparing the ingredients, cooking the noodles, and stir-frying the noodles. If you are looking for a new interesting dish to cook in a rice cooker, instant noodles might be a good idea to try.

How to Cook Stir-Fry Instant Noodles in a Rice Cooker by Kornravee Sailamul

2.4.6. Writing an Instructional Essay

Figure 2.3 shows someone drawing blood from another person's arm. Your task is to write an instructional process paragraph that someone can use to draw someone else's blood. Your final word limit is 250 words.

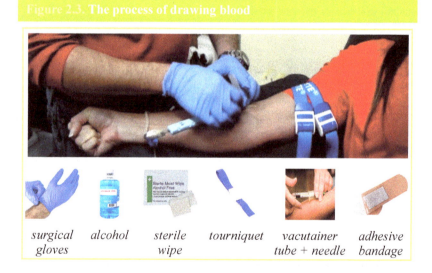

Figure 2.3. The process of drawing blood

surgical gloves   *alcohol*   *sterile wipe*   *tourniquet*   *vacutainer tube + needle*   *adhesive bandage*

Stage 1. Choose a Topic

The topic is "How to draw blood." Do some quick research on this subject to familiarize yourself with the process and the typical items that are used to do it. You may find it useful to watch some online videos or tutorials.

Stage 2. Pre-Writing Activity: Planning and Researching

You need to answer four questions before writing an instructional text. When answering these questions, think carefully about the details and assume very little. Keep everything in order and keep your instructions short, clear, and specific. Write only in the active voice. Keep your vocabulary simple. If you have to use technical vocabulary, then think about describing what the item looks like. That way, the person following your instructions can identify the object without having to research it.

Write down your answers to the following four questions. If you are not sure what each of the items listed below Figure 2.3 are, then do some more research. Only ask your teacher as a last resource.

1. What is the goal of this instructional process? (Be detailed.)
2. How many steps are involved in this process? Is there any danger involved with any of these steps?
3. What resources do you need at each step of this process? Do any of them need to be prepared beforehand?
4. When the task is complete, what next? Any recommendations or other memorable point(s) you want to leave the reader with?

Stage 3. Using a Sequence Chain for an Outline

One way to plan an instructional essay is to use a sequence chain. Use your answers to the four questions above to create a sequence chain of your own. Think about the essential details and specific words needed in each stage. You will need to be very specific because some steps in this process of taking blood from someone are potentially harmful or dangerous. If you have to use technical vocabulary, think about describing what the item looks like, especially if it needs to be combined with another item.

Stage 4. Write Your First Draft

Use your outline and write a first draft of no more than 250 words. Make sure you have included all of the equipment and steps required and have transitioned smoothly between steps. Also, be sure to use clear and concise language. Give it a title that is clear, and if possible also imaginative without being inappropriate, and that captures the essence of what you have written. Set the line spacing, paper size, margins, and font type and size according to the instructions given by your teacher or as specified in your course book or style guide.

-------------------- **SUBMIT FIRST DRAFT** ----------------------

Stage 5. Post-Writing Activity: Collaborative Peer Review

Now it is time to check your draft through peer review. Give the items needed to draw blood (your props) to two people. Read out your description and see if they can act out the process of drawing blood smoothly and safely.

Stage 6. Edit and Revise Your Draft

Edit your paragraph based on the feedback you got from the physical activity of trying to draw blood. Also, address any feedback the audience gives you. Ensure that the finished draft is under 250 words.

------------------- **WRITE SECOND DRAFT** --------------------

Stage 7. Let Your Revised Draft Sit a While and Then Proofread It Carefully

Do not forget to proofread the revised draft before you submit it, and try to finish well before any established deadlines. That way, you do not need to rush through last minute. It is also a good idea to give yourself a few days break from your revised draft before proofreading it. That way, you approach it as an unfamiliar reader would.

-------------------- **SUBMIT FINAL DRAFT** ----------------------

2.5. WRITING A DESCRIPTIVE ESSAY

2.5.1. Writing the First Draft

Stage 1. Choose a Topic

One of the best examples for witnessing all around descriptive details in action are in food and travel shows. These programs are usually hosted by strong personalities who work in busy kitchens or visit interesting places, while also taking part in unusual or challenging activities. In other words, we can write detailed descriptions of these programs in terms of people, places, and processes.

For this task, you will write a five-paragraph descriptive essay using a food or travel show as the source of your information. You are free to choose whichever show you wish, but make sure that it will be interesting to write about. For example, some of my previous students chose to describe the people, places, and processes in an episode of *An Idiot Abroad*, which is a British TV show produced by Ricky Gervais and Steve Merchant. The host, Karl Pilkington, never wanted to do a travel show and would much rather stay at home. It makes for entertaining viewing watching this reluctant host being forced to go outside of his comfort zone. Another interesting travel show is *Amazing Hotels: Life beyond the Lobby*. Popular food-oriented shows are *Restaurant Impossible* and several that involve cooking contests, including *The Great British Bake-Off*, *Kids Baking Championship*, *Beat Bobby Flay*, *Guy's Grocery Games*, and *Chopped*. An enjoyable show that combines both travel and food is *Gordon Ramsay: Uncharted*.

Stage 2. Pre-Writing Activity: Planning and Researching

Use a combination of techniques to make notes as you watch your chosen TV show. For instance, you could use a concept map to gather descriptive notes for your person, a spatial sketch for your description of the place, and a sequence chain to generate notes about the process (event).

Stage 3. Using a Template for an Outline

The students who wrote about *An Idiot Abroad* structured their essays as follows. Feel free to adapt this for your own purposes.

Introduction	Paragraph 1	**Hook**. Grab your reader's attention with something memorable. **Background information**. Introduce general topic. **Background information**. Introduce specific topic. **Present thesis.** Introduce the three main ideas you will cover in each body paragraph and give a reason why the reader should care.
Body paragraphs	Paragraph 2	CONTENT: DESCRIBING THE HOST'S APPEARANCE + PERSONALITY **Topic sentence**. → Supporting detail 1 → Supporting detail 2 → Supporting detail 3 **Concluding sentence** (*can also be used as a link to the next paragraph).
	Paragraph 3	CONTENT: DESCRIBING AN INTERESTING PLACE IN THE PROGRAM **Topic sentence**. → Supporting detail 1 → Supporting detail 2 → Supporting detail 3 **Concluding sentence** (*can also be used as a link to the next paragraph).
	Paragraph 4	CONTENT: DESCRIBING A PROCESS SOMEONE DID **Topic sentence**. → Supporting detail 1 → Supporting detail 2 → Supporting detail 3 **Concluding sentence** (*can also be used as a link to the next paragraph).
Conclusion	Paragraph 5	**Restate thesis**. Remind the reader what your central purpose for writing this essay was (i.e., reiterate why the topic is important). **Summarize**. Review the main points you described. **Final memorable point**. Address or reflect upon your essay in a memorable and thoughtful way that gives the reader something to think about).

Stage 4. Write Your First Draft

Use your outline and write a first draft of between 500–650 words. Make sure you describe your selected person's (the host's or other focal person's) personality as well as their appearance, and remember to "show, don't tell" where appropriate. Also, remember to include some figurative language in your draft and try to establish some kind of tone in your essay (e.g., sarcastic, optimistic, sincere, or amusing). Double-space your work so it easier to give feedback on, and set the paper size, margins, and font type and size according to the instructions given by your teacher or as specified in the course book or another style guide. Give your draft an imaginative title that reflects the content and tone of your essay.

2.5.2. Writing the Second Draft

Stage 5. Post-Writing Activity: Collaborative Peer Review

Now it is time to check your first draft through peer review. Swap drafts with one of your peers in class. Ask them to check what you have written. Check their draft in return and either make notes directly on their draft or in a separate document. For added feedback, use the scoring rubric at the end of the unit to grade the drafts. At the very minimum, your feedback should answer the following questions:

1. Is there a hook in the introduction? If not, suggest one.

2. Does the introduction clearly set the scene through giving an overview of the show (e.g., by moving from a general to specific focus on the topic)? Comment on how it does or does not do this.

3. Is there a clear and concise thesis statement in the introduction? What does it suggest will be the outcome of the essay? Moreover, does it give you an indication of the tone of the essay to come? If so, what will the essay's tone be?

4. Are there fully developed topic sentences at the start of each body paragraph? Put "TS?" next to any that are incomplete or unclear.
5. Is there a good balance between describing the focal person's appearance and describing their personality? What could be improved?

6. Underline at least one example of figurative language. Is it a good example?
7. How many senses are evoked in each body paragraph? Make suggestions for improvements.

8. What is the overall tone to the piece (if any)? What emotions does it evoke in the reader? Note how you felt after reading it.

Stage 6. Edit and Revise Your Draft

When your peer returns your draft (and possible score), read their feedback. Then reread, rethink, and rewrite your own draft. It is hard to write a perfect essay on the first try. It is therefore important that you get into the habit of editing and revising to improve your work. As you revise your first draft, incorporate the feedback from your peer and add any new ideas that may have come to you as you read their draft. Check your edits against the scoring rubric for descriptive writing at the end of unit. See if you can identify what the strong and weak points of your essay are.

Stage 7. Let Your Revised Draft Sit a While and Then Proofread It Carefully

It is a good idea to give yourself a break from your revised draft before proofreading it. That way, you approach it as an unfamiliar reader would. Also, before proofreading, it is usually a good idea to reread the instructions for the assignment or task rubric and/or to look at the grading criteria or scoring rubric again. This will help to ensure that you have not gone off task or missed something important during the revision process.

--------------------- **SUBMIT FINAL DRAFT** -----------------------

132 ESSENTIAL KNOWLEDGE AND SKILLS FOR ESSAY WRITING

APPENDIX 2A.
SCORING RUBRIC FOR DESCRIPTIVE WRITING

MICRO-LEVEL MISTAKES
→ One point deducted for every 5 micro-level mistakes: _____ divided by **5** =

IDEAS / CONTENT _____ out of **25** (5 points per item)
→ Title is imaginative and reflects the essay's contents
→ Introduction unveils topic and creatively grabs reader's attention
→ Images are included in relevant places. They are captioned and explained
→ Essay includes appeal to the five senses (taste, touch, sound, sight, smell)
→ Figurative language helps illustrate/explain/describe

ORGANIZATION _____ out of **25** (5 points per item)
→ Thesis sentence concludes introduction and reveals/suggests main point
→ Topic sentences start each body paragraph: one topic = one paragraph
→ Body paragraphs are well developed with supporting information
→ Body paragraphs flow seamlessly into each other
→ Conclusion relates to the introductory paragraph

WORD CHOICE _____ out of **25** (5 points per item)
→ Strong, active verbs are used throughout wherever necessary
→ Specific, detailed noun phrases are used wherever required
→ Adjectives are precisely chosen and well placed
→ No repetitive words, clichés, or general wordiness
→ Makes good use of circumstantial elements to add descriptive details

SENTENCE FLUENCY _____ out of **16** (4 points per item)
→ Variety of sentence lengths
→ Variety of sentence beginnings
→ Complete sentences (no run-ons or fragments)
→ Transition words and phrases are used where appropriate

CONVENTIONS _____ out of **4** (2 points per item)
→ Uses at least one kind of advanced punctuation (colon or semicolon)
→ Follows the instructions given in the task prompt or rubric

Total _____ out of **100**

DESCRIPTIVE WRITING   133

APPENDIX 2B. UNIT 2 ANSWER KEY

Exercise 2.1
Answers will vary so consult with your peers or teacher.

Exercise 2.2
Answers will vary but here are my similes:
Image 1: *The tree was like a giant makeup brush.*
Image 2: *The tree was as pink and fluffy as cotton candy.*
Image 3: *The bonsai was as a toy soldier rising from his grave.*

Exercise 2.3
1. Personified object = *wind / moon*;   Action = *whispering / gazing*
2. Personified object = *sun*;   Action = *beating*
3. Personified object = *flowers*;   Action = *dancing*
4. Personified idea = *deadline*;   Action = *creeping up*
5. Personified object = *engine*;   Action / trait = *coughing and spluttering / agonizing* (feeling pain)

Exercise 2.4
1. Simile: Literally – *the man was picking up lots and lots of plates.*
2. Simile: Literally – *the students in the class were being very loud and chaotic.*
3. Metaphor: Literally – *my bed was very soft and comfortable.*
4. Simile: Literally – *his arms were very skinny and pale.*
5. Simile: Literally – *those girls are very close and very similar.*
6. Metaphor: Literally – *she did not make any sounds or movement.*
7. Metaphor: Literally – *today was a series of ups and downs emotionally.*
8. Simile: Literally – *he made small, sharp movements that were very fast.*

134 ESSENTIAL KNOWLEDGE AND SKILLS FOR ESSAY WRITING

Exercise 2.5

1. Alliteration: *Radiant reds, peaceful purples, and gentle greens break up the barren blue backdrop.*
2. Hyperbole: *A wetsuit that could double as a yoga mat.*
3. Onomatopoeia: *Sssssss*; *usshh ..., usshh ... usshh*
4. Metaphor/Personification: *The reef itself is a sun-bleached homunculus.*
5. Simile: *descend slowly, like a teabag in a very large pot; Like a camera focusing in on its subject.*

Exercise 2.6

1. Enhancing qualifier (prepositional phrase): location: place (*where?*)
2. Enhancing circumstance (adverb): manner: quality (*how?*)
3. Enhancing qualifier (prepositional phrase): location: place (*where?*)
4. Enhancing qualifier (prepositional phrase): location: place (*where?*)
5. Enhancing circumstance (prepositional phrase): location: place (*where?*)
6. Enhancing qualifier (prepositional phrase): cause: purpose (*what for?*)
7. Enhancing qualifier (prepositional phrase): location: place (*where?*)
8. Enhancing circumstance (prepositional phrase): location: place (*where?*)
9. Enhancing circumstance (prepositional phrase): location: place (*where?*)
10. Enhancing circumstance (prepositional phrase): location: place (*where?*)
11. Enhancing circumstance (prep. phrase): manner: comparison (*how/like what?*)
12. Enhancing circumstance (adverb): manner: quality (*how?*)
13. Enhancing circumstance (prepositional phrase): location: time (*when?*)
14. Enhancing circumstance (adverb): manner: quality (*how?*)

15. Enhancing qualifier (prepositional phrase): location: place (*where?*)

You should have noticed how the adjectives did more than just add details to the nouns they modified. They helped the writer to (a) add their subjective stance toward the things they were describing and/or (b) narrow the descriptions, making them more specific. For example, in the first sentence, she states that the thermal bath is "an <u>unmissable</u> tourist attraction" – the adjective *unmissable* gives us an insight into how she evaluates the baths. Similarly, the use of *elegant* in "an elegant white building" (third sentence) tells us about her reaction to seeing the building, whereas the addition of *white* narrows the description of the building to a particular color.

Exercise 2.7
Answers will vary so consult with your peers or teacher.

Exercise 2.8 (answers will vary):
1. *For my birthday, he bought me a <u>white gold Pearlmaster 39</u>.*
2. *We ate at a <u>cute little restaurant in Soho</u>.*
3. *I have an <u>adorable little pug who has the face of an old man</u>.*
4. *Sonny bought a <u>lemon of a car</u>.*
5. *My place has a view of the <u>bustling waterway.</u>*
6. *The food was <u>to die for</u>.*
7. *The <u>pale crescent moon</u> was a wondrous sight at night.*
8. *We went on an awful trip around the island on <u>a rickety old longboat</u>.*

Exercise 2.9
Answers will vary so consult with your peers or teacher.

Exercise 2.10
The correct sequence of sentences is as follows:
<u>BODY PARAGRAPH 1.</u> 1 = a, 2 = d, 3 = f, 4 = b, 5 = e, 6 = c.
<u>BODY PARAGRAPH 2.</u> 1 = n, 2 = o, 3 = l, 4 = q, 5 = p, 6 = m.
<u>BODY PARAGRAPH 3.</u> 1 = I, 2 = h, 3 = g, 4 = k, 5 = j.

Exercise 2.11–2.14
Answers will vary so consult with your peers or teacher.

Exercise 2.15
The correct sequence of sentences is as follows:
<u>BODY PARAGRAPH 1.</u> 1 = d, 2 = a, 3 = c, 4 = b, 5 = e, 6 = f.
<u>BODY PARAGRAPH 2.</u> 1 = I, 2 = k, 3 = h, 4 = j, 5 = g.
<u>BODY PARAGRAPH 3.</u> 1 = m, 2 = l, 3 = n.

Exercise 2.16
Your answers will vary but the following connectors are found in the original essay:
1 = *The first step*, **2** = *Then*, **3** = *The second step*, **4** = *Add*, **5** = *Next*, **6** = *While waiting*, **7** = *When*, **8** = *Once*, **9** = *remove them*, **10** = *The last step*, **11** = *because*, **12** = *Then*, **13** = *After*, **14** = *Next*, **15** = *continue*, **16** = *After*.

Unit 3
NARRATIVE WRITING

Unit Goals

Upon completing this unit, you should be able to demonstrate the following knowledge and skills:

- Generate ideas and gather information for narrative writing.
- Use characterization and dialogue to move a plot forward.
- Establish the main components of a plot: setting the scene, rising action, climax, falling action, and resolution.
- Organize and sequence ideas to be presented in narratives.
- Write a narrative essay.

Definition

Consider the following quote from John Barthes' (1975) *An Introduction to the Structural Analysis of Narrative*:

> Narrative is present in myth, legend, fables, tales, short stories, epics, history, tragedy, drame (suspense drama), comedy, pantomime, paintings … stained-glass windows, movies, local news, conversation … It is present at all times, in all places, in all societies; indeed narrative starts with the very history of mankind; there is not, there has never been anywhere, people without narrative

… Like life itself, it is there, international, transhistorical, transcultural. (Barthes, 1975, p. 237)

In other words, narratives are universal to the human experience and are inextricably tied to the history of mankind. Indeed, some of the earliest evidence of cultures telling stories dates back 30,000 years (Chauvet, 1996).

A narrative is a story told through a narrator, and it is usually structured around a plot or plots. There is a sequence of actions and there is a clear beginning, middle, and end. In other words, a narrative has a series of details that will clarify for the reader what happened to who, when, where, and why? The plot deals with how these elements are grouped together and sequenced to form key conflicts, climaxes, and resolutions (how the story unfolds). Thus, a narrative is not to be confused with other storytelling formats, such as movies or video games, where the story is conveyed through the characters on the screen, primarily through their dialogue and actions. In addition, although some movies and video games do have narration in the form of an omniscient (all-seeing) narrator, the story unfolds on the screen and thus there is less room for our imagination to impact upon the scene, action, or emotions of the characters.

> **Narrative** *Telling the details of a story (who, what, where, when, and why?) through a plot (how a story unfolds).*
>
> **Plot** *How and when key conflicts are introduced and resolved: A series of action→ consequence→ action chains.*

The relationship between story and plot can be seen in Figure 3.1 (for a fuller description in relation to film, see Bordwell and Thompson, 2020, pp. 75–77).

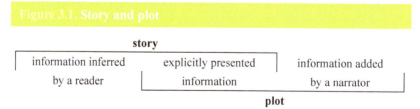

Figure 3.1 Story and plot

As the figure represents, a story unfolds through the interpretation of the reader, who pieces together the information presented by the narrator. The narrator chooses which information to present and which information to leave out, and thus generates a plot structure. The plot has five broad characteristics:

1. It involves a conflict, complication, or problem needing to be resolved.
2. It makes use of a central character through whom the conflict arises.
3. There is movement in time, sequenced through beginning, middle, and end.
4. Events are clearly connected, often with elements of cause and effect, and lead in a logical progression from beginning to end of the story.
5. It cycles through five rhetorical moves: *setting the scene, rising action(s), climax, falling action(s)*, and *resolution*.

Although there are no hard and fast rules for how a narrative should be written, there are several suggestions that can help you write an effective and appealing narrative paragraph, paragraph series, or essay. General guidelines for narratives include strong verbs; good dialogue; well-developed characterization; "show, don't tell"; and a sequence of actions or events that rise and fall, peaking at a central problem and ending with a resolution that leads to a satisfying conclusion or "crowning event," such as one that proves a point or provides a moral or lesson about life.

A good story is built to pull the reader along to its conclusion, often by including hints of what is to come. In addition, as for descriptions, narratives may deviate from grammatical norms. For instance, when reading a short story or a novel, you may come across fragments (e.g., single word sentences), split infinitives (*to boldly go*), sentences starting with coordinating conjunctions, paragraphs consisting of one sentence or one word, or the use of slang, contractions, and all capitals when representing dialogue.

140 ESSENTIAL KNOWLEDGE AND SKILLS FOR ESSAY WRITING

Let us look at an example of an opening paragraph from a student's narrative essay (Example 3.1). This paragraph is part of a narrative about a post-apocalyptic world filled with zombies. As you read it, try to spot as many deviations as you can.

3.1	Example of an opening paragraph from a narrative essay

A low mist hung in the morning air. There were no sounds. No birds. No traffic. Not even a rustling of trash in the deserted streets. Anna and Sean tiptoed forward, listening for any sounds. Any hint of activity. Any sign of danger.

They had no idea where the Deads were. All was silent and still. Disturbingly silent and still. This was bothering the two friends. They moved slowly but their hearts raced. They had no choice but to keep walking. Without medicine, Anna's wound would become infected quickly.

They stepped out of the alley and turned left on the main road.

"Zombies! Run! Run!"

Extract from *Find (Day 7)* by Vipavee Thongsuk

This introduction sets the scene, introduces two characters, and then builds to a central problem (a climax). It also raises the reader's curiosity about what will happen next: How will the two characters overcome their current predicament of being confronted with zombies? You will find out later in this unit when you read the rest of this essay.

In the sections which follow, we will build upon these basic elements of a plot and develop narratives that are more complex in their rhetorical structuring. We will also consider multiple characters, settings, dialogue, "golden details," and the all-important rise^fall plot structure, which is essential to most narratives and, without which, a narrative becomes a *recount* (a reporting or retelling of events).

3.1. KEY SKILLS

How you tell a story to your reader is just as important as what you tell them. This is known as the ***mode of narration***. The mode of narration includes choices about which tense you will primarily use (*narrative tense*) and the tone, style, and personal distance of your word choices and sentence structures (*narrative voice*). This unit primarily focuses on the latter: narrative voice (the narrator's style of telling the story).

The first section outlines how narrative perspective (3.1.1) can contribute to your narrative voice. This element reveals who is telling the story and thus sets up a relationship between the narrator, characters in a story, and the reader. The second section explores how *dialogue* (3.1.2), the spoken words of your characters, can contribute to your narrative voice by bringing your characters alive. The last section looks at how descriptive choices in *strong, vivid verbs* (3.1.3) and "*golden details*" (3.1.4) can bring your story world alive. Two other elements of narrative voice will be introduced as the unit progresses. These are *action* (action→consequence chains) and *exposition* (setting the scene), both of which help the narrator transition through time and space and thus help the story move forward.

3.1.1. Narrative Perspective

First-Person Narration

The narrator's perspective (or point of view) from which a story is told can originate with the speaker or writer. This is called *first-person narration*. First-person narration uses the pronoun *I* (as in the first example below) or, less frequently, *we* if the narrator is speaking as part of a group (as in the second example below):

> → *I* woke to the loud ding-ding from a message on my phone. *I* reached across the bed and slid the phone towards *me*.
>
> → "There was no possibility of taking a walk that day. *We* had been wandering, indeed, in the leafless shrubbery an hour in the morning."
>
> From *Jane Eyre* by Charlotte Brontë (1847/1998, p. 1)

First-person narration can also represent the perspective of a main character as if they are the one telling the story. A well-known

142 ESSENTIAL KNOWLEDGE AND SKILLS FOR ESSAY WRITING

example is the beginning of *David Copperfield* by Charles Dickens (1869/2009), which is shown in Example 3.2.

> **3.2 Example of first-person narration**
>
> Whether I shall turn out to be the hero of my own life, or whether that station will be held by anybody else, these pages must show. To begin my life with the beginning of my life, I record that I was born (as I have been informed and believe) on a Friday, at twelve o'clock at night. It was remarked that the clock began to strike, and I began to cry, simultaneously.
>
> Extract from *David Copperfield* (Dickens, 1869/2009, Chapter 1, paragraph 1)

In the above extract, Dickens uses first-person narration to set up the start of this novel as an autobiographical account. In the very first sentence, the reader is pulled into the life of the protagonist, David Copperfield, and this character is placed firmly at the center of the unfolding story—Dickens even switches from active to passive voice at one stage to avoid introducing anyone else (i.e., the person who told Copperfield about his birth).

In short stories and novels, first-person narration—*narration in I*—tends to emphasize the speaker or the narrator. This perspective is particularly useful when you want a story to unfold through the senses, thoughts, and feelings of the main character. Read Example 3.3, which is from *Jane Eyre* by Charlotte Brontë (1847/1998).

> **3.3 Example of first-person narration**
>
> I have told you, reader, that I had learnt to love Mr. Rochester: I could not unlove him now, merely because I found that he had ceased to notice me—because I might pass hours in his presence, and he would never once turn his eyes in my direction—because I saw all his attentions appropriated by a great lady, who scorned to touch me with the hem of her robes as she passed;
>
> Extract from *Jane Eyre* (Brontë, 1847/1998, p. 222)

Charlotte Brontë wrote this novel, *Jane Eyre*, from the first-person perspective. We accompany Jane as she moves through childhood, young adulthood, and on to her emotional relationship with Mr. Rochester. The use of first-person narration reveals all of Jane's inner thoughts, which helps us to understand her actions and motivations, including why she is attracted to Mr. Rochester.

Second-Person Narration

The point of view from which a story is told can also originate with the reader. This is called *second-person narration*. It uses the second-person pronoun *you*, as shown in the following examples:

> → *You* wake up to the loud ding-ding from a message on *your* phone. *You* reach across the bed and slide the phone toward *yourself*.
> → *You*'ve lived through COVID and all its variants. *You* might have caught it *yourself* and most likely know others who have succumbed. *You* are aware of all the controversy over vaccination and masking. *You* are tired of it all.

Second-person narration is a perfectly good theoretical construct—there is no grammatical reason not to use it—yet it remains rare and problematic in practice. It tends to shift emphasis away from the writer, even away from the story, and toward the reader. Addressed directly by the narrator, the reader is supposedly drawn into the story as a pseudo-participant. For this reason, it is most typically found in "Choose Your Own Adventure" type books. Bantam Books, for example, published 184 of these second-person point of view books. In these books, the reader takes on a role relevant to the adventure, such as a climber, doctor, or private investigator. At key points in the plot (usually every three or four pages), the reader is asked to make a choice between two or three options. The option they choose sends them to a certain page; thus, they have some control over the unfolding plot. Ultimately, the reader's choices lead to one of a number of possible endings (typically somewhere between 7 and 44).

Despite its limited appeal, second-person narration is occasionally used by authors to engage a reader. For instance, in the *Jane Eyre* extract above (Example 3.3), Brontë writes, "I have told *you*, reader." Another well-known example can be seen in the opening of *Moby-Dick* by Herman Melville (1851/2001). The novel starts by <u>addressing the reader</u> (*you* is understood) and then shifts to first-person narration:

144 ESSENTIAL KNOWLEDGE AND SKILLS FOR ESSAY WRITING

> **3.4   Example of shifting between second- and first-person narration**
>
> Call me Ishmael. Some years ago - never mind how long precisely - having little or no money in my purse, and nothing particular to interest me on shore, I thought I would sail about a little and see the watery part of the world. It is a way I have of driving off the spleen and regulating the circulation.
>
> Extract from *Moby Dick* (Melville, 1851/2001, p. 1)

Third-Person Narration

Finally, the point of view from which a story is told can also originate from outside the narrator. This is called *third-person narration*. It uses third-person pronouns (*he*, *she*, *it*, and *they*), named people, or other beings or entities that the writer enables to tell the story, or subject nouns describing those persons, beings, or entities, as shown below:

→ *Peter* woke up to the loud ding-ding from a message on his phone. *He* reached across the bed and slid the phone toward himself.

→ "*It* was the White Rabbit, trotting slowly back again, and looking anxiously about as *it* went, as if *it* had lost something." From *Alice's Adventures in Wonderland* by Lewis Carroll (1865/2008, Chapter IV, para. 1)

→ *The old house* had known and cared for many families. Over the years *it* had watched over a total of 17 children and their pets, including those belonging to *its* current occupants, the Reverend Perry Peterson and his wife Sarah.

Third-person narration tends to shift the emphasis away from the narrator (writer) and the reader, and toward the events and characters of the story itself. It is the most common form of narration and is probably the easiest form to use. Read the extract presented in Example 3.5 below. It is from *War and Peace* by Leo Tolstoy (1869/2001). Tolstoy uses a third-person perspective to put the reader on the outside, looking in.

NARRATIVE WRITING   145

> **3.5   Example of third-person narration**
>
> Just then another visitor entered the drawing room: Prince Andrew Bolkónski, the little princess' husband. He was a very handsome young man, of medium height, with firm, clearcut features. Everything about him, from his weary, bored expression to his quiet, measured step, offered a most striking contrast to his quiet, little wife. It was evident that he not only knew everyone in the drawing room, but had found them to be so tiresome that it wearied him to look at or listen to them. And among all these faces that he found so tedious, none seemed to bore him so much as that of his pretty wife.
>
> Extract from *War and Peace* (Tolstoy, 1869/2001, p. 19)

In this extract, we are introduced to Prince Andrew, a main character, and we learn that he is handsome with clean features. We then learn of the Prince's thoughts about the other guests (and his wife), but we never hear him saying or thinking these things directly. Instead, his thoughts and feelings are mainly implied through his actions.

3.1.2. Dialogue

In a narrative, a dialogue involves two or more characters talking. Dialogue is useful to show reactions between characters, express thoughts and emotions, and build characterization. Here are some basic guidelines for using dialogue:

→ Place quotation marks around the words spoken by one character.

→ If a different character begins to speak, start a new line. (In this way, it will be clear to your reader who is speaking at any given time.)

→ Write character's words exactly as they speak them, complete with slang and errors in grammar and pronunciation.

→ Separate dialogue tags (see below) from quoted speech by commas.

146   ESSENTIAL KNOWLEDGE AND SKILLS FOR ESSAY WRITING

The examples below illustrate how a writer can use dialogue in different ways. As you read them, pay attention to the punctuation and how the reader is able to know exactly who is speaking at any given time.

3.6 Example of using dialogue tags to create pause for thought
"The beer's nice and cool," the man said.
"It's lovely," the girl said.
"It's really an awfully simple operation, Jig," the man said. "It's not really an operation at all."
The girl looked at the ground the table legs rested on.
"I know you wouldn't mind it, Jig. It's really not anything. It's just to let the air in."
The girl did not say anything.
Extract from *Hills Like White Elephants* (Hemingway, 1927/2016, p. 51)

Ernest Hemingway was famous for his style of dialogue. He often used *dialogue tags* to break up speech and indicate that a character is pausing for thought. Example 3.6 is an extract from *Hills like White Elephants* (Hemingway, 1927/2016). It illustrates how dialogue can be used to establish a relationship between characters. In this section of a conversation, Hemingway sets up a clear power dynamic between *the man* and *Jig / the girl*, wherein the woman is feeling insecure and seeking reassurance from the man.

In the next extract (Example 3.7), which is from *Alice's Adventures in Wonderland* by Lewis Carroll (1865/2008), dialogue is used to establish the whacky nature of the character, the Cheshire Cat. Note the use of the em dash (—) to signal an interruption, and italics for emphasizing the intensity with which some words are said. Also note the use of commas next to the dialogue tags. In your own writing, you can also use three dots … to signal a trailing off to silence and/or a pause in speech.

NARRATIVE WRITING   147

3.7   Example of using dialogue to build a character

"Would you tell me, please, which way I ought to go from here?"

"That depends a good deal on where you want to get to," said the Cat.

"I don't much care where—" said Alice.

"Then it doesn't matter which way you go," said the Cat.

"—so long as I get *somewhere*," Alice added as an explanation.

"Oh, you're sure to do that," said the Cat, "if you only walk long enough."

Alice felt that this could not be denied, so she tried another question. "What sort of people live about here?"

"In *that* direction," the Cat said, waving its right paw round, "lives a Hatter: and in *that* direction," waving the other paw, "lives a March Hare. Visit either you like: they're both mad."

"But I don't want to go among mad people," Alice remarked.

"Oh, you can't help that," said the Cat: "we're all mad here. I'm mad. You're mad."

"How do you know I'm mad?" said Alice.

"You must be," said the Cat, "or you wouldn't have come here."

Alice didn't think that proved it at all; however, she went on. "And how do you know that you're mad?"

"To begin with," said the Cat, "a dog's not mad. You grant that?"

"I suppose so," said Alice.

"Well, then," the Cat went on, "you see, a dog growls when it's angry, and wags its tail when it's pleased. Now *I* growl when I'm pleased, and wag my tail when I'm angry. Therefore I'm mad."

"*I* call it purring, not growling," said Alice.

"Call it what you like," said the Cat. "Do you play croquet with the Queen to-day?"

"I should like it very much," said Alice, "but I haven't been invited yet."

"You'll see me there," said the Cat, and vanished.

> Extract from *Alice's Adventures in Wonderland* (Carroll, 1865/2008, pp. 71–72)

Now it is your turn to put what you have just learned into practice. As you complete the following exercise, think carefully about your use of dialogue tags and punctuation. Also feel free to use non-standard spelling and contractions to represent your characters' spoken words, and remember to create dialogue that sounds natural when it is read out loud.

> **Exercise 3.1. Writing dialogue**
>
> This exercise will help you create a dialogue-only scene. It illustrates why you should carefully choose who is interacting to maximize conflict, tension, and/or emotion.

In pairs, choose two inanimate objects that are usually paired together in order to function, such as shoes and shoelaces, knife and fork, pen and paper, padlock and key, tablet and stylus, or mobile phone and its charger. Write your selections below.

1.   2.

Now, imagine what kind of scene might unfold if your two items could talk to each other. What tensions might arise? What comedy might ensue? Might there be a secret love affair going on? Write a one-page dialogue between your inanimate items as though they could speak to each other. When you are finished, and if you are feeling brave, act out your dialogue for your peers.

3.1.3. Strong, Vivid Verbs

Good narratives make use of strong, vivid verbs to describe the action. Contrast *I drove to work* with *I raced to work*. Which one tells the reader more? This is one aspect of "show, don't tell." In other words, good story telling is immersive: it puts the reader into the heart of the action. What better way to do this than to make the reader imagine what is going on? If you simply tell them what is going on, then you are not really giving them much room to use their imagination, and thus the role of the narrator becomes a pointless one—they may as well just go and watch the movie version. Consequently, as in descriptive writing, consider using all five senses in your narratives—not just the sense of sight—to add details about what characters hear, smell, and physically feel as they move through your story-world.

NARRATIVE WRITING   149

Exercise 3.2 presents a range of activities. Think about how you would describe these activities to someone. In a story, you may want to focus on the action: that is, the verbs.

> **Exercise 3.2. Choosing strong, accurate verbs**
>
> Make a list of ten actions or states of being (verbs) that reflect what is happening in the images below. Go beyond the obvious choices and use a good thesaurus and/or dictionary to help you.

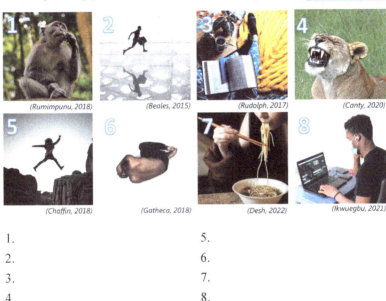

(Rumimpunu, 2018)   (Beales, 2015)   (Rudolph, 2017)   (Canty, 2020)

(Chaffin, 2018)   (Gatheca, 2018)   (Desh, 2022)   (Ikwuegbu, 2021)

1.   5.
2.   6.
3.   7.
4.   8.

Look at the words you have written down. Are they strong and/or specific? Do they accurately convey what is going on to the reader? Precise, vivid verbs help to draw the reader into the action. They can also be used to invoke emotions or give clues about a character's state of mind. For example, compare the following two sentences:

> → The boy was mad. He left the room and went upstairs.
> → The boy stormed out and stomped up the stairs.

Notice that the verbs *stormed* and *stomped* show the reader the boy's emotional state. We have also established a little bit of alliteration with the *st-* consonant cluster, which is, itself, an explosive sound when you physically produce it. Together, the words' connotations and the physical articulation and repetition of the sounds make the second sentence more interesting and emotive.

The next exercise will give you practice in selecting stronger, more vivid verbs.

Exercise 3.3. Using strong, vivid verbs

Next to each of the sentences below, suggest replacements for the underlined words or phrases. Suggest stronger, more vivid verbs/phrases so that you are showing and not telling.

1. The flower <u>moved</u> in the wind.

2. She <u>carefully left</u> the room.

3. Pam <u>got</u> out of bed at 05:00 am.

4. In an instant, the police <u>came</u> through the door.

5. He <u>ate</u> the cookie.

6. The lazy dog <u>walked</u> behind his owner.

7. Without hesitating, she <u>took</u> the money.

8. He was <u>scared</u> of snakes.

9. She <u>looked at him</u>.

10. She <u>told</u> him, "No. I <u>don't like</u> pizza"

Now go back and look at the list of eight words you used to describe the actions and states of being in Exercise 3.2. Can you improve upon any of these by making them stronger and/or more vivid?

Being able to choose strong, vivid words will help add descriptive power to your writing. Moreover, good descriptions can evoke strong emotional reactions from readers, especially when you make use of figurative language and strong words.

3.1.4. Golden Details

In novels, powerful descriptive elements are sometimes called *golden details*. Golden details are unique and elegant descriptions, which the reader will remember. In this section, you will read three such descriptions. As you read them, note how they describe things in such a way that they are completely original and unforgettable.

The first example of a golden detail (Example 3.8) is from *A Christmas Carol* by Charles Dickens (1843/1992). This book is about an elderly miser called Ebenezer Scrooge. He is a cruel and stingy man until he is visited by three ghosts (Christmas Past, Present, and Future). The ghosts show him the error of his ways, and he becomes a generous and kind man at the end of the story. In the following extract from the start of the novel, Dickens paints a picture of Scrooge as cold, distant, and solitary—not someone you would want to be friends with. Dickens does this through a combination of showing not telling, vivid language, and figurative language (metaphor and simile).

3.8   Example of golden details (1)

Oh! But he was a tight-fisted hand at the grindstone, Scrooge! A squeezing, wrenching, grasping, scraping, clutching, covetous old sinner! Hard and sharp as flint, from which no steel had ever struck out generous fire; secret, and self-contained, and solitary as an oyster. The cold within him froze his old features, nipped his pointed nose, shriveled his cheek, stiffened his gait; made his eyes red, his thin lips blue; and spoke out shrewdly in his grating voice.

Extract from *A Christmas Carol* (Dickens, 1843/1992, Stave One, para 6)

The next golden detail is from *Moby-Dick by* Herman Melville (1851/2001). This book is about the maniacal Captain Ahab and his quest to kill a monstrous white whale named Moby-Dick. The book is an allegory—a moral lesson—that aims to reveal the foolishness of unquestionably chasing that which can never be captured/obtained. In this extract, Captain Ahab and his crew have found the whale and are chasing it down.

152 ESSENTIAL KNOWLEDGE AND SKILLS FOR ESSAY WRITING

> **3.9 Example of golden details (2)**
>
> As they neared him, the ocean grew still more smooth; seemed drawing a carpet over its waves; seemed a noon-meadow, so serenely it spread. At length the breathless hunter came so nigh his seemingly unsuspecting prey, that his entire dazzling hump was distinctly visible, sliding along the sea as if an isolated thing, and continually set in a revolving ring of finest, fleecy, greenish foam. He saw the vast, involved wrinkles of the slightly projecting head beyond. Before it, far out on the soft Turkish-rugged waters, went the glistening white shadow from his broad, milky forehead, a musical rippling playfully accompanying the shade.
>
> Extract from *Moby Dick* (Melville, 1851/2001, p. 642)

As you read the previous extract, you might have experienced a feeling of impending doom, as if Melville was somehow building to an explosive encounter—the calm before the storm, to draw on a well-known analogy. Before reading the next example, look back at Example 3.9 and see if you can identify the word choices (particularly the adjectives and adverbs) that contribute to this feeling.

The final example of a golden detail (Example 3.10) is from a student essay by Noppanun Sookping. This extract is taken from another essay about Talad Thai, which was the focus of the first example in the previous unit (descriptive writing). That essay was called *The Blooming Bliss of Talad Thai*. The example below is called *The Irritable Nature of Talad Thai*. As you read the extract, think about the tone of the description, and how this student must have felt, both emotionally and physically, as he stood there looking at the sign. Also, think about how the rest of the essay probably unfolded.

> **3.10 Example of golden details (3)**
>
> The heat slapped my face as I stepped down from bus no. 510. I squinted my eyes and tried to regain focus. In front of me stood a huge greenish metallic billboard. Large white letters spelled out "Thai Market" in the Thai alphabet. What an original name, I thought. It was garish and rusty; its metallic supports were pitted and faded, like withered corn stalks burned and color-stripped by the scorching summer sun. The letters had started to peel off, as if they were trying to pull themselves free and escape. I sympathized with them.
>
> Extract from *The Irritable Nature of Talad Thai* by Noppanun Sookping

You probably felt, as I did, that the tone was somewhat ironic, and that the student was a bit of a reluctant visitor. Indeed, I took my class to this market on a writing assignment, and many of them did not want to go out in the midday heat. You probably also correctly guessed that the rest of the essay unfolded in much the same way, and that it stayed true to the sentiment expressed in its title.

Now that you have some understanding of what a golden detail is, Exercise 3.4 will give you practice in creating your own. Remember that in creating a golden detail, it is not so much about adding fancy words as it is about creating memorable descriptions that invoke the senses and feelings of the reader. So, be unique and be imaginative.

Exercise 3.4. Creating your own golden detail

Create your own golden detail describing an event, person, or thing of your choosing. Use the techniques you used in the last unit to help you. Compare your final draft with a classmate's.

3.2. ELEMENTS OF A STORY

3.2.1. Choosing a Good Topic

When choosing a topic for a narrative, draw upon your own experiences, interests, or imagination. Brainstorming ideas for short stories with friends or family is a good place to begin. At the very start of the writing process for narratives, you do not need a fully fleshed out plotline and developed characters. All you need is an idea that you think could be interesting if it were a focal point for a story. Think of your initial idea as a bag of rice. It is just the first component you need to make a meal. You then add in other elements, large and small—perhaps some chunks of meat, a pinch of salt, and some chilies. The result is a collection of elements: a finished product that is more than the sum of its parts, where each item is interconnected in some way.

The initial idea can be anything: an interesting character, a piece of dialogue, a place, a thing, or an event that to you is memorable and stimulating, and that you can imagine building a story around. Think about a point your story could prove or a possible life lesson it could teach the reader, and what dramatic events could be surrounding your initial idea or main character that could move from the initial idea through the plot. To be a true narrative there has to be some kind of complication or problem that your main character needs to overcome or solve in order for a change to take place. The change is most often a change in the main character but may also be a change in that character's context or world. The progression of the action should lead to a climax and a resolution that shows that change and draws a lesson or point from it as a conclusion to the narrative. If there is no change, then there is probably no basis for a satisfying conclusion in the form of a moral, a life lesson, a point proved, or other memorable outcome in the form of a crowning event.

Exercise 3.5. Choosing good topics

Write down three general ideas or topics that could make good stories. Remember that there must be some kind of conflict (internal/external) that creates a change in your main character.

TOPIC 1

TOPIC 2

TOPIC 3

3.2.2. Opening the Story

Writing the "Hook"

As you saw in the last unit, in real life, hooks are used to catch fish. In writing, hooks are used to catch the reader's attention. A hook is a sentence (or sentences) that gives the reader a reason to continue reading. It can be a relevant quotation, question, fact, definition, or anything interesting that attracts the reader's interest. Consider the examples of opening lines from famous novels given below.

> → "Call me Ishmael." From *Moby-Dick* by Herman Melville (Melville, 1851/2001, p. 1)
>
> → "The story so far: in the beginning, the universe was created. This has made a lot of people very angry and been widely regarded as a bad move." From *The Restaurant at the End of the Universe* by Douglas Adams (Adams, 1981, p. 1)
>
> → "We were somewhere around Barstow on the edge of the desert when the drugs began to take hold." From *Fear and Loathing in Las Vegas* by Hunter S. Thompson (Thompson, 1972, p. 1)
>
> → "It was a bright cold day in April, and the clocks were striking thirteen." From *Nineteen Eighty-Four* by George Orwell (Orwell, 1949, p. 1)
>
> → "Mother died today. Or maybe yesterday, I don't know." From *The Stranger* by Albert Camus (Camus, 1942/1946, p. 1)

Each of these examples makes the reader want to read on. The first one puts the reader straight into the story by engaging them in dialogue; the second and third ones are light-hearted and humorous and perhaps make the reader smile; the fourth and fifth ones create a mystery that makes the reader want to find out what is going on.

> **Exercise 3.6. Writing hooks**
>
> Write three hooks for a story about a student's first day at university. The conflict is that the student is really an alien from another planet, which has the potential for creating all kinds of complications and problems.

1.

2.

3.

Setting the Scene

After putting the reader "on the hook," the writer usually provides two or three sentences that take the reader "off the hook" and put them on to a topic or central idea that leads to a thesis suggesting the main point of the story to come. In a narrative, the writer usually provides information that the reader will need to understand the starting point of the story, such as when and where the story is taking place, who or what is involved, and perhaps why these characters find themselves in their current situation. As Blake Morrison states, "Beginnings matter. They always have …. And if it doesn't begin right, the suspicion is that the rest of it won't be right" (Morrison, 1999, para. 2). In Exercise 3.7, you will read an introductory paragraph from a student's five-paragraph narrative essay. As you read it, judge whether it sets the scene for an interesting story to follow.

Exercise 3.7. Analyzing an introductory paragraph

Read the extract below and answer the questions that follow. What kind of story will it be? You will find out later when I will ask you to sequence the accompanying body paragraphs.

It was the hottest night on record, and not even the breeze from the side canal helped take away the tiredness and anxiety of the lonely youths sitting in the bar. A girl with an unusually reddened face and bloodshot eyes sat alone in a shadowy corner. It was a dark corner with a dimly lit light, as far away from all the other patrons as possible. She exhaled clouds of cigarette smoke that were the color of neat whiskey. "Such a good combination for a f****d-up life," she thought. She could barely sit up straight but her hand still firmly gripped her phone. She stared at the phone's screen, occasionally looking up to puff out more smoke or suck down more brown liquid. Though dizzied, her eyes focused intensely on the face of a guy smiling up at her from the screen. It was not the look of hatred in her eyes. It was not the look of envy. It was not the look of pity. It was the look of longing. The longing of a girl who will never meet her loved one again.

Extract from Honey by Pitcha Dangprasith

1. Find the hook. Is it a question, quote, description, or something else?

2. What connecting information is between the hook and the thesis statement?

3. Underline the thesis statement. What points of development lead up to it?

The introduction in Exercise 3.7 sets the scene by firmly placing us in the middle of a conflict. We are introduced to an uncomfortable environment and an equally uncomfortable girl. Moreover, you have probably guessed that this is going to be a story about heartbreak. You will read the rest of this narrative later.

In the next exercise, you will write your own introductory paragraph to open a story. You can write in the space provided or you can write on a separate piece of paper, tablet, or computer. As this will be an introduction for a short essay, aim for about 150 words maximum.

Exercise 3.8. Setting the scene

Choose one of your topics from Exercise 3.5. Write a short introductory paragraph that includes a hook, sets the scene, and establishes a suitable tone for your upcoming story.

Topic:

Hook:

Setting the scene:

Now give what you have written to one of your peers. Ask them if your idea is interesting or not. Then ask them to comment on the effectiveness of your hook, and to tell you what kind of story they think is going to unfold. Also, ask them for their opinion on what kind of tone you have created. Do the same for them in return.

Writing a Thesis for a Narrative Essay

At the paragraph level, we have a topic sentence. At the essay level, we have a thesis statement. In a narrative essay, the thesis statement is not like the ones in descriptive, expository, or argument/opinion writing. A narrative thesis may begin the events of the story, or it may offer a moral warning or lesson learned, such as *I'll never do that again*, that relates to a conclusion to come. Alternatively, it may identify a theme that connects the story to a universal experience, such as a commonly accepted trope like *Every journey begins with a single step*.

> **Exercise 3.9. Writing thesis statements for narratives**

Look back at the topics you came up with for Exercise 3.5. Write potential thesis statements for each of the ideas you had written down. Compare your answers with those of a peer.

As you may have guessed, the opening paragraph of a narrative is typically used to set up aspects of what is to follow, such as what the story is about, who the characters are, where the story is set, and who is telling the story. Moreover, good writers will effectively build upon the initial hook by pulling the reader into the world they are creating. The writer sets up a kind of "contract" with the reader about what to expect—they are effectively saying, "if you come with me on this reading journey, you are going to have this kind of experience." For instance, narratives in a particular genre, such as thrillers, romance novels, or detective fiction, often make the reader very aware, right from the start, what type of story or genre they are reading.

We can lable narrative openings according to their purpose. Morrison (1999) categorizes the beginnings of stories as follows:

→ The **plunge** – sticks the reader into the middle of the action.
→ The **shocker** – a shocking surprise or crazy idea.
→ The **intriguing narrator** – first-person narrator who hooks you with a mystery.
→ The **epigram** – something memorable but short.
→ The **promise** – points to a future reveal.
→ The **omen** – a bad ending starts with a bad beginning.
→ The **particulars** – it is as if it the author is a news reporter in the olden days.
→ The **self-referral** – the narrator makes reference to themselves.

Exercise 3.10. Identifying openings

Read the five opening paragraphs that are shown below. The openings are written in different styles. They also use different modes of narration. Rate each one in the table as directed.

A. Alice was beginning to get very tired of sitting by her sister on the bank, and of having nothing to do: once or twice she had peeped into the book her sister was reading, but it had no pictures or conversations in it, "and what is the use of a book," thought Alice "without pictures or conversations?" – *Alice's Adventures in Wonderland* (Carroll, 1865/2008).

B. In the beginning God created the heaven and the earth. And the earth was without form, and void; and darkness was upon the face of the deep. And the Spirit of God moved upon the face of the waters. Then God said, "Let there be light": and there was light. – *The Bible* (King James Version, 1611/1989, Genesis 1:1-5)

C. It was the best of times, it was the worst of times, it was the age of wisdom, it was the age of foolishness, it was the epoch of belief, it was the epoch of incredulity, it was the season of Light, it was the season of Darkness, it was the spring of hope, it was the winter of despair, we had everything before us, we had nothing before us, we were all going direct to Heaven, we were all going direct the other way. – *A Tale of Two Cities* (Dickens, 1859/1994).

D. I am a sick man.... I am a spiteful man. I am an unattractive man. I believe my liver is diseased. However, I know nothing at all about my disease, and do not know for certain what ails me. – *Notes from the Underground* (Dostoyevsky, 1864/1996).

E. The studio was filled with the rich odour of roses, and when the light summer wind stirred amidst the trees of the garden, there came through the open door the heavy scent of the lilac, or the more delicate perfume of the pink-flowering thorn. – *The Picture of Dorian Gray* (Wilde, 1890/1994).

In the table below, score each of the above passages for the extent to which they accomplished the listed outcomes, using one star * for "hardly or not at all," two stars ** for "to some extent," and three stars *** for "to a great extent."

NARRATIVE WRITING   161

	A	B	C	D	E
I understand what the setting is					
I get a strong impression of the characters					
The narrator talks about themselves a lot					
I am put in the middle of the action					
I know what genre this novel is					
I want to read more					

Now, label each of the passages A–E above in terms of Morrison's (1999) eight categories. For example, does Text A represent a *plunge*, *shocker*, *epigram*, or another of his categories? If a passage does not seem to fit into one of Morrison's categories, place it in a category of your own.

TEXT A

TEXT B

TEXT C

TEXT D

TEXT E

If you are writing a narrative as a student assignment, you will generally be writing a short story or an essay that has 3–10 paragraphs, depending on the word limit and how you structure your story. Regardless of the overall length, the introductory part of your essay should include the three elements of hook, setting the scene, and thesis. All essays have similar, if not the same, components in their introductions; so it is a good idea to get into the habit of including them.

Exercise 3.11. Writing an identifiable opening

Revisit your answer to Exercise 3.8 above. Rewrite what you wrote so that it fits into one of Morrison's (1999) categories. Do not forget to set the tone as well as the scene.

3.2.3. Middle of the Story

The middle of a story can often be troublesome for authors. Beginnings and endings are easy to conceptualize, and the writer usually knows where the characters will start and how they will end up. It is the middle where a writer can run out of steam or lose focus as to where the story is heading or how to get there. When you find yourself drafting the middle part of a story, ask yourself the following questions to ensure you keep moving forward:

- What does my main character want to accomplish or gain at the end?
- What would the character(s) be likely to do in this current situation?
- Have I introduced complications or problems that my main character has not addressed yet?
- Have I introduced so many complications/problems that it is now impossible for my main character to overcome them?
- Am I getting closer to the climax? (The climax is the turning point in the story where the main character or the situation surrounding that character begins to change in a significant way.)

Many of these questions focus on the same issue, which is the chaining of events in terms of action⇨consequence⇨action⇨consequence sequences. These sequences of actions and consequences are very important to a story's progression, and they are driven by two key questions that help to move the story along: "What happens next?" and "How will this all end up?"

You can think of action⇨consequence chains in terms of stimulus and response. A stimulus is an external force, which in a story-world can be an event or piece of dialogue. For every stimulus, there is a desired or expected response, which is also typically external—your characters can do or say something. For example, your character is walking outside and it starts to rain heavily (stimulus). The expected response is for your character to react in some way—perhaps they will start running, open an umbrella, or take shelter. If your character did nothing, then you should explain to the reader why; otherwise, they may be puzzled as to why your character is not acting like a normal person would act. In other words, what should happen in the real world, should also happen in a story-world that a writer constructs. Thus, at the heart of most narratives, a chain of causes-and-effects, choices-and-outcomes, or actions-and-reactions is being played out: X happened, which caused Y; then Y caused Z, and so on, in a chain reaction or domino-like effect, as shown in the image below.

The following example is an extract from *Find (Day 7)* by Vipavee Thongsuk. This is a continuation of the story introduced in Example 3.1. That extract ended with Anna and Sean spotting a zombie hoard and Anna shouting "Zombies! Run! Run!" As you read the extract, underline the action/cause, and circle the resulting reaction/effect. At the end of the extract, note how Sean uses

the knife that he pulled out at the beginning of the extract. If he had not pulled out the knife at some point during the extract, then it may have seemed odd for him to be stabbing the zombie in the head at the end.

> **3.11 Action ⇨ consequence chain from a student's narrative**
>
> "Go!! Go!!" Sean shouted. He quickly pulled out a knife that he had found at the police station and turned to yell at Anna once again. "Go! I'll be right after you!"
>
> Anna started running but her weak legs crumpled. She fell to the ground. She tried to get up, but her arms gave way. A crawling zombie grabbed her left leg while another one approached her from behind.
>
> "No…! Please! Arhhhgg!!!!" Anna cried in pain when the zombie bit her shoulder. She instinctively elbowed it repeatedly until it fell on its back.
>
> Sean, hearing the scream, turned and ran toward Anna. He pulled the zombie off her and stabbed it in the head. He pushed the other zombie aside and stabbed it too.
>
> Extract from *Find (Day 7)* by Vipavee Thongsuk

Now that you have a basic idea of how a story can move forward through a chain of causes-and-effects, choices-and-outcomes, or actions-and-reactions, Exercise 3.12 will give you practice in establishing such chains.

> **Exercise 3.12. Setting up action⇨consequence chains**
>
> Below, I have provided an ending for Example 3.11. Write a likely series of actions and consequences (150–200 words) that could bridge the gap between Example 3.11 and my ending below. Compare your finished story with that of one of your classmates.
>
> Sean sat on the edge of the roof listening to the shuffling feet of the Deads below. He wiped his face with the back of his hand and looked to the blood red horizon. As he watched the sun slowly set, a solitary tear slid down his cheek. He sniffed. The tear fell onto the broken blade of the knife he held tight in his hand.
>
> <div align="right">Suggested ending to <i>Find (Day 7)</i> by Neil Bowen</div>

3.2.3. Closing the Story

The closer or conclusion of a story is usually also "the moral of the story," or it can be a surprise ending that is meaningful and relevant. The conclusion should include the closing action of the main event and the resolution of the conflict. In other words, the conclusion includes a reflection on and/or an analysis of (1) what happened during the falling action, and (2) the significance of the climax for the main character. For example, what lesson was learned? How did the event affect the protagonist's view on something? Did the climax cause something in their life to change?

Exercise 3.13. Analyzing a closing paragraph

The extract below is a closing paragraph from a student's narrative essay (the introduction can be seen in Exercise 3.7). Read it carefully and then answer the questions that follow.

Everything was a nightmare since her car crashed into a tree one month ago. The impact killed her instantly. And this place, this bar, is the only place she could exist. All the memories, all the precious moments she spent here with her loved one bound her soul to this place, and she had to relive it every day. A chain of suffering and torturing she could not escape. She looked at the phone screen once more. The time was approaching the exact moment when, 28 days ago, the impact happened. She began to cry ghostly tears. Slowly, her skull folded in on itself; blood poured down her face; her chest caved in; a rib ripped through her breastplate; both arms started twisting and contorting until they resembled the branches of the tree her car had hit almost a month ago. The song played on in the background… "So, for once in my life, let me get what I want. Lord knows it would be the first time." Through her broken jaw, the girl mumbled, "I will always be with you, honey."

Extract from *Honey* by Pitcha Dangprasith

1. What is unusual or unexpected about this final paragraph?

2. Are you left feeling something at the end? If so, what?

3. What is the resolution? (If there is one)

4. The song lyric has a double function. It not only builds up to the closing thought, but also serves to add a *macro-level* cohesive element (i.e., one that spans several paragraphs) to the conclusion. Look at the body paragraphs for this story (presented in Exercise 3.19). Find the other element that adds extra relevance to this quote. Write down your explanation of what is clever about the use of this quote at the end.

3.3. ELEMENTS OF A PLOT

In linguistic terms, sequencing individual events and actions in a story is relatively simple: you put them in order of when they occurred and make meaningful links between them. Sequencing time chronologically, from the first event to the last, is the most common and clearest way to tell a story. Writers sometimes work backwards in time (*reverse chronological order*) or jump around in time, but these ways of telling a story require greater skill to ensure that the reader can follow. Whether you choose to sequence events chronologically or not, use suitable transitions to tell the reader what happened first, next, and last. Consult Table 1.1 (Unit 1) for suitable conjunctive adjuncts for this purpose.

In a narrative, a new paragraph typically marks a change in scene, event, or speaker. In such instances, the easiest way to ensure that one paragraph flows into the next one is to create a link between the concluding sentence of one paragraph and the topic sentence of the next paragraph. For example, the end of one paragraph might be *I turned and looked back at the woman I left behind, hoping she would call for me to come back, but she was already walking away*. The start of the next paragraph might be *I have made many mistakes in my life*. Here, the writer has created an implicit link between the two paragraphs—namely, that leaving the woman was one of his mistakes. With this established, we might expect the writer to now elaborate on the mistake of letting the woman walk away and/or on the other mistakes he had made in his life.

Beyond sequencing, in order to establish a plot, and thus create a true narrative, there are number of elements that a writer needs to weave into an unfolding story. One of these is characterization: the development of the story's characters.

3.3.1. Characters

In Unit 2 (Descriptive Writing), you wrote a description of a person. You built up a description of physical appearance and personality, using "show, don't tell" to make your writing more engaging and appealing. In a narrative, you also build up descriptions of people. This is called *characterization*.

Some characters will be fully developed with complex emotions and histories. Others will be simple and may appear in just one or two scenes or events. For example, one popular form of narrative is the *quest*. A quest is a journey that a protagonist takes to overcome a problem or gain something that is missing (e.g., love or courage). The classic *Lord of The Rings* trilogy by J. R. R. Tolkien (1968) is a good example of a lengthy quest. In *The Lord of the Rings*, the hero, Bilbo Baggins must deliver a magical ring into the fires of Mordor to vanquish an evil threat. Along the way, he meets several characters, each of which performs specific roles or functions in the tale. These characters contribute to the plot in different ways, and thus characterization—the setting up of individuals in terms of their narrative functions—is an important part of storytelling.

One way to look at the role of characters is through the folktale, as in the research of Vladmir Propp. Propp (1928/1968) studied a hundred Russian folktales, and identified seven roles that were common to the tales:

- The **hero** (protagonist).
- The **villain** (antagonist; can be a person or a thing personified, such as a storm).
- The **helper**.
- The **donor** (provides a way to solve a problem [in folk tales it is usually via a magical gift]).
- The **princess** and **her father** (people who benefit from the Hero's quest).
- The **dispatcher** (the one who sends the hero on their way).
- The **false hero**.

These roles can be played by characters that are *flat*, *static*, *round*, and/or *dynamic*.

Flat characters are not developed enough to seem real or life-like. They have little to no personality, emotional reaction, or motivation, and are thus one-dimensional. They have only one trait—like a pancake with no toppings. Flat characters also do not change as the story unfolds and never experience internal conflict. Think of Gary the snail in the *SpongeBob* cartoon, or Crabbe and Goyle (henchmen) or Voldemort (villain) in the 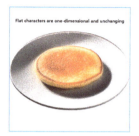 *Harry Potter* series. We use flat characters to create stability, mirror cultural stereotypes, and support the protagonist or antagonist.

A ***static character*** is similar to a flat character in that they also never learn a lesson or change as the story unfolds. The word *static* means staying still. Hence, these characters go nowhere in terms of development. In essence, we still have a pancake, only now we have a pancake with more layers and toppings. A static character can thus possess more life-like qualities, such as a strong personality, emotions, and motivations; yet these are typi- 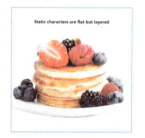 cally one sided, such as being very kind or very angry. In *SpongeBob*, this would be Plankton. In *Harry Potter*, this would be Draco Malfoy (villain). We use static characters to populate our story without overloading the reader in terms of character development. If every character in the story were changing as events unfolded, it might be difficult for a reader to keep up with them and follow the plot.

A ***rounded character*** is a complicated, life-like individual, with personality, goals, and history. Most heroes are rounded because it makes it easier for us to empathize with them. They have two or  more traits. Think of a box of chocolates—we have many choices and flavors, and some will appeal to most people. In *SpongeBob*, this would be SpongeBob. In *Harry Potter*, this would be Hermione Granger and Ron Weasley (who function as *deuteragonists*—secondary characters), Dumbledore (the helper), or Harry Potter (protagonist/ hero). We use rounded characters as the focal points for the plot: It is through rounded characters that conflict and change occur.

A ***dynamic character*** is, as the name suggests, one who changes in some way throughout the story, either through an internal or external conflict. The resultant change can be good or bad. Think of an ice cream. Over time, it changes states—it melts and becomes something different. Dynamic characters are usually central ones or play the leading role (protagonist). They are also multidimensional. For example, they may appear to be  brave, but inside they are terrified of everything. In *SpongeBob*, this would be Sandy the squirrel. In *Harry Potter*, this is Harry Potter, Hermione Granger, and Ron Weasley: Rounded characters are also often dynamic ones. The change in Harry, for example, is that he goes from a scared, unconfident boy who does not have many friends, to a very popular, courageous, and confident young man (i.e., the hero).

Exercise 3.14. Identifying types of characters

Select three main characters from one of your favorite novels or movies (other than one from Harry Potter). Identify which characters are rounded, flat, dynamic, or static, and give reasons. *Remember, characters can be rounded + dynamic, rounded + static, or flat + static.

Title of novel/movie:

Character 1:

Character 2:

Character 3:

170 ESSENTIAL KNOWLEDGE AND SKILLS FOR ESSAY WRITING

To ensure that characterization is consistent throughout a story, you can use a character diamond chart to list their key traits. A trait is a part of a character's overall personality, such as being bold, cowardly, secretive, or loyal. Whereas a character diamond is a screenwriting technique developed by David Freeman (Freeman, 2004), and you can use this technique to map your characters' distinctive qualities. Here, I introduce a four-sided shape for four key traits (see Figure 3.2 below), but you can also use a triangle (three key traits) or a pentagon (five traits), both of which are referred to by Freeman as "diamonds."

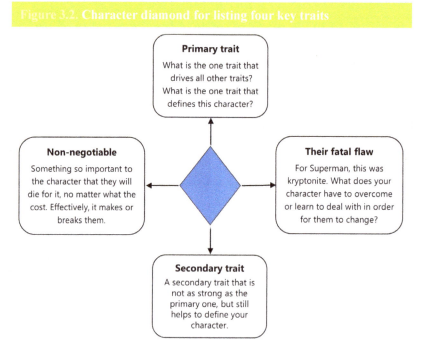

Figure 3.2. Character diamond for listing four key traits

I focus on four traits here because in the length of essays you will be asked to write, it would be difficult to squeeze in a five-trait character without confusing the reader. Use your character diamond as a reference point, so that every time your character performs an action or says a line of dialogue, they display one or more of the traits listed in the diamond.

NARRATIVE WRITING 171

Exercise 3.15. Creating a character diamond

Choose the most dynamic character from your list of answers to Exercise 3.14. Decide upon their four key traits and put these into the appropriate point of your own character diamond. Compare your character diamond with a classmate's diamond.

Chosen character:

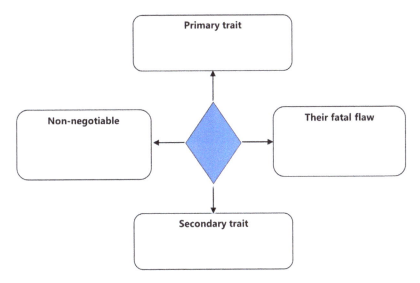

You may be familiar with the movie, *Willy Wonka and the Chocolate Factory* (Burton, 2005). If so, you may also be familiar with the story's hero, Charlie Bucket, and the four other children who, like Charlie, found a golden ticket in a Wonka chocolate bar. The following exercise asks you to describe those children.

If you do not know this movie and its characters, or if you simply want to refresh your memory, you may want to watch a clip from the movie. This can be a clip from the beginning of the movie or a clip from YouTube, such as *Willy Wonka and the Chocolate Factory: The Four Rotten Children* from the *Willy Wonka Channel*, which can be found at the following URL: https://www.youtube.com/watch?v=zslNn8Cd0-A

> **Exercise 3.16. Identifying character traits**
>
>
>
> For each of the characters listed below, write down their physical traits and personality traits in the spaces provided. List at least three physical traits for each character.
>
> AUGUSTUS GLOOP
>
> Physical traits:
>
> Personality traits:
>
> VERUCA SALT
>
> Physical traits:
>
> Personality traits:
>
> VIOLET BEAUREGARDE
>
> Physical traits:
>
> Personality traits:
>
> MIKE TEAVEE
>
> Physical traits:
>
> Personality traits:
>
> *Note how each character's physical traits feed into their personality in some way.

3.3.2. Rhetorical Structure: The Rise and Fall of a Narrative

A true story has a beginning, middle, and end. We often also learn something from our interpretation of it, for example, a life lesson or a moral in a fable or morality tale. If you have simply told the reader step-by-step what happened, then chances are you have written a recount, which is a type of descriptive writing. To be a true narrative, there must be more than just a retelling of events.

One popular form of narrative structure is that outlined by the sociolinguist, William Labov (for an overview, see Labov & Waletzky, 1967). Labov's description of narrative structure initially derived from his research on the language and discourse of African Americans in New York City. Although it mainly applies to oral narratives told in natural settings, some of its elements are suitable for five-paragraph essay writing, and so I draw upon elements of Labov's depiction of narrative structure in this section.

Another popular narrative pattern is that outlined by the Bulgarian narratologist, Tzvetan Todorov. Todorov (1971/1977) argued that most narratives are centered on a problem or disturbance in an otherwise relatively stable situation. Thus, a story consists of movement from *equilibrium* (state of balance) to *disequilibrium* (imbalance) and then back to *equilibrium* (new state of balance). This movement gives a story "meaning."

Drawing on the work of Labov and Todorov, we can depict the structure of many narratives as outlined in Figure 3.3:

Figure 3.3. General narrative structure

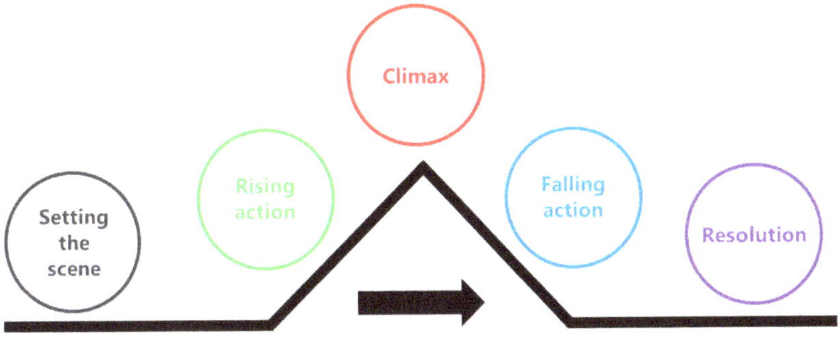

Starting on the left of Figure 3.3, we *set the scene* for our upcoming story—*orientation* in Labov's terms (Labov & Waletzky, 1967); *exposition* in Todorov's (1971/1977) terms. This rhetorical move would be similar to the introductory paragraph presented earlier on in this unit. This move introduces the audience to the initial equilibrium: a state of balance, normality, or stability.

We then move on to the *rising action* (*complicating action; disruption*). This rhetorical move (or stage) usually makes up the bulk of a narrative. Here, the tension is built up and the reader is expecting some dramatic event or turn of event in the story, such as a difficult problem being presented to the protagonist. In other words, an action–reaction chain of events is played out, such as small conflicts or complications. This stage thus represents the beginning of the disequilibrium, wherein the initial situation is disrupted, creating a problem, a quest for an answer, or a lack of something that needs to be obtained. These conflicts or complications can be internal, such as a mental or emotional struggle within a character; or they can be external, such as character vs. nature, character vs. character, character vs. society, character vs. technology, or character vs. supernatural.

The *climax* (*complication*) is shown as the peak of a triangle in Figure 3.3. This is to symbolize that it is often the most exciting part of a story. At this stage, three things should be happening: (a) The action should at its highest point; (b) the disequilibrium is usually at its tipping point; and (c), the reader should be emotionally involved.

The reader is then brought down through the *falling action*. Here, the protagonist begins to solve the problem, complete the quest, achieve their goal, or fulfill their desires. In this way, the disequilibrium (imbalance) slowly turns to equilibrium (balance).

The final stage is the *resolution* of the story: The "so what?" or the solution to the climax. Here, there is balance once again. The problem/quest/goal/desire has been addressed. Thus, a new state of affairs comes into being.

NARRATIVE WRITING 175

Exercise 3.17. Identifying narrative structure

Consider the fairy tale of Cinderella; try to identify the climax of this story, the following falling actions, and the final resolution that restores equilibrium.

* If you do not quite recall the story, you can review it from a printed or video version that you can easily obtain at a library or on the internet. Or you can view its ending portion in an animated film version of Cinderella (Jackson et al., 1950), which is available on YouTube https://youtube/Unx5x-XT3jw When you feel familiar with the story and its ending, complete the following questions:

1. What are the *three actions* taken after Cinderella loses her glass slipper that lead up to the climax?
   a)
   b)
   c)

2. What is the *climax* (the highest point of the action) and how do we know it?

3. What events signify that the *falling action has begun* and equilibrium is being restored?

4. What signifies the *resolution has begun*?

5. What is *the resolution* in the Cinderella story?

Let us now look at the structure of the whole story. In Cinderella, we have a clear example of a narrative with a beginning, middle, and end.

In the beginning, a clear state of equilibrium is set up—setting the scene—for the overall story—in which Cinderella (the protagonist: a rounded, dynamic character) is shown as living a difficult and sad life, and longing for happiness and true love. Following this, we have the first act, or narrative within a narrative. We see the sisters (antagonists: static, flat characters) preparing for an upcoming royal ball. However, we learn that Cinderella is not allowed to go to the ball, and even if she could, she has no fancy clothes to wear (*rising action* containing conflicts/complications for our protagonist). The fairy godmother (the helper) then arrives, signaling the *climax* of Act 1 (the turning point). The fairy godmother works her magic on Cinderella, gifting her with a beautiful gown and elegant glass slippers (*falling actions* for Act 1). The result of these falling actions is that Cinderella can now go to the ball (*resolution* of Act 1).

In the middle of the story, a new state of equilibrium is set up for a moment, and there begins Act 2. We see Cinderella happily attending the ball and all is going well: She is seen dancing with the prince and everyone at the ball is in awe of her beauty (**setting the scene** for Act 2). However, as it gets closer to midnight, she realizes that she must hurriedly make an escape before the fairy godmother's magic wears off, and we see her dashing for the exit (*rising action* containing conflicts/complications). During her escape, she loses one of her glass slippers (*climax* of Act 2), yet through a series of *falling actions*, she manages to get away in time (*resolution* of Act 2). The overarching narrative now returns to the previous state of equilibrium—a difficult and sad life for Cinderella—and thus Act 3 begins.

In Act 3, as we move toward the end of the story, the prince is now desperately searching for Cinderella. We see his servants and soldiers going from house to house, making all the women try on the glass slipper that Cinderella left behind (*rising actions*). Finally, they reach Cinderella's house, and despite the complaints of her family, she is asked to try on the slipper (*climax* of Act 3 and the overall story). The slipper fits. Cinderella is then whisked off to the palace, and she marries her prince in a grand ceremony (*falling actions*). The story ends with Cinderella and the prince heading off into the sunset to live happily ever after (overall *resolution*). A new state of equilibrium has now been made permanent, and the protagonist has found her true love (signifying changes in the protagonist's inner and external world).

NARRATIVE WRITING 177

Exercise 3.18. Checking concepts introduced so far

The questions 1–6 below check your understanding of the concepts introduced so far. Answer each question in your own words. Check your answers with your peers and teacher.

1. What happens during the *setting the scene* part of a narrative?

2. To what does the *rising action* refer?

3. List four types of *narrative conflict*.
    a)
    b)
    c)
    d)

4. What three things typically happen during the *climax*?
    a)
    b)
    c)

5. What happens during the *falling action*?

6. What does a story's *resolution* do?

3.3.3. Elements that Help Drive a Plot Forward

In a narrative, the unfolding events, interactions, dialogue, and characterization act as the evidence that supports your thesis. These elements realize the body of a narrative essay. They should be presented in a way that they contribute to each of the five main rhetorical stages of a narrative outlined above: setting the scene, the rising action, climax, falling action, and resolution.

Now that you are familiar with the main rhetorical structuring of a narrative, we can return to the narrative essay, *Honey*, introduced in Exercise 3.13. We have already analyzed its opening and closing paragraphs (its beginning and its ending) in Exercises 3.7 and 3.13. Now we will look at its body paragraphs (its middle) in Exercise 3.19.

Exercise 3.19. Analyzing the main body of a narrative essay

Paragraphs a–d contain the main body from the essay introduced in Exercise 3.7. Put the paragraphs in order so that they move through the rising actions and finish with the climax.

a. As she opened her eyes and transcended back into reality, those warm, dreamy feelings still lingered; they enameled her heart as the cigarette smoke had enameled her lungs. She sipped an almost empty glass. Her eyes drifted far away with no focus. The band started playing her favorite song from The Smiths, "Please, please, please let me get what I want." The lyrics of the song pierced her heart with cold and icy feelings. It was their favorite song and it reminded her of him. His face, his voice, his touch, his laughter. The memories haunted her as the song echoed through the bar. And, as if destiny was messing with her, the boy strolled into the bar, wearing a Nirvana T-shirt and with a Marlboro hanging from his mouth. He sat down not far away from her, ordered a drink, and smiled at the band that was playing his favorite song. He occasionally looked up at the band, puffed smoke, and went back to pondering. Tears started swelling up in her eyes; she could not keep it anymore. Now is the time to cry, he is right there, right in front of me, she thought. She stood up and walked through the crowd of people. She stood over him; hand reaching out to grab his shoulder.

b. Her hand went through his shoulder. He did not feel anything; he did not even flinch. His eyes were still lost in thought, pondering about things she could not know. He did not know she was standing right there. He did not see her nor did the other people. They all walked through her like thin air. The seat she was sitting in was in a closed off area. All the cigarettes she had smoked and all the booze she had drunk were simply a manifestation of her own imagination.

c. "Hi there, you like The Smiths? Morrissey is a bit of an asshole but he still writes good songs, right?" That was the first line he said to her. He had a face as neat as Al Pacino's, with eyes as sad as Dustin Hoffman's. She did not realize the volume in her earphones was so loud that he could hear it five feet away. "You've got good taste and everything, but you're gonna get kicked out of the library if you keep it this loud." He smiled at her, and that was that.

d. She had fallen for a guy before, but she had never fallen this hard for anyone so instantly. And before she knew it, she had started dating him. They would smoke weed all day, listen to alternative rock bands, and talk about their lives and their dreams – never going outside until the sun set. Wine and pizza were their routine dinner items. Their life together was like a warm, fuzzily, dreamy, hazy movie, uncut, unchronological, incomprehensible, yet still charmingly beautiful. So beautiful until it all came crashing down.

Main body of Honey by Pitcha Dangprasith

When reorganizing the above paragraphs, you should have noticed how the student slowly built to the climax. He did this through a series of events aided by characterization attached to his protagonist. The climax is then signaled via a "shocker"—a strong surprise. The closing paragraph to this story was presented in the last section, when we considered the resolution or "closer." So go back and look at that section if you need to remind yourself of how it all ended.

Overall, the story of *Honey*, by Pitcha Dangprasith, has all the elements required to create a plot, which are reproduced below as a reminder:

→ A *central character* for whom conflict/complication arises.
→ A *beginning*, *middle*, and *end*.
→ Events connected through *cause-and-effect*.
→ Five rhetorical moves (or stages): *setting the scene*, *rising action(s)*, *climax*, *falling action(s)*, and *resolution*.

When it comes to creating conflict for your own protagonist in a narrative, try to answer, the following three questions:

→ What will the change be that my protagonist goes through?
→ What will cause this change? (The answer to this usually reflects the climax.)
→ Who (or what) will cause problems for my protagonist?

In the student essay above, the protagonist's change is both external and internal, as the girl realizes that she is actually dead, and that she is now a ghost haunting her ex-boyfriend. The cause of this change (the climax) occurs in paragraph (b) when "Her

180 ESSENTIAL KNOWLEDGE AND SKILLS FOR ESSAY WRITING

hand went through his shoulder. He did not feel anything; he did not even flinch." This also represents the midpoint of the story in terms of both rhetorical structuring and approximate word count. With respect to who or what gets in her way, this is a little more complicated. The student writer has established a series of rising actions that focus on her memories intertwined with her watching the unfolding events in the bar. The combination of memories and unfolding events helps build her character and the tone as we head toward the climax. The combination of present and past also highlights the second necessary element for a plot: movement through time.

Many dictionary-based definitions of *plot* include something along the lines of *a series of dramatic events that start at a particular point and move forward in time to a final resolution*. This notion of plot is reflected in fairy tales that start with *Once upon a time* and end with *And they lived happily ever after*. How much time has elapsed between these two points will vary. It can be as little as a few minutes or hours—as in a one-scene or "slice of life" short story—or it can be as much as many decades or generations—as in some novels. As you will probably be writing short narratives on your writing course, it may be easier if your stories have short timeframes, too. However, your story may include the occasional *flash-back* to an earlier time or *flash-forward* to a later time, within an overarching timeframe, to help you build characterization. You can use *flash-backs* to refer to past events in your protagonist's life, and to create tension by moving between present dramatic events and past peaceful events, as in the student essay, *Honey*.

Honey also makes use of a *frame* (different from a *timeframe*, which is a span of time within which the action of a story takes place). More broadly, a frame is a literary device by means of/in which the author sets up opening and closing scenes that mirror each other: same location and moment in time. Within a frame, the author may choose to take the reader to other locations and times, creating stories within a larger story that ultimately leads back to its starting point. A frame is a useful device when the writer wants to bring the reader full circle. It creates a "rhetorical sandwich" through which the reader is given a clear opening and closing that starts and ends at the same point.

We can also see elements of connectedness and causality in the above narrative essay. In essence, we have a series of *causes and effects*—albeit in their simplest forms—reflecting simple action ⇨consequence⇨action⇨consequence chains. In *Honey*, the plot progresses through a series of actions and consequences that trigger subsequent actions and consequences, answering the all-important questions, "What happens next?" and "Where does it all lead to?"

The need for connectedness of events in a story highlights the fact that narratives, like other types of essays, must have some logic in the sequencing of information. Otherwise, your reader may not believe the world you are creating. For instance, if someone hits your protagonist over the head with a metal pipe, and the person simply goes "ouch," and continues as if nothing has happened, then you will probably lose all credibility with your reader. In other words, be realistic with the consequences of the actions in your stories—unless you are writing about some superhuman being.

In Exercise 3.14, you chose your favorite character from a movie or novel and wrote down their character traits in a character diamond. Write that character's name in the space below:

Name of character:

Exercise 3.20. Identifying the four elements of a plot

With reference to your character written above, answer questions 1–6 below. Discuss your answers with a peer, preferably one who has seen the movie or read the novel.

1. What was your character's initial *state of equilibrium* (setting the scene)?

2. What were some of their *internal/external conflicts* (rising action[s])?

3. Who or what got in the way of your character (usually found in the *rising actions*)?

182 ESSENTIAL KNOWLEDGE AND SKILLS FOR ESSAY WRITING

4. What signaled the *climax* in their story (point at which the rising actions peaked)?

5. What was the *major change* in this character at the end of the story (resolution)?

6. What caused the change (*falling action[s]*)?

3.4. WRITING A NARRATIVE ESSAY

3.4.1 Writing the First Draft

Stage 1. Choose a Topic

For this task, I will give you the general topic so that you can discuss elements such as characterization and conflicts with your peers. Your goal is to write a post-apocalyptic short story (one day long) set in a location and time of your choosing. For example, perhaps a disaster has happened and most people have not survived, such as an alien invasion, an asteroid hitting the Earth, or a nuclear war caused by hypersonic missiles.

Your story should have a protagonist and an antagonist—that is, a minimum of two characters—but note that an antagonist does not need to be a human. You should also follow the narrative arc of setting the scene, rising action(s), climax, falling action(s), and resolution. Most importantly, your story must be interesting.

Stage 2. Pre-writing Activity: Generating Ideas

As you have probably gathered, a narrative takes more planning than a description. You need to figure who your characters will be, what conflicts they will encounter, where these conflicts (events) will take place, and how they will proceed to a climax and resolution. To get you started, provide short answers to questions 1–10 below. This will help populate your story-world and generate key elements for your plot.

1. When and where does the story take place (setting the scene)?

2. Who is your main character (protagonist)? Fill in a character diamond for them.

3. What will their initial state of equilibrium be?

4. What kind of change will this character or the character's world undergo?

5. Are there any other characters (animate or inanimate; flat, dynamic, static, etc.)?

6. What will their role be (e.g., antagonist, helper, etc.)?

7. Will there be conflict and how will this be represented (rising action[s])?

8. What will signal the climax (the point at which the rising actions reach a peak)?

9. What will cause the change (falling action[s])?

10. How will the story end (resolution or new state of equilibrium)?

Stage 3. Outlining

The outline below is a suggestive one for a five-paragraph narrative essay. You can have more (or fewer) paragraphs—the choice is yours. However, use this outline as a starting point. It will help you to sequence the most important parts of your narrative and to establish the plotline (the sequence of events that reflect the rise and fall movement that span each side of your climax). If you

184   ESSENTIAL KNOWLEDGE AND SKILLS FOR ESSAY WRITING

need or want to, you can split the climax and falling action(s) into separate paragraphs.

Introduction	Paragraph 1	CONTENT: INTRODUCE YOUR STORY **Hook**. Grab your reader's attention with something memorable. **Set the scene**. Establish the state of balance, normality, or stability that your protagonist is living in (the equilibrium). **Present thesis**. Give the reader an indication of what type of narrative it will be (e.g., quest, inner conflict, external conflict, etc.).
Body paragraphs	Paragraph 2	CONTENT: RISING ACTION(S) **Supporting details**. Start disrupting the equilibrium by introducing internal or external conflicts and/or complications (*don't forget to "show, don't tell" and to use dialogue and character traits to help move the plot forward). **Concluding sentence**. It should be evident at this stage that the equilibrium has been disrupted (*can also be used as a link to the next paragraph).
	Paragraph 3	CONTENT: RISING ACTION(S) **Supporting details**. Continue with the internal or external conflicts and/or complications and build to the climax (*don't forget to "show, don't tell" and use dialogue and character traits to help move the plot forward). **Concluding sentence**. It should be evident at this stage that the climax is coming in the next paragraph (*can also be used as a link to the next paragraph).
	Paragraph 4	CONTENT: CLIMAX + FALLING ACTION **Supporting details**. Present the climax. **Supporting details**. Present the falling action(s); your main goal is to show how the protagonist or the protagonist's world is returning to a state of equilibrium after the climax. **Concluding sentence**. It should be evident at this stage that a problem is being addressed, a quest is ending, a goal is being achieved, or a desire is being fulfilled (*can also be used as a link to the next paragraph).
Conclusion	Paragraph 5	CONTENT: CONCLUDE YOUR STORY **Restate thesis**. Indicate that a new equilibrium has been achieved. **Resolution**. Present the crowning event or the lesson learned. **Evaluation**. What is the result of this new equilibrium?

Stage 4. Drafting

Use your outline and write a first draft of 500–650 words. Make sure you have gone through all the necessary stages for a narrative and have not just written a recount. Remember, a narrative reflects a series of dramatic events that create a change in the protagonist or the protagonist's world.

Give your essay a title that is imaginative and captures the essence of what you have written. Set the line spacing, paper size, margins, and font type and size according to the instructions given by your teacher or as specified in the course book or another style guide. Do not forget to put your name or student ID as a running header.

3.4.2. Writing the Second Draft

Stage 5. Post-Writing Activity: Collaborative Peer Review

Now it is time for peer review. Swap your draft with one of your peers in class. Ask them to check what you have written. Check their draft in return and make notes either directly on their draft or in a separate document. For added feedback (and fun), use the general scoring rubric at the end of the unit to grade each other's essays. At the very minimum, the feedback should answer the following questions:

1. Is there a hook in the introduction? If not, suggest one.

2. Does the introduction clearly set the scene by establishing a state of equilibrium? If not, what could the author elaborate upon or edit?

3. After the introduction, are there a series of actions-and-reactions (rising actions) that also represent conflicts or complications for the protagonist?

4. Do these action–reaction sequences flow seamlessly into one another? Give suggestions on how this section of the plot could be improved in terms of content and/or mechanics (e.g., punctuation, sentence length, or other features).

5. Is there clear evidence of a climax (a turning point in the story)? Underline this point in the essay and write "Climax?" next to it.

6. What is the resolution of the story at the end? In other words, what change occurred in the protagonist, or in some part of their life or world, that has been a shift from disequilibrium (through rising actions) to equilibrium (through falling actions)?

7. Throughout the essay, is there evidence of strong, vivid word choices? Circle any words that you think are vague or weak.

8. Is there at least one example of figurative language? Is it a good example?

9. How many senses are evoked throughout the narrative?

10. What is the overall tone of the piece? What emotions does it evoke in the reader?

Stage 6. Edit and Revise Your Draft

When your peer returns your draft (and possible score), read their feedback. Then reread, rethink, and rewrite your own draft. As you revise your draft, incorporate the feedback from your peer and add any new ideas that may have come to you as you read their draft. Check your edits against the scoring rubric for narrative writing at the end of this unit. See if you can identify the strong and weak points of your essay.

Stage 7. Let Your Revised Draft Sit a While and Then Proofread It Carefully

Give yourself a break from your revised draft before proofreading it. That way, you approach it as an unfamiliar reader would. Also, before proofreading, it is usually a good idea to reread the instructions for the assignment or task rubric and/or to look at the grading guidelines or scoring rubric again. This will help to ensure that you have not gone off task or missed something important during the revision process.

---------------------- SUBMIT FINAL DRAFT ----------------------

188 ESSENTIAL KNOWLEDGE AND SKILLS FOR ESSAY WRITING

APPENDIX 3A.
SCORING RUBRIC FOR NARRATIVE WRITING

MICRO-LEVEL MISTAKES
→ One point deducted for every 5 micro-level mistakes: _____ divided by **5** =

IDEAS / CONTENT _____ out of **30** (6 points per item)
→ Topic is interesting and engaging
→ Conflict and suitable resolution are included
→ An appealing picture of the action and the people are presented
→ Dialogue and sensory details are used to good effect
→ The reader wants to know what happens next at each stage

ORGANIZATION _____ out of **30** (6 points per item)
→ Story has a clear beginning, middle, and end
→ Plot is sequenced as rising action(s) – climax – falling action(s) – resolution
→ Easy to follow events with clear (and realistic) action-consequence chains
→ Transition words and phrases are used to connect ideas
→ Dialogue is realistic and easy to follow

STYLE AND TONE _____ out of **10** (5 points per item)
→ Writer creates a tone and a mood that fits the topic
→ Writing shows the writer's personality or individual style

WORD CHOICE _____ out of **15** (5 points per item)
→ Essay contains specific nouns, vivid verbs, and colorful modifiers
→ Writer uses sensory details and figurative comparisons where appropriate
→ There are no repetitious words, clichés, or general wordiness

SENTENCE FLUENCY _____ out of **10** (5 points per item)
→ Sentences flow smoothly from one idea to the next
→ Writer uses a variety of sentence lengths and structures

CONVENTIONS _____ out of **5** (2.5 points per item)
→ Writer applies basic rules of grammar, usage, and mechanics
→ Paper is presented according required to format

Total _____ out of **100**

NARRATIVE WRITING   189

APPENDIX 3B. UNIT 3 ANSWER KEY

Exercise 3.1
Answers will vary so consult with your classmates or teacher.

Exercise 3.2
Answers will vary, but you may have something similar to the following:

1 = contemplate, **2** = sprint, **3** = reading, **4** = chuckle

5 = leap, **6** = curl up, **7** = chow down, **8** = surf (the internet)

Exercise 3.3
Answers will vary, but here are my choices for stronger, more vivid verbs:

1. The flower <u>danced</u> in the wind.
2. She <u>tiptoed</u> out of the room.
3. Pam <u>slithered</u> out of bed at 05:00 am.
4. In an instant, the police <u>smashed</u> through the door.
5. He <u>devoured</u> the cookie.
6. The lazy dog <u>waddled</u> behind his owner.
7. Without hesitating, she <u>snatched</u> the money.
8. He was <u>petrified</u> of snakes.
9. She <u>glared</u> at him.
10. She <u>screamed at</u> him, "No. I <u>hate</u> pizza"

Answers will also vary for this part of the exercise, but you may have something similar to the following:

1 = pondering, **2** = racing, **3** = captivated by, **4** = celebrating,

5 = leaping, **6** = throwing in the towel, **7** = wolfing down,

8 = pored over

Exercise 3.4–3.6
Answers will vary so consult with your classmates or teacher.

Exercise 3.7
1. The hook is a description (setting the scene): "It was the hottest night on record."

190 ESSENTIAL KNOWLEDGE AND SKILLS FOR ESSAY WRITING

2. There is mainly a description of a person, the place they are in, and activities they are engaged in (i.e., the writer is establishing an equilibrium for their protagonist).

3. Thesis statement: "It was the look of longing. The longing of a girl who will never meet her loved one again." The points of development relate to characterization. The writer is attempting to get the reader to empathize with his protagonist.

Exercise 3.8–3.9
Answers will vary so consult with your classmates or teacher.

Exercise 3.10 (probable answers)
TEXT A: The plunge.
TEXT B: The promise.
TEXT C: The particulars.
TEXT D: The omen / self-referral.
TEXT E: The promise.

Exercise 3.11
Answers will vary so consult with your classmates or teacher.

Exercise 3.12
Answers will vary, but the most likely chain of events involve Anna dying, Sean breaking his knife somehow, and then Sean escaping into a building, where he takes refuge on the roof.

Exercise 3.13
1. The paragraph reveals a shocking twist in the story – the girl is actually a ghost.
2. Answers will vary, but most people will probably feel shocked and maybe also sad.
3. The resolution is that she has accepted her fate.
4. The lyrics are a reference to the song they talked about when they first met.

Exercise 3.14–3.15
Answers will vary so consult with your classmates or teacher.

Exercise 3.16

AUGUSTUS GLOOP

Physical traits: *light skin, red hair, and blue eyes. Quite tall but fat/chubby, wears traditional German clothes.*
Personality traits: *gluttonous.*

VERUCA SALT

Physical traits: *dark, straight hair, icy blue eyes and pale skin, long-sleeved navy-blue blazer, beige tights, and white ankle-length socks and black shoes.*
Personality traits: *very spoilt.*

VIOLET BEAUREGARDE

Physical traits: *thin, pale skinned, short straight blonde hair, blue eyes, wears a light blue tracksuit with blue and white trainers.*
Personality traits: *very competitive.*

MIKE TEAVEE

Physical traits: *short brown hair, fair skinned, rosy cheeks, green eyes, grey t-shirt with a skull on it under a long-sleeved black shirt, dark grey sweatpants, and black sneakers.*
Personality traits: *easily angered, a bit of a know it all and seeks attention.*

Exercise 3.17

1. The three main actions that are taken after Cinderella loses her slippers are as follows:
   a) The prince sends out a proclamation that he is trying to find the woman who lost a glass slipper at the ball.
   b) The prince sends out a delegation to go from house to house to find the woman who fits the glass slipper.
   c) The stepsisters try on the glass slipper at their house but it does not fit them.
2. Cinderella tries on the glass slipper and it fits.
3. The prince proposes to Cinderella and then he takes her to the palace.
4. Cinderella marries the prince.
5. Cinderella and her prince live happily ever after.

Exercise 3.18

1. The author provides key information that the reader needs to understand the starting point of a story. This usually involves answering who and/or what will be involved in the upcoming story and when and where it takes place.
2. A series of events that build toward the climax (central point of interest/conflict).
3. Conflict can be with self, others, nature, society, technology, or any other external force.
4. During the climax, the three things that typically occur are: (a) the action is at its highest point; (b) disequilibrium is at the tipping point; and (c) the reader should be emotionally invested.
5. The disequilibrium (imbalance) is slowly transformed into equilibrium (balance), as the protagonist addresses the main complication.
6. The resolution reinforces the new state of equilibrium and leaves the reader with a feeling of completion.

Exercise 3.19

Answers will vary so consult with your classmates or teacher.

Exercise 3.20

1 = c, **2** = d, **3** = a, **4** = b.

Exercise 3.21

Answers will vary so consult with your classmates or teacher.

Unit 4
EXPOSITORY WRITING

Unit Goals

Upon completing this unit, you should be able to demonstrate the following knowledge and skills:

- Recognize distinct kinds of expository writing.
- Organize and sequence expository writing using appropriate rhetorical structuring and sentence level connectors.
- Use Venn diagrams and concept maps to brainstorm and organize ideas.
- Write compare/contrast, classification, and cause-effect essays.

Definition

Expository essays deal with facts, ideas, and beliefs. Their purpose is to define, explain, analyze, compare, and/or contrast a topic or topics. In order to accomplish each of these functions, there is a corresponding number of expository text-types, each of which calls for somewhat different language choices and organizational patterns. This chapter will cover the most common types you are likely to encounter in your undergraduate studies: compare/ contrast, classification, and cause-effect.

> **Define** *Describe the meaning and exact limits of something.*
>
> **Explain** *Make something clear or easy to understand.*
>
> **Analyze** *Examine something in detail in order to reveal non-obvious things about it.*

194 ESSENTIAL KNOWLEDGE AND SKILLS FOR ESSAY WRITING

A *compare/contrast essay* can explore similarities, differences, or similarities and differences. A subtype of compare/contrast is the advantages/disadvantages essay. We can classify it as a subtype because it is very similar to compare and contrast, only there is one topic and we compare its good and bad points.

A *classification essay* sets up relationships between things, people, places, or ideas. In this type of writing, we group things, people, places, or ideas together. This grouping, which is based on some shared feature, allows us to classify something into neatly demarcated categories. This type of writing draws heavily on tax-onomies (systems of classification, e.g., types of animals or plants), relationships of subordination (being a member of a class, e.g., a *hammer* as a type of *tool*), superordination (being an overarching class, e.g., *tool* being a class that includes *hammer*, *saw*, etc.), and meronymy (being a part of a larger whole, e.g., a *finger* being a part of a *hand*).

The final type of expository writing we will look at is the *cause-effect essay*. Fortunately, once you know the basic principles for writing the other two types of exposition, then it just a matter of applying those principles to a slightly different organizational pattern: one that makes use of causal-conditional conjunctions to portray cause-effect relationships.

Example 4.1 illustrates expository writing and is characteristic of the kind of text found in a scientific textbook.

4.1   Example of an expository paragraph

Clouds and fog are formed when moisture becomes visible in the air. This moisture comes from the saturation of water vapor (gas) in the air. Saturation occurs when the amount of water vapor present is more than the surrounding air can hold. Saturation can be achieved in two ways: (a) **evaporation**, wherein the moisture accumulates from sources of water evaporating from the Earth's surface; or (b) **condensation**, wherein the surrounding air temperature drops, altering the ratio of air molecules to water vapor. The only difference between clouds and fog is the altitude. A cloud is visible moisture that occurs at or above 50 feet; fog is visible moisture that occurs below 50 feet.

The Formation of Clouds and Fog by Neil Bowen

This is typical expository writing. It is full of technical vocabulary, nominalizations, and precise details. It also includes examples of the following elements (and more):

CAUSE-EFFECT

→ Clouds and fog are formed when moisture becomes visible in the air.
→ Saturation occurs when the amount of water vapor present is more than the surrounding air can hold.
→ … the moisture accumulates from sources of water evaporating from the Earth's surface
→ … the surrounding air temperature drops, altering the ratio of air molecules to water vapor.

COMPARISON

→ The only difference between clouds and fog is the altitude.

CLASSIFICATION

→ A cloud is visible moisture that occurs at or above 50 feet; fog is visible moisture that occurs below 50 feet.

4.1. KEY SKILLS

4.1.1. Elaborating, Enhancing, and Extending upon Details

A common issue when students begin writing expository texts is that they simply list a number of facts or pieces information. Your teacher may then ask you to add more detail, so you proceed to add more nouns and adjectives, thinking that expository writing is just like descriptive writing. However, an exposition calls for an extension or elaboration of supporting details and not just enhancement of existing ones. An effective way to ensure that you have good supporting details is to ask the following questions of your topic (X):

• What does X consist of?

- How is X best explored with regard to my main idea? (i.e., what kind of relationship exists: compare/contrast, classification, cause–effect?)
- Can I give a give a specific example of X?

For instance, instead of just writing, *It takes confidence to talk in front of a class of students*, elaborate upon the topic of public speaking as shown in Example 4.2.

4.2 Example of elaborating on a topic

1. One of the biggest phobias people have is public speaking. 2. Speaking in front of a large audience can be nerve wracking as all the attention is on you. 3. You have to be able to talk clearly and have something interesting to say. 4. For example, if you stand in front of an audience and start mumbling about what you had for breakfast, people would probably stop listening or may even laugh at you.

The Phobia of Public Speaking by Neil Bowen

In this example, Sentence 1 is the topic sentence of the paragraph. Sentences 2 and 3 elaborate on the topic of fear of public speaking. Sentence 4 then gives an example, which helps the reader visualize the process of speaking in front of an audience.

Exercise 4.1. Elaborating on a topic

For each of the three statements below provide two elaborating details and one example. Vary the connectors you use and try not to be repetitive with your word choices.

1. Studying face-to-face is better than online learning.

2. Motorbike drivers should always wear a helmet.

3. Most Westerners are not aware that there are many types of noodle.

4.1.2. Connecting Ideas: Transitions

Two of the more challenging aspects of writing expository essays is (a) *connecting the details* and (b) the *overall organization*. To connect individual sentences, you can use some of the conjunctive adjuncts introduced in Table 1.1, Unit 1. The most useful of these I reproduce below in Table 4.1 while also adding some of my own:

Table 4.1. Useful adjuncts for expository writing		
Adjuncts for Comparisons (Similarities)		
In addition	Correspondingly	Compared to
Similarly	Just as	As well as
Likewise	In the same way	At the same time
Adjuncts for Contrasts (Differences)		
However	On the contrary	On the other hand
Even though	In contrast	Although
Unlike	Conversely	While
Adjuncts for Causes (c) and Effects (e)		
Since (c)	The reason is (c)	As a result of (e)
Because of (c)	Consequently (e)	Thus (e)
Results from (c)	Therefore (c)	Hence (e)

4.1.3. Rhetorical Structure: Block Method or Point-by-Point Method

Most five-paragraph expository essays follow two basic overall structures. These are the *block method* and the *point-by-point method*. The outlines below are tailored for a compare/contrast essay. The first one (block method) focuses on each of the subjects being compared/contrasted. The second one (point-by-point method) focuses one by one on the similarities and/or differences between the subjects.

Neither method is necessarily better than the other is. It is simply a matter of what you have chosen to focus on. Once you have chosen the appropriate method, you can use the relevant outline to help you organize the overall structure of your expository essay. As the unit progresses, you will learn to tailor these outlines to fit other expository essays.

Block Method

In the ***block method***, for a compare/contrast essay, each body paragraph addresses one of the subjects from your pair of subjects and compares/contrasts aspects that they share. Thus, your focus is on the subjects that are being compared/contrasted across paragraphs. For example, if you are going to compare Honolulu (subject 1) and Singapore (subject 2), items that you might compare and contrast are things like population, climate, lifestyle, cost-of-living, etc. These are your shared aspects, which you would first address for one of the subjects (e.g., Honolulu) and then address for the other subject (e.g., Singapore). The block method outline for a five-paragraph compare/contrast essay is shown below.

Introduction	**Paragraph 1**	CONTENT: INTRODUCE YOUR ARGUMENT **Hook**. Grab your reader's attention with something memorable. **Background information**. Introduce general topic. **Background information**. Introduce specific topic. **Present thesis.** Present the subjects and indicate whether they will be compared, contrasted, or both).
Body paragraphs	**Paragraph 2**	CONTENT: DISCUSS ASPECTS OF SUBJECT 1 **Topic sentence for subject 1**. *Aspect A* – detail(s) + example(s). *Aspect B* – detail(s) + example(s). *Aspect C* – detail(s) + example(s). **Concluding sentence** (*can also be used as a link to the next paragraph).
	Paragraph 3	CONTENT: DISCUSS ASPECTS OF SUBJECT 2 **Topic sentence for subject 2**. *Aspect A* – detail(s) + example(s). *Aspect B* – detail(s) + example(s). *Aspect C* – detail(s) + example(s). **Concluding sentence** (*can also be used as a link to the next paragraph).
	Paragraph 4	CONTENT: OPTIONAL REFLECTION This paragraph is optional and is often used to reflect on the comparisons/contrasts you have made—for example, by recounting an experience that illustrates it.
Conclusion	**Paragraph 5**	CONTENT: CONCLUDE YOUR ESSAY **Restate thesis**. Remind the reader what your central purpose for writing this essay was (i.e., reiterate why the topic is important). **Summarize**. Review the main points you compared/contrasted. **Final thought**. Address or reflect upon your essay in a memorable way.

Exercise 4.2 presents a body paragraph from a student's essay that uses the block method. The essay compares two periods of

political protests in Thailand: those in 2013 (subject 1) and those in 2020 (subject 2). The body paragraph in the exercise covers subject 2 (i.e., it gives one aspect and some supporting details for the 2020 protests).

Exercise 4.2. Analyzing a block method paragraph

Read the paragraph and then answer the questions that follow. As you read the paragraph, pay attention to the transitions between sentences.

In response to the 2020 protests, the government took a number of different tactics from those used previously. First, they used high-pressure water trucks to attack protestors (Post Reporters, 2020). Second, they sent armed forces to arrest the protesters. Third, the government enacted an emergency decree in Bangkok. At the same time, the media were banned from broadcasting news about the demonstrations (Anonymous, 2020). However, in contrast to ten years ago, social media quickly became the tool of the masses, and that enabled information, including the telling of the movement of troops, to be easily disseminated in real time.

References
Anonymous. (2020, July 30). *Thailand's ban on fake, distorted news, fearmongering begins Friday, as media threatened with censorship.* Thai PBS World. https://www.thaipbsworld.com/thailands-media-restrictions-begin-friday-with-ban-on-fake-distorted-fearmongering-news/

Post Reporters. (2020, Oct 17). *Water canon blast rally.* Bangkok Post. https://www.bangkokpost.com/thailand/politics/2003475/water-cannon-blast-rally

Paragraph 2 from *Two Decades of Protests: What is Different Now?* by P. Srihased

1. What is the main idea stated in the topic sentence (i.e., what is the main aspect the writer will contrast in this paragraph?)

2. How many points of contrast do they include in this paragraph? List them below.

Note how some of their examples have in-text citations to a source. In this type of essay, you may need to provide references to attribute original sources of information.

Point-by-Point Method

In the ***point-by-point method*** for a compare/contrast essay, subjects are compared and/or contrasted to each other within each paragraph. Each body paragraph contains details on one aspect for both subjects. For example, suppose you have decided to use the point-by-point method to compare/contrast the <u>facilities</u> (an aspect) of *Airport-1* and *Airport-2* (your two subjects). You might start by comparing/contrasting the <u>seating areas</u> (feature 1 of their shared aspect), giving specific details about each airport's seating capacity, quiet spaces, type of seating, etc. Once you have covered this feature in sufficient detail for each airport, you may then want to write about another feature related to the facilities (feature 2 of their shared aspect), such as <u>access to changing rooms</u>, <u>showers</u>, or <u>restrooms</u>. Thus, the focus is on the similarities and/or differences between the subjects in the same paragraph: One shared aspect of both subjects is mentioned in the same paragraph. The five-paragraph outline for this method is shown below.

Introduction	**Paragraph 1**	<u>CONTENT: INTRODUCE YOUR TOPIC</u> **Hook**. Grab your reader's attention with something memorable. **Background information**. Introduce general topic. **Background information**. Introduce specific topic. **Present thesis**. Present the subjects and indicate whether they will be compared, contrasted, or both.
Body paragraphs	**Paragraph 2**	<u>CONTENT: DISCUSS ASPECT A FOR BOTH SUBJECTS</u> **Topic sentence for Aspect A**. *Aspect A (Feature 1)* – give at least two details. *Aspect A (Feature 2)* – give at least two details. **Concluding sentence** (*can also be used as a link to the next paragraph).
	Paragraph 3	<u>CONTENT: DISCUSS ASPECT B FOR BOTH SUBJECTS</u> **Topic sentence for Aspect B**. *Aspect B (Feature 1)* – give at least two details. *Aspect B (Feature 2)* – give at least two details. **Concluding sentence** (*can also be used as a link to the next paragraph).
	Paragraph 4	<u>CONTENT: DISCUSS ASPECT C FOR BOTH SUBJECTS</u> **Topic sentence for Aspect C**. *Aspect C (Feature 1)* – give at least two details. *Aspect C (Feature 2)* – give at least two details. **Concluding sentence** (*can also be used as a link to the next paragraph).

EXPOSITORY WRITING   201

Conclusion	Paragraph 5	CONTENT: CONCLUDE YOUR ESSAY **Restate thesis**. Remind the reader what your central purpose for writing this essay was (i.e., reiterate why the topic is important). **Summarize**. Review the main points you compared/contrasted. **Final thought**. Address or reflect upon your essay in a memorable way.

In the next exercise, there is a body paragraph taken from a student essay that uses the point-by-point method. The essay's topic is a comparison of two Thai kings: Ramkhamhaeng of Sukhothai (subject 1) and Mangrai of Lanna (subject 2).

Exercise 4.3. Analyzing a point-by-point method paragraph

Read the paragraph and answer the questions that follow. Note how the student has given good examples, and how some of these examples have citations sources.

The two kings' most noticeable distinction is their strategies towards the Kingdom's expansion. King Ramkhamhaeng took a diplomatic approach. Rather than engaging in battles, for example, he successfully expanded his kingdom with diplomatic tactics. Specifically, several kingdoms allied with him or voluntarily succumbed to him. His diplomacy skills also greatly contributed to the civilization of Thailand. He promoted overseas trade and accepted foreign cultures and business, such as the industry of Chinese ceramic pottery called Sangkalok, which later became essential in his kingdom's economy (Mishra, 2010, pp. 37–38). In contrast, although King Mangrai was also diplomatic, he adopted more strategies that were confrontational. When he ascended to the throne of Ngoenyang, for example, he demanded that surrounding principalities pay homage to him and subjugated those who refused. With this strategy, he managed to attain numerous principalities; consequently, he was able to establish a new kingdom called "Lanna" and its capital Chiang Mai in the north of Thailand (Prachakitkorachak, 1961, pp. 281–295).

References
Mishra, P. P. (2010). *The history of Thailand*. ABC-CLIO.
Prachakitkorachak, P. (1961). พงศาวดารโยนก. Silapabunnakan.

Paragraph 2 from *The Great Kings* by P. Srihased and V. Thongsuk

202 ESSENTIAL KNOWLEDGE AND SKILLS FOR ESSAY WRITING

1. What is the main idea stated in the topic sentence? (i.e., what is the main aspect the author compares and contrasts in this paragraph?)

2. What is the difference between these two kings with regard to this aspect?

3. What is the difference between the block method and the point-by-point method?

4.2. COMPARE/CONTRAST

4.2.1. General Guidelines for Compare/Contrast Writing

Choosing a Good Topic

A compare/contrast essay should be undertaken in order to *make a novel point* or *serve a specific purpose*. Often such essays do one of the following:

- **Clarify** an unknown or not well-understood subject or pair of subjects.
- Lead to a **fresh insight** or new way of viewing a subject or pair of subjects.
- Bring one or both of the subjects into sharper **focus**.
- Show that one of the subjects is **better** than the other is.

The *same points* should be discussed for both subjects; it is not necessary, however, to give both subjects the same degree of development if only one of them is the writer's primary interest.

After choosing your topic, consider the following three questions:

1. Will you be covering similarities (comparing), differences (contrasts), or both?
2. Will you focus on one of the subjects more than you focus on the other?

EXPOSITORY WRITING   203

3. What does your audience want or need to know? For example, if you are comparing two airports, the average reader will not care about the length of runways or who designed the airports—though an audience of engineers or architects might be interested in these things. Most readers will want to know about customer-service features such as parking, shuttle services, food outlets, and duty-free shopping.

Exercise 4.4. Choosing good topics

Brainstorm ideas for compare/contrast essays. Think of pairs of people, places, and things that would make for an interesting compare/contrast topic for a reader (not just yourself!). Compare your completed list with those of your peers.

1. PEOPLE   and
2. PLACES   and
3. THINGS   and

Using a Venn Diagram to Generate Ideas

A ***Venn diagram*** is a graphical tool for showing relationships among things or finite groups of things. Pictured below, the circles that overlap have something in common (i.e., a shared trait, aspect, or feature). Circles that do not overlap do not share any traits with each other.

In pairs, choose one of your topics and fill in a Venn diagram. Use your Venn diagram to indicate areas of overlap and difference in

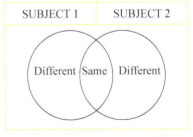

your two subjects. Decide on at least three aspects that are different (contrast) for each subject and three aspects that are the same (compare).

204 ESSENTIAL KNOWLEDGE AND SKILLS FOR ESSAY WRITING

Writing a Thesis Statement

A thesis statement for a compare/contrast essay is relatively simple. You state your topic, which includes the two subjects of your essay; give an indication that you will be comparing and/or contrasting them; and introduce what aspects you will be focusing on. The thesis may be stated in one sentence or two but rarely more than two.

The examples below of thesis statements are taken from three compare/contrast student essays. You will see that they are written in different styles but all achieve the same purpose. I have also provided you with the connecting sentences that lead up to the thesis statement when they are needed to understand the thesis.

> **4.4 Example of thesis statement (1)**
>
> This essay explores how two political protests in Bangkok (2010 and 2020) had similar goals but two different responses from the military.
>
> From *Two Decades of Protests: What is Different Now?* by Peerada Srihased

This first thesis statement (above) is straightforward but formulaic, in the form of *this essay is about such and such*. It thus lacks originality and suggests an essay that will present information as a list-like review of facts.

> **4.5 Example of thesis statement (2)**
>
> They were close companions who were similar in two ways: Both started their lives studying under the same master and ascended to the throne around the same time. Yet despite these similarities, the two Kings had distinctive approaches to achieving their goals, which affected Thailand in different ways.
>
> From *The Great Kings* by P. Srihased and V. Thongsuk

This second thesis statement (underlined above) is more original and promises a more in-depth analysis. We have already encountered some of the corresponding body paragraphs in Exercises 4.2 and 4.3.

> **4.6 Example of thesis statement (3)**
>
> The debate over whether public or private employment is better is never-ending. <u>Understanding the similarities and differences between each can help you make a decision on which is more suitable to you. Some primary things you have to consider are benefits, competition, and types of job.</u>
>
> From *Public Sector vs Private Sector Employment* by Kanyarat Nakapiw

This last thesis statement (underlined above) is given in two logically linked sentences. These announce the purpose and the interest for the reader of doing the comparison/contrast as well as the aspects to be discussed. Note how this third essay could be very easily changed into an advantages/disadvantages essay, a text-type that we will discuss later.

Now that you recognize a compare/contrast thesis statement, Exercise 4.5 will give you practice in writing your own thesis statements for compare/contrast essays.

> **Exercise 4.5. Writing compare/contrast thesis statements**
>
>
>
> Look back at the topics you came up with for Exercise 4.4. Write potential thesis statements in the spaces below for each of your topics. Remember to be clear, concise, and original.
>
> 1. Thesis statement on comparing and/or contrasting *people*:
>
>
> 2. Thesis statement on comparing and/or contrasting *places*:
>
>
> 3. Thesis statement on comparing and/or contrasting *things*:

Other Elements in the Introduction

In addition to thesis statements, compare/contrast essay introductions include other elements we have covered in previous units—namely, a hook and connecting sentences, as illustrated in the next exercise, Exercise 4.6.

Exercise 4.6. Analyzing a compare/contrast introduction

Read the paragraph below and think about how the writer establishes the territory, the importance of the topic, and the reader's interest. Then answer the questions that follow.

Many people think that a psychopath and a sociopath are the same. To be perfectly honest, it is quite hard to spot the differences between these two personality types, even for someone with a background in psychology. Their labels rhyme, and they both represent deviant tendencies, but there are a lot of differences hidden under the surface. In the following paragraphs, we will take a psychological trip into the minds of sociopaths and psychopaths, who may or may not be "mentally ill" and may or may not be "fit to live in our society." We will dig deep into the core traits that separate them and discover what the real differences between these two personality disorders are.

Introduction from *Who is More Dangerous?* by Pitcha Dangprasith

1. Do you think this is a good introductory paragraph? Give reasons for your answer.

2. Which part of the paragraph comprises the thesis statement? What is unusual and original about it?

3. What will the tone of this essay likely be? Give examples of how the writer has achieved this tone.

Good Supporting Details

Each of the body paragraphs in your compare/contrast essay should be tied to the thesis statement. Remember that the topic sentence in each paragraph can help you do this. You will also need to present evidence or support in the form of accurate, up-to-date, well-researched information. So be prepared to cite authoritative sources as needed (for information about referencing see section 5.13, Unit 5).

4.2.2. Sequencing a Compare/Contrast Essay

Without clear transitions between the aspects you are discussing, the overall structure of a compare/contrast essay will break down. Transitions between paragraphs and sentences are thus very important in this type of essay. Exercise 4.7 will give you practice in organizing and correctly sequencing compare/contrast content.

Exercise 4.7. Sequencing compare/contrast elements

The sentences below are from the student essay comparing and contrasting sociopaths and psychopaths. Put the sentences in the correct order. What organizing method was used by this student?

First, psychopaths do not have feelings; they cannot feel love, sadness, or even guilt.

- [ ] a. Therefore, their feelings and expressions are just mere impersonation of others', and thus they often struggle to touch the concept of being "human."
- [ ] b. However, not feeling all of these things is quite a different story.
- [ ] c. They do not care about others. They are driven only by their own pleasure.
- [ ] d. Being human is to feel the present, past, future, and all the emotions life puts you through; to be able to learn from scrapes and bruises; to laugh, to cry and to love.

You may wonder, what about sociopaths?

- [ ] a. Sociopaths do have feelings, even if this is just 20–30 percent of the levels of normal people. Nevertheless, they do have them.
- [ ] b. It can be assumed that this comes from their deviant brain structures. Psychopath's brains, for example, lack the almond-shaped nuclei called "amygdala," which is the part of the brain responsible for creating and understanding emotions.
- [ ] c. They are able to fall in love, feel guilt, and even be sympathetic towards others; whereas psychopaths are only able to feel just one thing: superiority.
- [ ] d. In contrast, sociopaths' brains are 100 percent complete and function normally as for other people. Therefore, they are able to touch the concept of "genuine" feelings.

Paragraphs 2 and 3 from *Who is More Dangerous?* by Pitcha Dangprasith

A Strong Conclusion

In a complex essay, such as one that features the organizing method of compare/contrast, the conclusion is a very important part of the essay. Since a reader will often go straight to the conclusion to get an overall view of an essay's content, you should spend a reasonable amount of time planning and writing it. In fact, it is good practice to spend just as much time and effort writing the conclusion as you did the introduction.

As a general guideline, for the conclusion of a compare/contrast essay, summarize and synthesize the main points that you have compared and contrasted in each body paragraph, and reflect on their significance. At a minimum, your conclusion should accomplish the following goals:

- Restate why the topic is important.
- Review the main points of your argument.
- Address or reflect upon your thesis statement.
- Make a memorable point to leave the reader with something to think about.

The following exercise is based on the concluding paragraph from a five-paragraph compare/contrast essay. Not only will it provide you with a good example of a concluding paragraph for a compare/contrast essay, but it will also give you practice in recognizing the main elements listed above.

Exercise 4.8. Analyzing a concluding paragraph

Read the extract below, which is taken from a student essay. It is the conclusion to the same essay as the body paragraphs you saw in Exercise 4.7. Answer the questions that follow.

Psychopaths and sociopaths often do not know what is wrong with them and carry on with their lives without realizing that they are mentally ill, resulting in worsening personalities and, in worst-case scenarios, murder. Are they normal? No, they are not; they are ill, mentally ill. That makes it even more important for you not to feel disgusted by them, even if their actions are terrible. Try to understand that they cannot help themselves:

It is not their fault. Be open-minded. For any psychopaths or sociopaths who have just realized that they are one, I hope this essay has provided some needed information about your personality disorder. And to them I say this: Remember, being a psychopath or a sociopath is not your fault; sometimes it just happens, and there is no stopping it. Even though there is still no cure for your disorder, there is still time to stop you from falling into a dark abyss.

Conclusion from *Who is More Dangerous?* by Pitcha Dangprasith

1. Has the author restated why the topic is important? If so, how?

2. How many main points of comparison and contrast has the author reviewed?

3. How has the author reflected upon the thesis statement?

4. Who is the author speaking to in this concluding paragraph? Do you think this is effective? Why or why not?

5. What memorable point(s) does the author leave the reader with? What is your reaction to this ending?

6. Is the essay unified?

4.2.3. Writing a Compare/Contrast Essay

Stage 1. Choosing the Topic

For this task, you will write about two cities of your choice. Think about what the purpose of comparing/contrasting two cities might be, and then select two that you would enjoy writing about.

Stage 2. Pre-writing Activity: Using a Venn Diagram

Here are some aspects that you might compare and contrast between the two cities: *climate, population, size, location, cost of living, friendliness of locals,* and *famous landmarks.* Do some research on your two cities and fill in a Venn diagram to explore the similarities and differences.

Stage 3. Outlining

Look at the items (aspects) you have listed for each of the cities (subjects). Think about removing items that do not contribute well to addressing your purpose in comparing/contrasting those cities.

Choose one of the compare/contrast outlines introduced above (block method or point-by-point method), and fill in the details where indicated. Once you have finished populating your outline, give it to one of your peers. Ask them to answer the following questions about it:

1. Is the thesis statement clear? If not, suggest how to improve it.
2. Does the writer use the block or point-by-point method? Is this method effective for the type of focus they have? If not, suggest why they should change it.
3. Does each topic sentence clearly state the point of comparison? If not, make suggestions for improvement.
4. What is the best part of the outline?

Stage 4. Drafting

Make any necessary changes to your outline using the feedback from your peer. Use your updated outline and write a first draft of 500–650 words. Make sure you have a brief thesis statement in the introduction and a concluding remark at the end. Give your draft a title that is imaginative and captures the essence of what you have written. Set the line spacing, paper size, margins, and font type and size according to the instructions given by your teacher or as specified in the course book or another style guide. Do not forget to put your name or student ID as a running header.

--------------------- **SUBMIT FIRST DRAFT** -----------------------

Stage 5. Post-Writing Activity: Collaborative Peer Review

Swap drafts with one of your peers in class. Ask them to check what you have written. Check their draft in return and make notes either directly on their draft or in a separate document. For added feedback (and fun), use the scoring rubric at the end of the unit (Appendix 4B) to grade each other's essays. At the very minimum, the feedback should answer the following questions:

1. In one sentence, what is the essay about?

2. Identify the hook. Is it effective? Make suggestions for improvements if needed.
3. Is there a clear topic sentence in each body paragraph? Underline any topic sentence that needs improvement.
4. List the main details that the writer compares/contrasts. Are they easy to identify?

5. Are the comparisons/contrasts supported with examples? Put an asterisk (*) next to details that perhaps need more supporting information.
6. Does the writer use connectors correctly? Highlight any incorrectly used connectors, and indicate places where specific connectors could be added.
7. Does the writer rephrase the thesis in the conclusion?
8. In the conclusion, is there an opinion or a suggestion about the two subjects?
9. Do you agree with the writer's final words? If not, why not?

212 ESSENTIAL KNOWLEDGE AND SKILLS FOR ESSAY WRITING

Stage 6. Edit and Revise Your Draft

When your peer returns your draft (and possible score), edit and revise your essay according to their feedback. Check your edits against the scoring rubric for expository essays. See if you can identify your strong and weak points.

-------------------- **WRITE SECOND DRAFT** --------------------

Stage 7. Let Your Revised Draft Sit a While and Then Proofread It Carefully

Give yourself a break from your second draft before proofreading it. That way, you approach it as an unfamiliar reader would. Also, before proofreading, it is usually a good idea to reread the instructions for the assignment or task rubric and/or look at the grading criteria or scoring rubric again. This will help to ensure that you have not gone off task or missed something important during the revision process.

-------------------- **SUBMIT FINAL DRAFT** --------------------

4.2.4. Writing about Advantages and Disadvantages

Another way to compare and contrast something is to talk about its **advantages** (positive points) and **disadvantages** (negative points). This type of writing is most useful when you are not making a comparison of two things; you have one topic but you want to compare the good and bad aspects of it to answer questions such as, *Should I buy the new iPhone?*

The next exercise includes a student paragraph on the advantages of working for a private company in Thailand. As you read it, pay attention to how she moves between ideas and uses supporting details to enhance the aspects she is covering.

> **Exercise 4.9. Analyzing an advantages paragraph**

Read the example below of a student paragraph about why she wants to work for a private company (she is focusing on advantages). After reading it, answer the questions that follow.

The best option for me when I graduate is working for a private company, because it can give many advantages and is exciting. Firstly, the work in a private company is challenging. For example, you have to compete with other companies, so you need to continually learn new knowledge and come up with great ideas. Another reason is you have to work against a tight deadline; this is very important, because if your work is not finished, your colleagues cannot finish the next part after yours, and then the whole work is delayed. Secondly, you need to have excellent communication skills. Moreover, because working for a private company requires working as a team like an ant army or bee colony, you have to communicate with many people to get your work done. In addition, a private company can provide you with a high salary, and if you are a real gem, every company is going to want you. That is why you can negotiate with them to get a desirable salary. These reasons are why I would choose working with a private company; it is a great opportunity to challenge yourself and grow as a person!

Working for a Private Company by Natthaladda Thammachak

1. What are some of the supporting details?

2. Is there any place where you would like more explanation or detail? If so, where?

3. Does the conclusion end with a suggestion, an opinion, or a prediction?

4. If this paragraph were part of a larger comparison/contrast essay, what might the rest of the essay be about?

An essay that only reviews advantages (or disadvantages) can be seen as rather one-sided and unbalanced. Thus, in most cases, both advantages and disadvantages would be considered. The writer may argue that the advantages outweigh the disadvantages, or vice versa, or that they are more or less in balance.

Go back to the compare/contrast essay you did on the two cities and consider how you would revise it to focus on the advantages/disadvantages of one of those cities. What point could you make based on the relative advantages/disadvantages of the two? Discuss your ideas with a peer.

Exercise 4.10. Writing about advantages and disadvantages

In pairs, choose a topic and write it in the space below. One of you write a 100–150 word paragraph about its advantages. The other write a 100–150 word paragraph about its disadvantages.

Topic:

*Read each other's paragraphs and add one idea to the other person's paragraph.

4.3. CLASSIFICATION

Classification is another type of expository essay. When you classify something, you characterize it in relation to other things, people, or ideas. In this type of writing, you group together things, people, ideas, etc., based on some shared feature(s). In other words, you classify them by putting them into *categories*. You can also place these categories into *hierarchies* (taxonomies) to show how the items and groupings are related to one another in terms of subordination and superordination.

For example, animals can be grouped together into classes based on the distinctive features that they share. For instance, the first superordinate classification of animals is based on those with a backbone (*vertebrates*) and those without a backbone (*invertebrates*). Within the class of vertebrates, there is a further distinction between *warm-blooded* and *cold-blooded* vertebrates, as shown in Figure 4.3.

Warm-blooded is a subcategory of vertebrates whose membership is restricted to animals that maintain a constant warm body temperature. Within this category are mammals and birds. When we get down to this level of classification, animals are distinguished via their morphology (bodily components and structure). In simple terms, this means to be considered as a member of group X, the subject must have the distinctive features A, B, etc. For birds, this primarily means having feathers and a beak.

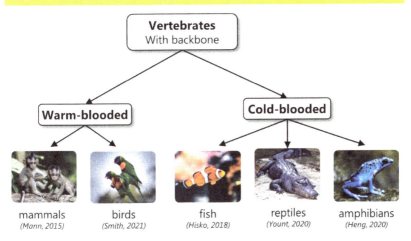

Figure 4.3. Classification system for vertebrates

What is the purpose of classification? Humans classify, categorize, and taxonomize all manner of things because it helps to organize and make sense of a complex world. Some of the things we classify exist in the physical world (e.g., plants and animals) or are abstracted from these (e.g., shapes and colors), while others are more complex abstractions (e.g., forms of government such as capitalism, communism, Marxism, and libertarianism). These things are not physical objects but nonetheless we consider them as things we can describe and classify.

4.3.1. General Guidelines for Classificatory Writing

Choosing a Good Topic

Classification is most commonly found in business, science, advertising, and opinion writing by essayists and journalists (i.e., editorials). In advertising and opinion writing, topics can be subjective, humorous, or even sarcastic.

To create an interesting essay, it is advisable not to choose obvious topics. Obvious topics might include types of cars (e.g., hatchback, sedan, convertible) or dogs (e.g., Poodles, Labradors, Alsatians). However, you may want to choose an obvious topic if you can introduce a quality or feature for classifying them that readers are not likely to know about (e.g., cars with new kinds of power sources, new cross-breeds of dog, or cars/dogs classified in some kind of novel, humorous way, such as type of owner). Moreover, as with most types of writing, you should choose a topic that will be of interest to you and your audience, and feel free to use your imagination. Feel free to be creative and original, and to enjoy the process of creating an interesting classification essay. Consider in Example 4.6 the introductory paragraph to a student's classification essay on types of Instagram girls.

4.6 Example of an introductory paragraph for a classification essay

If you do not have an Instagram account, how weird are you? You would be especially weird if you were a teenage girl. This is because Instagram users of the world are mostly made up of young girls trying to represent their selves through their posts; but are they being true to themselves or are they just selling their t*ts and a** for likes? As you read on, try not to laugh at these three types of basic-b*****s on Instagram as you may find yourself thinking, "Eh, that's me!" or "I know a girl like that."

Introduction from *Three Types of Basic-B*****s on Instagram* by P. Wongbuakaew

---

As you read the above example, you should have noticed that the tone of the essay is set right from the start, when the hook asks a somewhat deprecating, yet humorous question. The student then goes on to introduce the topic (types of female Instagram users) while continuing with the humorous tone established at the start.

When writing a classification essay, be clear and consistent as to how you are grouping things. There are three steps to effective classification:

- Put things into useful categories.
- Use only one organizing principle or criterion.
- Give clear examples that fit into each category—be sure to give an equal number of examples for each category.

Number 2 in the list above can be quite tricky to master at first. However, there are two basic rules that can help you with this step.

RULE 1. Once you have established your categories, make sure that there is only *one organizing principle.* An organizing principle is how you will sort the groups. More specifically, how will you classify the subject of your essay in terms of distinct characteristics or properties? These characteristics or properties define an item as belonging to category A, B, or C. For example, will you put things into groups based on distinct time periods (chronological differences); distinct sizes, shapes, or colors (physical differences); or some other *single criterion* according to which your categories differ in measurable or observable ways?

RULE 2. Create categories that are broad enough and that can be comprehensively subdivided to cover everything you are classifying. For example, we can classify mobile phone owners as *iPhone (iOS) users* or *Android users.* However, these two types of users do not cover all possible types of mobile phones or phone operating systems. What about those using Windows Phone or Linux phones or other, lesser-known mobile operating systems which nonetheless make up a large number of owners when grouped together? To cover the majority of mobile phone owners, you would need at least the following three subcategories:

A. **iOS users** (e.g., those using Apple iPhones).
B. **Android users** (e.g., those using Samsung phones).
C. **Other users**, which includes those who use less common operating systems, such as Windows Phone (e.g., Nokia Lumia), Linux (e.g., Fairphone 2), or BBS (Blackberry phones).

Exercise 4.11 will give you practice in considering the purposes served by classification, that is, why you might want to classify something, and how you might group things into distinct categories.

> **Exercise 4.11. Identifying a purpose**
>
> Write down a purpose for classifying each topic below (i.e., why might you need to classify these things?). Then give one or more qualities/features that can be used to delineate the categories.

1. TYPES OF TINDER USERS

Purpose:

Three defining qualities/features:

2. TYPES OF PAYMENT FOR GOODS

Purpose:

Three defining qualities/features:

3. TYPES OF PEOPLE IN A GYM

Purpose:

Three defining qualities/features:

When you have selected a topic for a classification essay, make sure you have a specific purpose for your classification and good ideas for describing and labeling your categories that fit your purpose. For example, do you want your categories to make a social comment (e.g., about Tinder or gym membership) or give advice (e.g., to people thinking of using Tinder or joining a gym)? The answer to this question will surely affect your classification system and category labels. One past student observed different types of monks on her travels, and decided that she would like to make a social commentary on these differences, based on her evaluation of their behavior. Rather than labeling them *good monks*, *bad monks*, and *those in the middle*, she grouped the monks she had seen into the three descriptive categories of *the sweeper*, *the hitchhiker*, and *the pretender*. She then went on to describe and evaluate their behavior in relation to those category labels. This system of classification made for an original and interesting essay.

EXPOSITORY WRITING   219

4.3.2. Sequencing a Classification Essay

The body paragraphs in classification essays have two main functions: to outline a distinct category and to give specific details and examples of that category. To introduce the categories, you can use phrases such as, *The first kind/type/group…*, *The second kind/type/group…*, and similar constructions. After you have introduced the category, you can then use elaborating transitions of *exposition* and *exemplification*—some of which were introduced in Table 1.1 (Unit 1) but are further expanded upon in Table 4.2:

Table 4.2. Expository and exemplifying transitions		
Such as	For example	For instance
To illustrate	To demonstrate	As an illustration
A case in point	This is exemplified in/by	Specifically

Classification essays can sometimes come across as fragmented or list-like because they group sets of things into individual paragraphs. For this reason, in addition to transitions between individual sentences, it is important to provide transitions linking the paragraphs (or categories) of a classification essay together. Do not just start a paragraph by stating something like *The second type is exemplified by…*. Start the paragraph instead by relating the categories/paragraphs to each other in some meaningful way, such as *Unlike type A, as described in the preceding paragraph, type B is … [some contrasting property]*.

Exercise 4.12 will help you to select appropriate connectors for a classification essay. The exercise contains the body paragraphs from a student's essay on classifying types of Instagram users—you encountered the introductory paragraph for this essay in Example 4.2 above. In this essay, the student also decided to include images from Instagram to show the reader examples of each of the categories she outlines. Although I have removed these because of copyright issues, it might be a good idea for you to include images in your assignments if they add value to your work, but check with your teacher first and be sure to correctly attribute the source of any images you use.

220 ESSENTIAL KNOWLEDGE AND SKILLS FOR ESSAY WRITING

> **Exercise 4.12. Sequencing classificatory elements**
>
> The paragraphs below are from a student essay classifying types of female Instagram users. Underline all the connecting words and phrases and then answer the questions that follow.

The first major type of b***h on your Instagram timeline is "The Selfie B***h". Is there anything else on their timeline except for selfies? Absolutely, NOT! Ninety percent of the photos on this chick's Instagram are of her in full makeup face—usually with irrelevant captions, such as "thinking about pizza" or lyrics from popular songs, and accompanied by a #selfieoftheday. However, what is most annoying on her profile is that she does the same face in almost every post, as exemplified in Figure 1. Specifically, her selfies are always taken from the same angle, making you wonder what she is hiding. Is there a mole? A pimple? A wonky eye? The only thing that changes is the background. The rest of her posts (10%) are mirror selfies, which are only done to show off a cool new iPhone case or spandex mini dress—the dresses show a little cleavage to gain more LIKES from her "perv" followers.

A similarly self-obsessed type of b***h you will find while scrolling down your Instagram feed is "The Rich B***h". You cannot even imagine how much she has spent to announce her crazy luxury lifestyle through her posts on Instagram! Wearing head to toe Hermes, Chanel, or Louis Vuitton is a must in every post. A case in point is the b***h shown in Figure 2. For this type of Instagram user, a post without hi-end products is a terrible mistake. However, no matter how much she tries to be gorgeous in her pictures, the only thing that attracts her followers' attention is the Ferrari logo on the bonnet of the car. Another feature that sets The Rich B***h apart from other Instagram chicks is that she is always on an outrageously expensive vacation. There are photos of her cross-legged, sitting on her private yacht and holding a glass of "KRUG CLOS D'AMBONNAY 1998" in her hands, along with quotes like "GOOD VIBES HAPPEN ON THE TIDES". The question that immediately comes to my mind is, "Does she not have work to do?" but The Rich B***h is #toorichtocare.

In contrast to the first two self-obsessed b***hes, "The Café B***h" is somewhat mellow and outward looking. For instance, I have no idea why, but she always seems to be looking away from the camera, smiling or laughing at a cup of Caramel Macchiato (Figure 3). She divides her posts between showing love for coffee, beautiful cafe scenes, and delicately arranged desserts and bakeries on a marble table and accompanied by #goodfoodgoodmood tags. There are seemingly no cafes in the world that she has not visited, yet her outfit is still well matched with the cafe scene in every photo. You cannot deny that her pictures look good, but you also cannot help but wonder how long it took her to stage all of these photos… #getalife.

> Body paragraphs from *Three Types of Basic-B*****s on Instagram* by
> P. Wongbuakaew

1. What are the three categories that this student created?

2. What is the organizing principle (criterion) by which she classified each type into its own unique category?

4.3.3. Rhetorical Structure

The simplest way to organize a classification essay is to use the block method. Using this method, the essay will contain an introductory paragraph that ends with a thesis statement; body paragraphs that explore each category in turn and provide good examples; and a concluding paragraph that ends with a memorable point.

Introduction	Paragraph 1	CONTENT: INTRODUCE YOUR TOPIC **Hook**. Grab your reader's attention with something memorable. **Introduce general topic**. **Introduce specific topic**. **Present thesis**: Name what you intend to classify, describe the basis of classification, and label the categories you will be using.
Body paragraphs	Paragraph 2	CONTENT: DEFINE AND EXPLAIN YOUR FIRST CATEGORY **Topic sentence for Category 1**. *Defining Feature A* – give at least one detail + example. *Defining Feature B* – give at least one detail + example. **Concluding sentence** (*can also be used as a link to the next paragraph).
	Paragraph 3	CONTENT: DEFINE AND EXPLAIN YOUR SECOND CATEGORY **Topic sentence for Category 2**. *Defining Feature A* – give at least one detail + example. *Defining Feature B* – give at least one detail + example. **Concluding sentence** (*can also be used as a link to the next paragraph).
	Paragraph 4	CONTENT: DEFINE AND EXPLAIN YOUR THIRD CATEGORY **Topic sentence for Category 3**. *Defining Feature A* – give at least one detail + example. *Defining Feature B* – give at least one detail + example. **Concluding sentence** (*can also be used as a link to the next paragraph).

		CONTENT: CONCLUDE YOUR ESSAY
Conclusion	Paragraph 5	**Restate thesis**. Remind the reader what your central purpose for writing this essay was (i.e., reiterate why the categorization is important). **Summarize**. Review the main points you detailed. **Final thought**. Address or reflect upon your essay in a memorable way.

4.3.4. Writing a Classification Essay

Stage 1. Choosing the Topic

Using the guidelines given above, choose an interesting topic for a Classification Essay. Write the purpose for your essay in the space below.

Stage 2. Pre-Writing Activity: Using a Concept Map

Brainstorm ideas for categories using a concept map (illustrated in Figure 4.4 for the Instagram essay example above). As you draw your own concept map, think about specific details defining each category and examples you can use to illustrate them. Make sure that each of your categories is distinct and show no overlapping features. Also, give them clear, concise, and original labels.

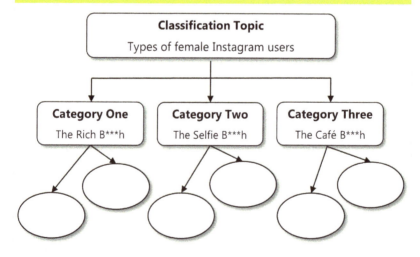

Figure 4.4. Concept map for types of female Instagram users

Stage 3. Outlining

Look at the items (details) you have listed. Think about removing any that perhaps do not contribute to the overall theme or feeling you are trying to create. Fill in a block method outline using the template in the previous section as a guide.

Stage 4. Drafting

Use your outline and write a first draft of 500–650 words. Before you start drafting your essay, write your thesis statement in below and show it to your teacher or peer.

Make sure you have all the necessary details in the introduction and a concluding remark at the end. Give your draft a title that is imaginative and captures the essence of what you have written. Set the line spacing, paper size, margins, and font type and size according to the instructions given by your teacher or as specified in your course outline or chosen style guide.

--------------------- **SUBMIT FIRST DRAFT** -----------------------

Stage 5. Post-writing Activity: Collaborative Peer Review

Swap drafts with one of your peers in class. Ask them to check what you have written. Check their draft in return and make notes either directly on their draft or in a separate document. For added feedback (and fun), use the scoring rubric at the end of the unit to grade each other's essay. At the very minimum, the feedback should address 1–5 below.

1. Write the thesis statement below. Underline the categories the author is describing.

2. Does the writer give equal space to each category or group? If not, please comment.

3. Is each body paragraph developed with sufficient detail?

4. In your opinion, what is the best part of this essay, and why?

5. Which part of this essay is the least effective? How could the writer improve it?

Stage 6. Edit and Revise Your Draft

When your peer returns your draft (and possible score), edit and revise your essay according to their feedback and answers to the questions above. Check your edits against the scoring rubric for classification essays. See if you can identify your strong and weak points.

-------------------- **WRITE SECOND DRAFT** ---------------------

Stage 7. Let Your Revised Draft Sit a While and Then Proofread It Carefully

Give yourself a break from your revised draft before proofreading it. That way, you approach it as an unfamiliar reader would. Also, before proofreading, it is usually a good idea to reread the instructions for the assignment or task rubric and/or look at the grading criteria or scoring rubric again. This will help to ensure that you have not gone off task or missed something important during the revision process.

--------------------- **SUBMIT FINAL DRAFT** ----------------------

4.4. CAUSE-EFFECT

As a student, if you go out and get drunk the night before a test, you probably will not do so well on the test. This is an example of a ***cause-effect relationship***. This type of relationship is the focus of a cause-effect essay, which sets out to describe how one event or set of events (the cause or causes) lead(s) to a separate event or set of events (the effect or effects)—or conversely, how an effect or set of effects results from a specific cause or set of causes.

There are three kinds of cause-effect essays. The only difference between them is what the writer decides to focus on.

As one option, a writer can decide to focus on the *causes* because there is single effect that is quite obvious and straightforward, but there are multiple causes of that effect. The writer then explores in detail a number of causes that lead to the same effect. This results in a ***focus-on-causes essay***.

As a second option, a writer might decide to focus on the *effects* because there is a single cause that is quite obvious and straightfor-ward, but there are multiple effects stemming from that cause. The writer then explores in detail how a number of effects stem from the same cause. This results in a ***focus-on-effects essay***.

The third possibility is that neither causes nor effects are obvious or straightforward, so that a ***mix of both*** approaches is appropri-ate. In this mixed type of cause-effect essay, it is not a good idea to describe both causes and effects in the same paragraph, as this can get quite complicated and hard to follow for a reader. Instead, causes and effects are best described in separate paragraphs or sequences of paragraphs. This more complex type of essay may therefore call for more than five paragraphs to develop the discus-sion of both causes and effects fully.

226 ESSENTIAL KNOWLEDGE AND SKILLS FOR ESSAY WRITING

4.4.1. General Guidelines for Cause-Effect Writing

Choosing a Good Topic

To create a good cause-effect essay, choose an actual cause-effect relationship and not a correlational relationship. For instance, consider the following syllogism (logical paradigm):

→ *Many people are wearing sunglasses.*

→ *Many people are eating ice cream.*

→ *Therefore, wearing sunglasses causes people to eat ice cream.*

Clearly, this is faulty logic, and it is easy to spot the error. It is more likely that people are eating ice cream because it is hot outside, and people are wearing sunglasses to shield their eyes from the sun. In the faulty syllogism above, we have missed out several important events or facts in our chain of reasoning. As this example illustrates, it is important that you focus on the actual event(s) or fact(s) that link cause and effect. Otherwise, you may just be looking at a correlation.

A correlation is a connection that is not one of cause and effect, but just a close association of two variables or phenomena. For example, since the 1950s, both education levels and obesity have increased significantly, yet there is no direct causal link between the two. Yet there is a positive correlation: the simultaneous increase (or decrease) of two variables along the same time scale. A negative correlation is one where the two variables go in opposite directions (i.e., as one variable goes up, the other one goes down). For example, the colder it is, the earlier people go to bed; students who spend less time on social media spend more time studying; as people increase their exercise, they eat less junk food.

When selecting a topic for this type of essay, consider the following questions:

- What is the result of something (the effect)?
- Is there one, clear effect, or are there several?
- Is there one, clear cause, or are there several?

EXPOSITORY WRITING 227

> **Exercise 4.13. Identifying good topics for cause-effect essays**
>
> Consider the topic suggestions in 1–8 below. Put an "X" in the box next to those that would not make good cause-effect topics. Try to identify what type of writing or essay would better suit those topics (e.g., descriptive, instructional, etc.).

1. Reasons why the earth's weather has changed in the last century ☐
2. Sydney versus Hawaii as a holiday destination ☐
3. A visit to a relative ☐
4. Why many people don't like studying online ☐
5. Explaining how to lose weight ☐
6. Why only a small percentage of people buy newspapers ☐
7. How to get a scholarship ☐
8. Why there are more males than females in China ☐

Exercise 4.14 will give you practice in generating cause-effect topics. Put some thought into your selections, as you will be using these topics for more exercises as the unit progresses.

> **Exercise 4.14. Choosing a good topic**
>
> In groups of three or four, discuss possible topics for cause-effect essays that are current, researchable, and manageable. Write down four possible essay topics in the spaces provided.

1.
2.
3.
4.

Include a Clear, Concise, and Well-Written Thesis Statement

In this type of essay, you may want to add an opinion to your thesis, but make sure it is worded carefully and it is not too strong. In the examples below of thesis statements for cause-effect essays, note that some of them do not explicitly include the words *cause* or *effect* as these can be implied from the statements. You may, however, want to state how many causes/effects your essay will cover (i.e., give numbers).

Example thesis statements for a focus-on-causes essay:

→ The main causes of teacher burnout seem to be class size, excessive administrative work, and constantly updated curricula.
→ Many people prefer to use delivery services for three important reasons.

Example thesis statements for a focus-on-effects essay:

→ Most people are not aware of the positive effects of meditation.
→ Playing video games for too long can be bad for child development, especially during adolescence.

Exercise 4.15. Writing thesis statements for cause-effect essays

Write thesis statements for the four topics that you came up with in Exercise 4.14. Vary your answers so you have some focus-on-cause and some focus-on-effect thesis statements. After you finish, compare your thesis statements with those of your peers.

Write a Complete Introduction

In the introductory paragraph, a writer starts with a hook to grab a reader's attention. The writer then sets up the background and/or context for the thesis. In this way, the writer establishes the importance of the topic. This is done through connecting or supporting sentences that bridge between the hook and the thesis. At the end of the introduction, the writer presents their thesis statement. Typically, this location is where the reader will be expecting a thesis statement. However, you can put it in a different location within the introduction, if it seems appropriate.

The following exercise is based on an introductory paragraph from a student essay on the causes and effects of stomach cancer. This was part of a group essay written by three students. The paragraph has all of the components that were mentioned above. The exercise will help you to recognize and evaluate these components in an introductory paragraph for a cause-effect essay.

Exercise 4.16. Analyzing an introductory paragraph

Read the introductory paragraph below that is taken from a cause-effect essay and answer the questions that follow. Discuss your answers with your peers.

An estimated 9.6 million people died of cancer in 2018—about one-sixth of deaths worldwide according to the WHO (2018). Cancer is caused by abnormally developing cells, and it can happen in any part of your body. One of the lesser-known types of cancer is stomach cancer: "A deadly cancer that is often overlooked" (Sirimontaraporn, 2015, p. 3). Yet, stomach cancer is the third most common cause of cancer-related death, and it spreads even faster than colon cancer (Sirimontaraporn, 2015). It is caused by two main factors: heredity and environment, and its effects can be divided into three stages: early stage, chemotherapy, and beyond chemotherapy.

References

Sirimontaraporn, N. (2015). *Stomach Cancer – A Deadly Cancer That Is Often Overlooked.* Samitivej Hospitals. https://www.samitivejhospitals.com/article/detail/stomach-cancer-Deadly-Cancer

World Health Organization. (2018, Sep 12). *Cancer.* http://www.who.int/cancer/en/

From *The Causes and Effects of Stomach Cancer* by A. Wichai, T. Maneechai, and I. Suprapas

1. What kind of hook does this introduction use?

2. How do the writers establish the importance of the topic?

3. Why is the thesis statement a good one?

After you have decided on a topic, you need to decide if you will focus more on the causes or the effects. The easiest way to do this is to make a list of causes and effects, and then consider what supporting information would be needed to show the connections between them. It is often easier to let the supporting details decide what type of essay will work best, rather than trying to figure it out from the topic alone.

> **Exercise 4.17. Brainstorming using a list**
>
> Choose one of your topics from Exercise 4.14. Make a list of causes and effects in the spaces below. Then decide whether the resulting essay would be focus-on-cause, focus-on-effects, or focus on both causes and effects?

Causes   **Effects**

4.4.2. Sequencing a Cause-Effect Essay

Some of the key conjunctive adjuncts in cause-effect/effect-cause writing are enhancing ones that signal causal-conditional relations (see Table 1.1, Unit 1, or Table 4.1 in this unit). Some others are presented in Table 4.3 in the form of syntactic frames, where you simply replace X or Y as needed and add additional modifiers, such as modal verbs, mood adjuncts, or comment adjuncts to qualify your statements:

Table 4.3. Syntactic frames for cause-to-effect and effect-to-cause

Cause to effect		
X is the cause of Y	X results in Y	X affected Y
X influences Y	X is the reason for Y	X produced Y
X leads to Y	One cause of Y is X	
Effect to cause		
Y is the effect of X	One of the effects of X is Y	Y was the outcome of X
Y can be attributed to X	Y occurred because of X	A key factor of Y is X
A consequence of X is Y	Y is a result of X	

In Exercise 4.18, I have given you the first two body paragraphs for the student essay introduced in Exercise 4.16, *The Causes and Effects of Stomach Cancer*. The following two body paragraphs discuss two causes: heredity and environment.

Exercise 4.18. Choosing transitions and connectors

Insert an appropriate conjunction, conjunctive adjunct, or connecting phrase into each of the spaces below. Use Table 1.1 (Unit 1), 4.1, or 4.3 if you need help.

As you are reading the extract, make note of how the topic sentences tie into the thesis statement presented in Exercise 4.16, and how the supporting details all tie into their respective topic sentences.

(PARA. 2) Heredity is a significant cause of stomach cancer. Stomach cancer can be inherited through genetics by the mutation of CDH1, a gene located on chromosome 16 that encodes a protein called E-cadherin (World Health Organization, 2018). This protein functions as a link that connects cells and tissues together. [1] _____ whenever the CDH1 mutate, E-cadherin tends to malfunction, which, [2] _____ causes a hereditary condition called Hereditary Diffuse Gastric Cancer (HDGC) that increases the risk of stomach cancer. Descendants have a 50% chance to inherit the mutant gene from ascendant carriers. [3] _____ , three-fourths of them are prone to developing stomach cancer (nostomachforcancer.org, n.d.).

(PARA. 3) [4] _____ stem from external chemicals and one's behavior. [5] _____ a greater exposure to radiation or pollution leads to a greater risk of stomach cancer. [6] _____ a research article on radiotherapy for patients with cervical cancer reveals that the patients who took more radiation doses had more risk of stomach cancer (Kleinerman et al., 2013). [7] _____ according to a paper on the relationship between air pollution and stomach cancer, the penetration of nitrogen oxides throughout the atmosphere from automobiles increases the risk of gastric cancer (Nagel et al., 2018). [8] _____ environmental problems and people's lifestyles can increase the risk of stomach cancer. People who eat too many salty foods but reject fruits and vegetables, [9] _____ tend to have more risk of the disease. Those who usually drink alcohol and smoke either cigarettes or tobacco are [10] _____ more likely to have stomach cancer (Cancer Research UK, 2016).

References

Cancer Research UK. (2016, August 3). *Causes and risks of stomach cancer*. https://www.cancerresearchuk.org/about-cancer/stomach-cancer/causes-risks

Kleinerman, R. A., Smith, S. A., Holowaty, E., et al. (2013). Radiation dose and subsequent risk for stomach cancer in long-term survivors of cervical cancer. *International Journal of Radiation Oncology, Biology, Physics*, *86*(5), 922–929. https://doi.org/10.1016/j.ijrobp.2013.04.010

Nagel, G., Stafoggia, M., Pedersen, et al. (2018). Air pollution components and incidence of cancers of the stomach and the upper aerodigestive tract in the European Study of Cohorts of Air Pollution Effects (ESCAPE), *International Journal of Cancer, 143*(7), 1632–1643. https://doi.org/10.1002/ijc.31564

World Health Organization. (2018, Sep 12). *Cancer*. http://www.who.int/cancer/en/

Paragraphs 2 and 3 from *The Causes and Effects of Stomach Cancer* by A. Wichai, T. Maneechai, and I. Suprapas

4.4.3. Rhetorical Structure

The simplest way to outline a cause-effect essay is to use the block method:

Introduction	Paragraph 1	CONTENT: INTRODUCE YOUR TOPIC **Hook**. Grab your reader's attention with something memorable. **Introduce general topic**. **Introduce specific topic**. State why it is important to write about. **Present thesis**. Indicate if your essay will be focusing on causes and/or effects.
Body paragraphs	Paragraph 2	CONTENT: DEFINE AND EXPLAIN YOUR FIRST CAUSE/EFFECT **Topic sentence for effect / cause 1**. *Supporting sentence* – detail(s) + example(s). *Supporting sentence* – detail(s) + example(s). **Concluding sentence** (*can also be used as a link to the next paragraph).
	Paragraph 3	CONTENT: DEFINE AND EXPLAIN YOUR SECOND CAUSE/EFFECT **Topic sentence for effect / cause 2**. *Supporting sentence* – detail(s) + example(s). *Supporting sentence* – detail(s) + example(s). **Concluding sentence** (*can also be used as a link to the next paragraph).

EXPOSITORY WRITING   233

	Paragraph 4	CONTENT: DEFINE AND EXPLAIN YOUR THIRD CAUSE/EFFECT **Topic sentence for effect / cause 3**. *Supporting sentence* – detail(s) + example(s). *Supporting sentence* – detail(s) + example(s). **Concluding sentence** (*can also be used as a link to the next paragraph).
Conclusion	Paragraph 5	CONTENT: CONCLUDE YOUR ESSAY **Restate thesis**. Remind the reader what your central purpose for writing this essay was (i.e., reiterate why the topic is important). **Summarize**. Review the main points you detailed. **Final thought**. Address or reflect upon your essay in a memorable way.

For the body paragraphs presented in Exercise 4.18, the student authors used the block method. They continued to use the block method for the rest of this essay, where they wrote seven paragraphs in total: one introductory paragraph, five body paragraphs, and one concluding paragraph. The first two body paragraphs—presented in Exercise 4.18—were focus-on-cause (Paragraphs 2 and 3). The students then switched to focus-on-effects for the next three body paragraphs (Paragraphs 4, 5, and 6, as shown in Exercise 4.19).

Exercise 4.19. Identifying supporting sentences and additional details

Read the three body paragraphs presented below, which focus on some of the effects of stomach cancer, and answer the questions that follow. Note how the paragraphs are almost of equal length, reflecting their equal importance.

Patients with stomach cancer encounter its effects to varying degrees. In the early stages, people might not recognize the disease because the symptoms look like other less serious diseases. However, the digestive system of gastric cancer patients will not function as well as before. While eating, patients will have more difficulty swallowing food, but they feel fuller faster and become bloated more often. They will also feel pain in their stomach and chest while the food is being digested. Some might get heartburn, or acid reflux, which occurs when some of the digested food returns to the esophagus. Moreover, these patients will burp more frequently and sometimes vomit a little blood (NHS, 2018).

234 ESSENTIAL KNOWLEDGE AND SKILLS FOR ESSAY WRITING

After being diagnosed with stomach cancer, chemotherapy—a systematic treatment to treat or prevent further cell mutation and division—will be chosen as the primary treatment. According to Cancer Research UK (2016), it is the most frequently used method. However, chemotherapy might result in many possible short-term side effects, both physical and mental. As stated by American Cancer Society (2017), patients may show symptoms such as nausea, fatigue, hair loss, and/or hearing loss. Chemotherapy may lead to mental illness as well; for example, depression or an anxiety disorder may arise because of stressful treatment procedures. Although effects will eventually vanish after the patient is completely done with the treatment, some after-effects may emerge if there is any following treatment session (American Cancer Society, 2017).

In later stages of stomach cancer, patients may need to undergo major surgery, which can detrimentally affect the patient's life. The scale and type of surgery depends on the size and the location of the tumor, which can mean removing parts of or the entire stomach. In some case, surgery might result in an anastomotic leak, causing the patient to experience breathlessness and severe chest pain. In addition, without parts of the stomach, the patient often faces malnutrition. Consequently, they will be required to adjust their diet and take supplements, such as calcium, vitamin D or iron (Cancer Research UK, 2016). In the final stage of stomach cancer, when mutated cells have spread to other parts of the body and medications are no longer effective, patients can choose to continue with hospitalization or return home to their loved ones.

References

American Cancer Society. (2017, December 15). *Living as a stomach cancer survivor*. https://www.cancer.org/cancer/stomach-cancer/after-treatment/follow-up.html

Cancer Research UK. (2016, August 3). *Causes and risks of stomach cancer*. https://www.cancerresearchuk.org/about-cancer/stomach-cancer/causes-risks

NHS. (2018, August 20). *Stomach cancer*. https://www.nhs.uk/conditions/stomach-cancer/

Paragraphs 4, 5, 6 from *The Causes and Effects of Stomach Cancer* by A. Wichai, T. Maneechai, and I. Suprapas

EXPOSITORY WRITING 235

1. What are some of the effects of stomach cancer that the writers describe?

2. As described in the second and third paragraphs, how do chemotherapy and major surgery figure in the cause-effect chain of stomach cancer?

Fully Address the Thesis Statement in Your Conclusion

A reader will often go straight to the conclusion to get an overall view of an essay. The concluding paragraph is therefore an important part of your essay. Exercise 4.20 is a good example of a concluding paragraph for a cause-effect essay. It is the conclusion of a seven-paragraph student essay. You have already read the rest of this essay in Exercise 4.16 (introduction), 4.18 (paragraphs 2–3), and 4.19 (body paragraphs 4–6).

Exercise 4.20. Analyzing a concluding paragraph

Read the extract below. This extract is the concluding paragraph from the cause-effect essay presented in previous exercises. Answer the questions that follow.

Even though stomach cancer is not very well known, it is as deadly as the other types. Considered the fifth most common cancer—after lung, liver, breast, and colon cancer—stomach cancer has killed a large number of people. Worse than that, it is often too late for many patients who are diagnosed with stomach cancer to be cured. Therefore, everyone should become aware of the hidden danger of this disease and get a check-up as soon as possible. The earlier they find out that they have this cancer, the more chance they will have to get treatment before it is incurable. When people understand how easily one can have stomach cancer, they will become more concerned about their behaviors and adopt healthier lifestyles to prevent the causes of this ailment.

From *The Causes and Effects of Stomach Cancer* by A. Wichai, T. Maneechai, and I. Suprapas

236 ESSENTIAL KNOWLEDGE AND SKILLS FOR ESSAY WRITING

1. Have the authors restated why the topic is important? If so, how?

2. How many main points of cause-effect have they reviewed?

3. How have they reflected upon their thesis statement (look back to Exercise 4.16)?

4. What type of memorable statement do they end with?

Overall, these students have covered everything stated in their thesis statement (see Exercise 4.16) and provided adequate support in each body paragraph for each of their main ideas. They have then brought everything full circle with a concluding paragraph that draws practical implications about the information they have provided.

4.4.4. Writing a Cause-Effect Essay

Stage 1. Choosing the Topic

For this exercise, you will write a cause-effect essay that focuses on causes, effects, or both. The first stage is to choose an interesting topic. You can use one of your topics from Exercises 4.14 and 4.15, or you can choose a new one. Write your topic below.

Stage 2. Pre-writing Activity

Brainstorm ideas for causes and effects. Put them in the lists below.

Causes   **Effects**

Stage 3. Outlining

Look at the items (details) listed above. Carefully consider if the focus of your essay should be causes or effects, or possibly both. If you have more effects, then perhaps you should outline a focus-on-effects essay with one cause. If you have more causes, then perhaps you should outline a focus-on-causes essay with one effect. If you have an equal number of causes and effects, perhaps consider including both approaches in your essay—if you are up for the challenge.

Before creating your outline, consider removing any item that perhaps does not contribute to the overall theme or may be less interesting than the other items. When you are happy with your chosen items, fill in an outline template as per the one shown in section 4.4.3, using focus-on-effects, focus-on-causes, or both approaches.

POST-OUTLINING ACTIVITY: COLLABORATIVE PEER REVIEW

Give your outline to one of your peers. Ask them to respond to points 1–4 below.

1. Can you tell if this will be a focus-on-causes or focus-on-effects essay? If not, suggest how the writer can make the purpose clearer (unless, of course, the topic needs a focus on both causes and effects).
2. Are each of the topic sentences related to the thesis? If not, underline the ones that need revising.
3. Is there a clear link between the supporting details and their respective topic sentences in each paragraph? If not, underline the ones that need replacing or clarifying.
4. I think the best part of the outline is …

Stage 4. Drafting

Use your outline and write a first draft of 500–650 words. Make sure you have a brief thesis statement in the introduction and a concluding remark at the end. Give your essay a title that is imaginative and captures the essence of what you have written. Set the

238 ESSENTIAL KNOWLEDGE AND SKILLS FOR ESSAY WRITING

line spacing, paper size, margins, and font type and size according to the instructions given by your teacher or as specified in your course book or style guide.

-------------------- **SUBMIT FIRST DRAFT** ----------------------

Stage 5. Post-Writing Activity: Collaborative Peer Review

Now it is time to check your draft through peer review. Swap drafts with one of your peers in class. Ask them to check what you have written. Check their draft in return. For added feedback (and fun), use the scoring rubric at the end of the unit to grade each other's essays. At the very minimum, the feedback should answer the following questions:

1. What is the essay about?

2. Look at the introduction. Do the supporting details flow smoothly from the hook to the thesis statement? If not, make a suggestion as to what needs to be changed.

3. Do all of the topic sentences tie into the thesis statement in some way? If not, underline the ones that need revising.

4. Are the supporting details related to each of their respective topic sentences? If not, underline the ones that need revising.

5. Is it easy to understand how the causes and effects are connected? If not, underline any confusing sentences and suggest what needs to be changed.

6. Are there any examples of wordiness? If so, circle them and suggest a way to fix the problem.

7. Is the thesis restated/rephrased in the conclusion? Moreover, is it clear?

Stage 6. Edit and Revise Your Draft

When your peer returns your draft (and possible score), edit, and revise your essay according to their feedback and answers to the questions above. Check your edits against the scoring rubric for expository essays. See if you can identify your strong and weak points.

-------------------- **WRITE SECOND DRAFT** ---------------------

Stage 7. Let Your Revised Draft Sit a While and Then Proofread It Carefully

It is a good idea to give yourself a break from your revised draft before proofreading it. That way, you approach it as an unfamiliar reader would. Also, before proofreading, it is usually a good idea to reread the instructions for the assignment or task rubric and/or look at the grading criteria or scoring rubric again. This will help to ensure that you have not gone off task or missed something important during the revision process.

--------------------- **SUBMIT FINAL DRAFT** -----------------------

240   ESSENTIAL KNOWLEDGE AND SKILLS FOR ESSAY WRITING

APPENDIX 4A.
SCORING RUBRIC FOR EXPOSITORY WRITING

MICRO-LEVEL MISTAKES

→ One point deducted for every 5 micro-level mistakes: _____ divided by **5** =

INTRODUCTION _____ out of **10** (2.5 points per item)

→ Title is imaginative and reflects the essay's contents

→ Hook creatively grabs reader's attention

→ Linking sentences clearly introduce the topic

→ Introduction establishes what type of exposition the essay will be

THESIS _____ out of **10** (2 points per item)

→ Offers a thought-provoking idea

→ States why the topic is important to write about

→ Is clear, concise, and well placed

→ Does not simply announce the essay structure (i.e., list-like structure)

→ Is not too general or too broad

DEVELOPMENT/SUPPORT _____ out of **35** (7 points per item)

→ General topic sentences start each body paragraph

→ Thoroughly compares/contrasts, classifies, or establishes cause-effect

→ Body paragraphs provide sufficient examples and evidence

→ Content is interesting and supported with reference where needed

→ Supporting details are relevant and tied to thesis

ORGANIZATION/STRUCTURE _____ out of **15** (5 points per item)

→ Transition words and phrases effectively link sentences and paragraphs

→ Paper exhibits sophistication in structure and is not merely a list

→ Information is well placed in terms of importance

GRAMMAR / STYLE _____ out of **20** (5 points per item)

→ Variety of sentence lengths and sentence beginnings

→ Complete sentences (no run-ons or fragments)

→ Observes the conventions of plain language usage

→ Exhibits correctly used advanced punctuation (colon, dash)

CONCLUSION _____ out of **10** (5 points per item)

→ Thesis not merely restated

→ Summarizes and ends with an appropriate memorable point

Total _____ out of **100**

APPENDIX 4B. UNIT 4 ANSWER KEY

Exercise 4.1
Answers will vary so consult with your classmates or teacher.

Exercise 4.2
1. … *a number of different tactics from those used previously.*
2. (i) Used high-pressure water trucks to attack protestors; (ii) sent armed forces to arrest protesters; (iii) enacted an emergency decree; (iv) banned media from covering the protests; (v) social media became the tool of the masses.

Exercise 4.3
1. The main idea is the different strategies that the two kings used.
2. King Ramkhamhaeng was more diplomatic and less confrontational than King Magai,
3. The block method compares/contrasts subjects across paragraphs (one paragraph = one subject), whereas the point-by-point method compares both subjects in one paragraph (one paragraph = two subjects).

Exercise 4.4–4.5
Answers will vary so consult with your classmates or teacher.

Exercise 4.6
1. It is a good paragraph. It has an interesting hook (it makes me want to read on) and aims to connect the reader with the writer by putting them on an equal footing in which they are both learning about these two personality types. Moreover, even though it is a serious topic, the tone is playful. This makes it stand out from other student essays, which are often very "academic" and serious.
2. The thesis is stated in the last two sentences. The use of inclusive *we* suggests that author and reader will be taking a journey together—*a psychological trip*, as the author states.

242 ESSENTIAL KNOWLEDGE AND SKILLS FOR ESSAY WRITING

3. As already noted, the tone is a playful and informal one, signaled by phrases such as *To be honest*, *psychological trip*, *dig deep*, and the general simplicity with which the author writes (it is almost conversational at times).

Exercise 4.7
1 = c, **2** = a, **3** = d, **4** = b, **5** = a, **6** = c, **7** = b, **8** = d.
The organizing method was the block method.

Exercise 4.8
1. Yes, he has restated why the topic is important via the non-finite dependent clause, *resulting in worsening personalities and in worst-case scenarios, murder*.
2. None. He has instead decided to expand upon the central importance of the topic. The bulk of his conclusion is in fact new information expressing the author's sympathy for psychopaths and sociopaths.
3. He has decided to focus on the shared aspect of psychopaths and sociopaths—even though the body of the essay was written to contrast them—namely, that they are mentally ill, a point addressed in the thesis statement, and that their condition is not their fault, a new point.
4. The writer addresses the general reader, *you*, and then addresses any readers who are themselves psychopaths or sociopaths.
5. The final memorable points are addressed to those who suffer from these personality disorders: If you are psychopath of sociopath, you can get help. The essay ends up having an important purpose of alerting psychopaths and sociopaths to their illness and urging them to get help.
6. The essay lacks unity because the introduction, body paragraphs, and essay title do not connect well to the conclusion. This is because the conclusion has a purpose different from comparing/contrasting the two types of psychological disorders. It is possible that the writer intended this to be a "surprise ending." However, it is also possible that he changed his mind

about the essay's purpose while writing. If this happens to you, it is a good idea to revise your essay to reflect the new purpose in the introduction, the thesis statement, and possibly also in the body paragraphs.

Exercise 4.9

1. Supporting details = examples of three things you will learn (in response to challenges): new knowledge, how to work to deadlines, how to communicate effectively. An example of a material benefit: a higher salary if you work hard.
2. Answers will vary, but I feel there is a slight imbalance regarding the salary aspect.
3. A prediction (your life will be adventurous).
4. It might review the advantages/disadvantages of another employment option.

Exercise 4.10–4.11

Answers will vary so consult with your peers or teacher.

Exercise 4.12

1. The three categories are *The selfie b***h*, *The rich b***h*, and *The café b***h*.
2. The organizing principle was the content of pictures they typically post.

Exercise 4.13

1, 6, 7, and 8 would make for poor topics.

Exercise 4.14–4.15

Answers will vary so consult with your peers or teacher.

Exercise 4.16

1. The hook is a "shocker" in the form of a very large statistic.
2. The writers establish the importance of the topic through the following two sentences: *One of the lesser-known types of cancer is stomach cancer: "A deadly cancer that is often overlooked" (Nathavut, 2015, p. 3). Yet, stomach cancer is the third most common cause of cancer-related death.*

244 ESSENTIAL KNOWLEDGE AND SKILLS FOR ESSAY WRITING

3. The thesis very clearly outlines that they will be covering two causes (*heredity and environment*) and that effects will be grouped into three stages (*early stage, chemotherapy, and beyond chemotherapy*).

Exercise 4.17
Answers will vary so consult with your peers or teacher.

Exercise 4.18 (possible answers—yours may vary somewhat)
1. *Therefore*, **2.** *Subsequently/unfortunately*, **3.** *Moreover/ Unfortunately*, **4.** *(Some) other causes* **5.** *First/Notably*, **6.** *For instance/For example/Supporting this relationship*, **7.** *In addition/As another example*, **8.** *Besides*, **9.** *for example/ Instance*, **10.** *also*

Exercise 4.19
1. <u>BODY PARA. 1.</u> Problems with ingesting and digesting food, including difficulty swallowing, bloating, stomach and chest pain, heartburn or acid reflux, frequent burping, and vomiting blood;
   <u>BODY PARA. 2.</u> Nausea, hair loss, hearing loss, and mental illness;
   <u>BODY PARA. 3.</u> Reduction in stomach function; breathlessness and severe chest pain
2. Chemotherapy and major surgery are performed as a result of the cancer, and they in turn cause many types of effects.

Exercise 4.20
1. Yes, via the dependent clause, *it is as deadly as other types*.
2. They have focused on only the overall effect of stomach cancer, which is death. They have decided instead to build to a memorable final point warning of the danger of this type of cancer. They deem the topic very important, and so they want to affect people's behavior by the information they have provided, rather than just summarizing it.

EXPOSITORY WRITING   245

3. They have reflected on their overall thesis with the statement: *everyone should become aware of the hidden danger of this disease and get a check-up as soon as possible.*

4. It is a cause-effect statement asserting the power of knowledge (cause) to change behavior (effect): *When people understand how easily one can have stomach cancer, they will become more concerned about their behaviors and adopt healthier lifestyles to prevent the causes of this ailment.*

Unit 5
ARGUMENT/OPINION WRITING

Unit Goals

Upon completing this unit, you should be able to demonstrate the following knowledge and skills:

- Recognize the elements of a successful argument/opinion essay.
- Qualify claims so it is more difficult to argue against them.
- Develop warrants to link relevant evidence to a claim.
- Organize and sequence elements of a Toulmin argument.
- Write an argument using grounds and warrants as your support.

Definition

The argument (or opinion) essay is one of the more complex types of writing tasks. It requires writers to express their opinion, interpretation, insight, analysis, explication, personal reaction, evaluation, and/or reflection on a timely issue/topic, and to do so through logical appeals and measured claims that are firmly based on sound evidence,

> **Argument** *Consists of a claim—which may be an opinion—that is supported by credible evidence and logical reasoning.*
>
> **Opinion** *A belief or view that someone holds on a topic, not necessarily based on what is true or logical.*

warrants, and backing. Thus, writing an argument differs from persuasive writing, wherein "you can select the most favorable evidence, appeal to emotions, and use style to persuade your readers. Your single purpose is to be convincing" (Kinneavy & Warriner, 1993, p. 305).

A good argument generally requires in-depth knowledge about the subject you are writing, and the recognition of others' opinions besides your own. Consequently, this type of writing often requires you to research a topic by collecting, generating, and evaluating evidence from primary and secondary sources. Once you have good sources, you can establish a position on a topic by linking the evidence (grounds) to your opinions (claims) through logical reasoning (warrants). Thus, critical thinking skills go hand-in-hand with an ability to build a strong argument. This unit will give you practice in developing these skills alongside the knowledge you need to write successful argument essays.

Good evidence together with *logical reasoning* gives a writer *sufficient means* to claim what they want to claim. Note that a writer builds a good argument by taking up a position that is supported by the evidence, rather than finding evidence that supports their pre-existing opinion. Otherwise, they may find themselves succumbing to confirmation bias—that is, using only evidence that supports their opinion and ignoring any evidence that does not support it—which does not lead to balanced claims or a strong argument being made. Let us look at an example.

248   ESSENTIAL KNOWLEDGE AND SKILLS FOR ESSAY WRITING

> **5.1   Example opening from an opinion essay**
>
> After the government, again, disappointed everyone with poor Covid-19 relief, the latest news about the donation-made millionaire taxi driver had Thai people rejoicing with glee. We have always been too generous: From medical equipment fundraising to flood relief, we never stop donating money. However, I condemn such "generosity" as shortsighted, which merely sweeps numerous problems under the rug.
>
> First, it is not that surprising that Thais donate out of altruism, since the idea is rooted in Buddhist doctrines. Through the tenth Jataka, taught in schools, we learn how to "truly"' give. In the Buddhist story, the soon-to-be Gautama Buddha sacrificed all his belongings to others, including his wife and children, for a step closer to nirvana. This tale has frequently been used to brainwash Thais into giving blindly. We believe that donating money equals "doing good". We reach nirvanic orgasm through our donations, and we think we are making virtuous gifts. However, without any form of critical thinking as to where our money is going, we are committing grave sins. The people's sufferings will still be endless, since, through donations, we are concealing the root cause of this charitable madness: systemic corruption and institutional greed.
>
> Extract from *A Wakeup Call to Generous Money Donors* by
> Iwarin Suprapas

In the above extract, the student introduces her short argument/opinion essay on the downside of blindly giving money to charity. You can see how she injects a strong personal voice into her writing, and you are in no doubt as to how she feels about the topic. She also contextualizes the argument using information that her immediate audience will be familiar with, making it personally appealing to those about whom she writes. In other words, she has framed her upcoming argument in light of who she expects her main audience/readership to be. Being aware of who your audience is, and what they may or may not know about your topic, should be one of the first things you consider when planning your argument.

5.1. KEY SKILLS

5.1.1. Modal Verbs, Modal Adjuncts, and Comment Adjuncts

A key difference between an argument essay and the other essays covered so far is that it includes complex ***interpersonal meanings.*** These types of meaning relate to the writer offering or soliciting some form of social relationship, such as offering their personal views on a proposition or soliciting the reader's agreement to their opinion.

In terms of language choices, a writer's position—that is, their *stance* or *appraisal*—on something can be realized by elements such as modal verbs, mood adjuncts, and comment adjuncts.

Modal Verbs

You will probably already be familiar with modal verbs. These are one main aspect of modality in English. Modal verbs can be used to position a proposition or proposal along a range of choices between "it may be true" and "it must be true." For example, consider the following continuum of modal verbs and their equivelant mood adjuncts (adverbs):

A Continuum of Probability
may/might be --------------- should be -------------- must be *(modal verbs)*
possibly ---------------------- probably ------------ certainly *(mood adjuncts)*

Moreover, by combining modal verbs with **mood adjuncts**, you can create gradations in stance that are even more delicate, further refining your position on a proposition or proposal. This is illustrated below (also see Halliday & Matthiessen, 2014, p. 179).

Possible
it may/might be true --   *its possibly true -----*   *it may/might possibly be true*
Probable
it should be true -------   *it's probably true ---*   *it should probably be true*
Certain
it must be true ---------   *it's certainly true ---*   *it must/will certainly be true*

250 ESSENTIAL KNOWLEDGE AND SKILLS FOR ESSAY WRITING

Modal verbs are relative easy to understand, and you probably have a good idea already about how to use them. Mood adjuncts— as their name suggests—are closely associated with the mood of a sentence. Thus, mood adjuncts are tightly tied to the *finite element* (the tensed main verb or auxiliary, which is the central element that controls the mood of a sentence).

Mood Adjuncts

As you saw above, mood adjuncts can be used to make assessments along a continuum of probability (The students have *possibly/probably/certainly* finished their homework by now). Other types of mood adjuncts can be used for different forms of gradation, such as degrees of frequency (*sometimes/usually/always* true), intensity (*hardly/quite/totally* true), or time (it will *eventually/soon* be true).

In terms of their position in a clause, a mood adjunct is most commonly inserted before the verb phrase, as in (a) below, or after the finite element of a verb phrase, as in (b). A mood adjunct can also take thematic prominence for added affect at the start of a clause (although this is rare with adjuncts of intensity), as in (c) below, or at the end of a clause as a kind of afterthought, as in (d) below.

a) The students probably have not finished their homework. (*Neutral*)
b) The students have probably not finished their homework. (*Neutral*)
c) Probably, the students have not finished their homework. (*Thematic*)
d) The students have not finished their homework, probably. (*Afterthought*)

Exercise 5.1. Varying the position of mood adjuncts

Show the four positions for mood adjuncts by rewriting statements 1–4 below to include an adjunct of probability (do not use the same mood adjunct more than once).

1. The student will gain marks for effort.

Afterthought:

2. Marks will not be given for effort.

Neutral:

3. The teacher will award some points for effort.

Thematic:

4. Effort will not be rewarded.

Neutral:

Comment Adjuncts

A comment adjunct is a word or phrase that adds commentary by a writer (or speaker). As Halliday and Matthiessen (2014) note, "there is no very clear line between [comment adjuncts] and the mood Adjuncts … The difference is that comment Adjuncts are less tightly tied to the grammar of mood; they are restricted to 'indicative' clauses (those functioning as propositions)" (p. 190).

Table 5.1 below contains some common English words/phrases that can function as comment adjuncts. It is from Halliday and Matthiessen (2014, p. 191). As shown in the table, comment adjuncts can be used to indicate a perspective or take a stance on a proposition in terms of (a) being *assertive* or *qualificative* on the whole clause, or (b) showing *wisdom, morality,* or *typicality* with regard to the grammatical subject. Comment adjuncts can also be used to indicate a perspective or take a stance on a speech function (e.g., making a statement or asking a question) in terms of commenting on a declarative (giving the writer's angle) or on an interrogative (seeking the reader's angle) with respect to being *persuasive, factual, valid,* or *personally engaging.* When using speech functional comment adjuncts, be aware that they are generally restricted to initial (thematic) or final position (afterthought) in the clause.

252 ESSENTIAL KNOWLEDGE AND SKILLS FOR ESSAY WRITING

Table 5.1. Examples of comment adjuncts

Type					Examples
Propositional	on whole clause	assertive	natural		*naturally, inevitably, of course*
			obvious		*obviously, clearly, plainly, of course*
			sure		*doubtless, indubitably, no doubt*
		qualificative	prediction	predictable	*unsurprisingly, predictably, to no one's surprise*
				surprising	*surprisingly, unexpectedly*
			presumption	hearsay	*evidently, allegedly, supposedly*
				argument	*arguably*
				guess	*presumably*
			desirability	luck	*luckily, fortunately*
				desirable: hope	*hopefully*
				undesirable	*sadly, unfortunately*
			amusement		*amusingly, funnily*
			significance		*importantly, significantly*
	on Subject	wisdom	& positive		*wisely, cleverly*
			& negative		*foolishly, stupidly*
		morality	& positive		*rightly, correctly, justifiably*
			& negative		*wrongly, unjustifiably*
		typicality			*characteristically, typically*
Speech-functional	un-qualified	persuasive	assurance		*truly, honestly, seriously*
			concession		*admittedly, certainly, to be sure*
		factual			*actually, really, in fact, as a matter of fact*
	qualified	validity	general		*generally, broadly, roughly, ordinarily, by and large, on the whole*
			specific		*academically, legally, politically, ethically, linguistically,*
		personal engagement	honesty		*frankly, candidly, honestly, to be honest*
			secrecy		*confidentially, between you and me*
			individuality		*personally, for my part*
			accuracy		*truly, strictly*
			hesitancy		*tentatively*

Copyright © 2014 Adapted from *Introduction to Functional Grammar* by Halliday, M. A. K., & Matthiessen, C. M. I. M. Reproduced by permission of Taylor and Francis Group, LLC, a division of Informa plc.

Exercise 5.2 includes an extract from a student's argument/opinion essay about why true-crime documentaries do not appeal to Thai people. It will give you practice in selecting appropriate modal verbs, mood adjuncts, and comment adjuncts. For the latter, you should make use of Table 5.1.

Exercise 5.2. Choosing appropriate indicators of mood

Fill in each of the spaces below with an appropriate indicator of mood (modal verb, mood adjunct, or comment adjunct). The information in the square brackets tells you which type of modal verb, mood adjunct, or comment adjunct would be appropriate.

It is absurd that westerners are so obsessed with true crime documentaries. "It's factual, just, and fun," the fanatics [1]   [comment adjunct: typicality] say, but we all know that is nonsense. [2] [comment adjunct: factual], in Thailand, true crimes are not that popular. This is not solely because of the genre itself, but because of a [3] [comment adjunct: typicality] Thai way of thinking.

To begin with, true crime documentaries are two thumbs down. If I were to rate them, they [4]   [modal verb] [5]   [mood adjunct] get rotten tomatoes, what with their dull plots and mudflat characters.

A three-year old [6]   [modal verb] [7]   [mood adjunct] predict their plot: a crime occurred and somewhat [8]   [comment adjunct: prediction] the suspect was captured. Sometimes it turns out that some of them were [9]   [comment adjunct: negative morality] accused. Yet, somehow, there is always a common motif: Both murderers and the accused are [10]   [comment adjunct: negative morality] harassed by the police and the media. Can you see the [11]   [comment adjunct: assertive] clear pattern here? Fellow criminals committing murders, or not, are fighting against the same authorities.

This is why the characters in each of these documentaries are flat and identical, especially the antagonists. [12] [desirability: undesirable], these characters are not epic. They are [13]   [comment adjunct: persuasive] twisted and bent. Typical heroes, like police officers are turned into villains, while the original villain is turned into a protagonist. This [14] [modal verb] not have happened if we had used a post-modern point of view to look at their narrative structure. However, [15]

[comment adjunct: desirability: undesirable], this is a "true" crime documentary. [16]   [comment adjunct: personal engagement], It makes no sense.

> Extract from *A Sweeping Obsession for True Crime... We Thais Just Don't Get it!* by Iwarin Suprapas

5.1.2. General Guidelines for Writing an Argument/Opinion Essay

When writing an argument/opinion essay, it is important to outline exactly what the issue is and why the reader should care about it. Once this has been established, the writer presents a logical and cohesive argument followed by a strong conclusion. Many argument essays start out by providing excellent descriptions of a problem and arguments to support the writer's claims, but then fail to give a strong conclusion. A good argument will finish with a forward-looking and original solution. Remember that the conclusion is the last part of your essay that a reader will read—sometimes, they may even jump to the conclusion after reading your introduction—so put as much time and effort into writing your conclusion as you do the rest of your essay.

Choosing a Good Topic

Selecting the right topic is a very important first step in writing an argument/opinion essay. Choose the wrong topic and you may end up "flogging a dead horse" (that is, spending a lot of effort trying to influence people on a "dead" or already settled issue). Choose a topic that is current, debatable, researchable, and—perhaps most importantly for a student essay—manageable. It is also often best to avoid PARSNIP topics (politics, alcohol, religion, sex, narcotics, *-isms*, and pork—i.e., "red meat" issues). These topics stir up emotions and do not necessarily lend themselves to logical claims or opinions. Also, try to avoid moral issues, as they tend to be based on what people view as right and wrong (value claims), and thus they are often rooted in deep-seated beliefs rather than potentially changeable opinions.

A *timely topic* is one that has emerged in recent times or in the past and has been reinvigorated due to a new development or event. You might choose a topic that is a current hot issue in science, technology, medicine, society, or another area. Perhaps choosing one that is relevant to your own life and interests will help you stay motivated. Choosing a long-standing topic like abortion, legalizing marijuana, or the death penalty is risky, as these have been debated over and over for years, and repeating the same arguments that have been made before will make for an unoriginal essay on a worn-out topic. Moreover, to make an original argument on these topics as reviewed in the current context would be a challenging enterprise.

A *debatable topic* is one that is not a settled issue and has two or more valid viewpoints. For instance, arguing that a company should not use automation in manufacturing is a moot point since it is already prevalent and has improved the manufacturing process immensely. However, an argument could be made that some forms of automation have increased unemployment rates.

A *researchable topic* is one that you can actually research: Can you find valid, authoritative, and/or credible information on the topic? In relation to automation, for instance, you can research what has happened in manufacturing sectors that have become highly dependent on these mechanical aids, and how this may have affected employment rates in the immediate area. This may lead to you finding objective data to support a claim as to whether or not automation has led to increased unemployment.

A *manageable topic* is one that can be done within the available time and word limit you have been given. Continuing with the example above, debating the broad issue of automation in manufacturing would probably call for a book-length treatment of the topic; and, even then, you might not be able to conclude it decisively. Therefore, you would have to narrow your scope to something more manageable, such as a specific effect in a geographical area and/or a specific manufacturing sector.

> **Exercise 5.3. Choosing a good topic**
> In groups of three/four, discuss topics for argument essays that are interesting, current, debatable, researchable, and manageable for you. Write down three possible topics in the spaces.

1.

2.

3.

Include a Clear, Concise, and Well-Written Thesis Statement

If you do not have a solid thesis statement, the content of your essay will probably be difficult to pin down. Think of your thesis as an anchor, and your argument as the boat attached to it. Without an anchor, your boat will drift off into the ocean and be lost forever. Anchor your argument to your thesis and do not let it drift away from you. In other words, use your thesis statement to keep you focused and on topic.

A thesis statement for an argument/opinion essay should be one or two sentences long. It should present the main idea and make a claim about your issue. This is the central claim for your essay, and thus it should be clear and direct. There are several ways arguments can be presented (see below), and you will need to decide among them. You'll need to decide, in other words, if you want to present one side of the issue (a *Classical/Aristotelian argument*), both sides (*Rogerian argument*), or if you want to base your argument primarily on the evidence (*Toulmin argument*). Finally, a thesis for an argument/opinion essay should not directly announce what your essay will be covering. Instead, it will make an assertion that suggests the points of your argument and give the reader some indication of what the content of your essay will be. For instance, compare the following two statements:

ARGUMENT/OPINION WRITING 257

> ✗ In this essay, I will persuade you that Thais do not like true crime documentaries because of a number of reasons.
>
> ✓ "In Thailand, true crime documentaries are not popular. This is not solely because of the genre itself, but because of a characteristically Thai way of thinking." From *A Sweeping Obsession for True Crime... We Thais Just Don't Get it!* by Iwarin Suprapas

The first example of a thesis statement above tells the reader quite forcefully that *I will persuade you...* First, it is never a good idea to tell anyone that you will persuade them of anything—you should always give them the option to make up their own mind. All you can do is try to convince them that your claim or opinion is more valid than an alternative claim or opinion, and even then, there is no guarantee that they will agree with you. Second, remember the definition at the start of this unit—an argument essay is not simply a persuasive essay. By using this phrase, the student misleads the reader as to the kind of essay to expect. Third, the first thesis statement is quite vague in that it simply states *because of a number of reasons*. Contrast this with the second thesis statement, which gives the reader some kind of hint as to the direction the author will be taking the reader—the reader will be learning something about *a characteristically Thai way of thinking*. There is also no mention of the author being certain about their ability to do anything to the reader.

Exercise 5.4. Writing thesis statements for arguments

Write thesis statements for the three topics that you came up with in Exercise 5.3. Remember to be clear and concise, and to give an assertion, not an announcement.

Write a Complete Introduction

In the introductory paragraph of an argument, after presenting the hook, a writer sets up the background and/or context for the upcoming argument by reviewing the topic in a general way. In this way, the writer ***establishes the territory*** to be explored in the essay. Next, the writer introduces the specific topic (narrowing the essay's scope) and explains why readers should care about this particular topic. In this way, the writer ***establishes the importance*** of the topic to be explored. The writer then presents the thesis statement. The content and scope of the thesis statement should provide a suitable framing of the issue and of the argument to come.

Exercise 5.5 presents an example of an introductory paragraph from a student's argument/opinion essay. The rest of this essay focuses on why celebrities should be afforded the same privacy rights as everyone else. Before you read the extract, note how the title makes use of one of the most memorable lines from the *Lord of the Rings* movies—a line that later became the basis of a very popular internet meme: The first half of the student's title is from when Gandolf stands before Balrog and says "You shall not pass" (Jackson, 2001). Give your essays similarly imaginative titles but make sure they also reflect the content of your essay, as the second part of this student's title does.

Exercise 5.5. Analyzing an introductory paragraph

Read the following example of an introductory paragraph from a student's argument/opinion essay. Then answer the questions that follow in the spaces provided.

In 2007, the picture of Britney Spears' baldhead was published in every newspaper. In 2014, nude pictures of Jennifer Lawrence were flying all over the internet. For more than 10 years, Korean superstars' homes were under surveillance by hidden micro cameras installed without permission. In 1997, the Princess of Wales died in an accident because paparazzi were chasing her. From Hollywood stars to Eastern celebrities to British Royals, privacy has gone out the window. Such invasions of privacy violates celebrities' rights, sabotages their careers and health, and can even take away their lives. I think it is time celebrities are given more rights to protect their privacy.

Introduction from *You Shall not Pass! Celebrities' Privacy is Theirs to Hold* by I. Suprapas

1. How does the writer establish the relevant background or territory within which the topic will be explored?

2. How does the writer establish the importance of the topic?

3. Discuss with a partner if the thesis statement is a good one or not.

Transition Clearly and Logically between Paragraphs

Transitions are like cement. They hold the bricks of your essay wall together. Without clear transitions between sentences that show the relationships between ideas and propositions, the overall structure of your essay will break down. Transitions between paragraphs are also important when building an argument; so, in addition to the sentence-level transitions covered in previous units, you can construct paragraph-level transitions by wording the concluding sentence from one paragraph in such a way that it leads into the topic sentence of the next paragraph.

The extract below is taken from a student essay. It is another argument essay about celebrity privacy. Notice how the author ties in the concluding sentence of the first body paragraph (1) to the upcoming topic sentence of the second body paragraph (2) by repeating words, reformulating phrases, and making inferential connections. Note how he does the same when moving between body paragraphs (2) and (3).

5.2   Example method for tying paragraphs together

… While most of society might assume that fame and power would protect these celebrities from intusions of privacy, or that deprivation of privacy is a fair price that every celebrity should pay, these are faulty assumptions. In truth, privacy is a luxury many celebrities are yearning for, and they should be treated with respect like ordinary people. (Intro para.)

One of the reasons why celebrities deserve to have their privacy recognized is because there is still a belief among the general public that privacy violation is a well-deserved predicament of being famous.… [in the original draft, supporting details/sentences can be found here] …. Ultimately, this belief among the general public is partially why celebrities' private lives continue to be targeted and threatened by benefiting parties, such as paparazzi, stalkers, etc. (1)

Apart from the public's belief in the deserved cost of being famous, which contributes to the continuity of celebrities' privacy invasions, the demand for access to public figures' private lives can also have drastic consequences for the targeted celebrities. … (2)

Extract from *Celebrity Privacy: when privacy is buried by fame* by Noppanun Sookping

Populate Each Paragraph with Sufficient Evidence (Data) + Reasons (Warrant)

When writing an argument essay, stick to the "one topic, one paragraph" rule. This will make it easy for the reader to follow your train of thought. Each of your body paragraphs should also tie into the thesis statement in your introduction through their respective topic sentences and supporting details.

It is also important to link the evidence in a body paragraph to its topic sentence through sound, logical reasoning: Explain how and why the evidence you have presented supports the main idea expressed in the topic sentence. In other words, provide sufficient warrant (reasoning) that links the evidence (grounds) within a paragraph to the paragraph's individual claim (topic sentence) and the essay's overall claim (thesis statement).

Some argument essays will include differing points of view regarding the topic. In such a case, depending on your word limit, you may want to consider dedicating one or two body paragraphs to opposing viewpoints, then discuss why those viewpoints are incorrect, invalid, untrue, or less worthy than the one you are arguing. In these paragraphs, you briefly outline the strongest, most relevant counterargument(s), present evidence that refutes the counterargument(s), then explain why your argument better fits the evidence you just presented. Such a paragraph would constitute a rebuttal. More on this later.

Use Relevant, Reliable, and Balanced Evidence

To construct a solid argument, you need to present accurate, up-to-date, well-researched information as evidence. *Relevant* information that can serve as evidence is current and relates specifically to your issue. *Reliable* (or *credible*) information that can serve as evidence is from authoritative and trustworthy sources (e.g., government, scientific, academic, or balanced news sources).

Some of the evidence you find will support your claim; some of it will counter your claim. You should never exclude any relevant and reliable information when presenting an argument, as this is misleading and therefore unethical. Selectively choosing evidence that supports your viewpoint is called ***cherry-picking***—you are picking the most delicious looking cherries off the tree and ignoring the rest. Not only is this unethical, but it can leave glaring weaknesses in your argument's support structure. If the opposing side is aware of any evidence that you have left out, they can (and will) use it to pick apart your argument. Therefore, it is important to not leave out any potentially strong pieces of evidence and to conduct a thorough search of all the available relevant and reliable sources. If you find there is more evidence for the counterclaim side, then perhaps you should consider changing your initial claim.

A key issue when choosing evidence is "What constitutes a good source?" When searching the internet, for example, you will find an abundance of potential sources you could use as evidence in your essay. That being the case, how do you judge which sources you will use and which sources you will not use, that is, which ones are the most relevant and credible? There is not enough space here to explore such issues in depth. However, Exercise 5.6 will help you to develop a basic awareness of the relevance and reliability of sources.

In the table below the following exercise box, there are six documents (A–F). These documents were produced by different authors/ organizations between 2010 and 2022. The table also includes a brief summary of each document's content. Each of these documents is a potential source of evidence to be used in an argument/ opinion essay on the health risks associated with cell phone use. Your task is to rank these sources in terms of relevance and reliability using a scale of 1 to 4. Put your rankings in the last two columns on the right hand side of the table.

Exercise 5.6. Evaluating sources

Rank the sources below for relevance and reliability on a scale of 1–4, with 1 being "highly relevant/reliable" and 4 being "not relevant/reliable." Then answer the questions that follow.

Document	Author(s)	Summary of content	Published	Ranking (1–4) Relevance Reliability
A. *high school textbook*	science teachers	Explains how cell phones and electro-magnetic radiation work in neutral academic terms.	02-10-2017	
B. *public info text*	National Protection Agency	States that there is no evidence that cell phone use causes cancer but recommends precautions.	01-09-2010	
C. *popular science article*	research reporter	Cites researchers who argue that radiation from cell phones pose serious health risks.	15-07-2021	
D. *debate article*	phone industry engineer	Argues against the popular science article (above). Claims that health risks related to cell phone use are exaggerated.	20-07-2022	
E. *polemic*	journalist	Cites research that cell phone use causes cancer and claims there is a conspiracy involving businesses and politicians to conceal it.	15-11-2011	

F. *news article*	journalist	Interviews a person with a brain tumor who thinks that it was caused by heavy cell phone use.	04-04-2020

Questions of relevance

1. Which source(s) is/are the most relevant, and why?

2. Which source(s) is/are the least relevant, and why?

Questions of reliability

3. Which source(s) is/are the most reliable, and why?

4. Which source(s) is/are the least reliable, and why?

5. What makes the remaining sources less or more reliable than the ones you selected above? (i.e., explain why you did not choose the mid-range sources.)

6. Discuss with a peer what other kinds of relevant and reliable sources you could use in an essay about the health risks from cellphones. Find three examples of relevant and reliable ones.

Whether specific sources are cited in your essay or eliminated as not sufficiently relevant or reliable is a decision which you must make—and which you will be judged on by readers.

Fully Address the Thesis Statement in Your Conclusion

A conclusion for an argument must be logical and backed by the information the writer has provided. In your conclusion for an argument essay, be careful of overgeneralizing, and use appropriate indicators of modality to make accurate and measured claims. Do not introduce any new evidence at this stage. Instead, summarize and synthesize the main point or concluding statement from each of your body paragraphs. Overall, your conclusion should do the following things:

- Restate why the topic is important.
- Review the main points of your argument.
- Address or reflect upon your thesis statement.
- Make a final memorable point.

The following exercise presents a concluding paragraph from an argument/opinion essay on why celebrities should be afforded the same privacy rights as everyone else (you have already seen the introductory paragraph for this essay in Exercise 5.5). Exercise 5.7 will help you to recognize and evaluate each of the elements listed above, as well as provide you with an example of a concluding paragraph from a short essay.

Exercise 5.7. Analyzing a concluding paragraph

Read the extract below and answer the questions that follow. Pay attention to how the student uses concessive relations (i.e., *despite*, *nevertheless,* and *after all*) to qualify her statements.

After exploring both sides of the issue, it is reasonable to say that celebrities should be able to fend off most privacy violations. Despite miscellaneous claims that the invasion of celebrities' privacy is acceptable, whether as a duty or against basic rights, adequate evidence, theories, and case studies aptly rebut those claims. The invasion of celebrities' privacy can indeed handicap their fundamental rights, as well as disrupt their careers and trigger mental illnesses. Nevertheless, as long as there are people reading and yearning to discuss celebrities' private lives, the paparazzi will have more stories ready to be published. Therefore, it is for us, the devourers of the media, to stop allowing a celebrity's privacy to be raided only just to feed our curiosity. After all, they are only human, just like the rest of us.

From *You Shall not Pass! The Celebrities' Privacy is Theirs to Hold* by Iwarin Suprapas

1. Has the author restated why the topic is important? If so, how?

2. How many main points of the argument have they reviewed?

3. How have they reflected upon their thesis statement?

4. What memorable point is made at the end?

Now that you should be able to identify the core elements of a concluding paragraph for an argument/opinion essay, Exercise 5.8 will test your ability to create these elements. The exercise contains an extract from John F. Kennedy's infamous *Moon Speech*, which he delivered at Rice University, Houston Texas on September 12th, 1962.

Exercise 5.8. Writing a concluding paragraph

The extract below is from a famous speech delivered by U.S. President, John F. Kennedy. Your task is to write a six-line concluding paragraph for this speech.

We set sail on this new sea because there is new knowledge to be gained, and new rights to be won, and they must be won and used for the progress of all people. For space science, like nuclear science and all technology, has no conscience of its own. Whether it will become a force for good or ill depends on man, and only if the United States occupies a position of pre-eminence can we help decide whether this new ocean will be a sea of peace or a new terrifying theatre of war...

... But why, some say, the moon? Why choose this as our goal? And they may well ask why climb the highest mountain? Why, 35 years ago, fly the Atlantic? Why does Rice play Texas? We choose to go to the moon. We choose to go to the moon in this decade and do the other things, not because they are easy, but because they are hard, because that goal will serve to organize and measure the best of our energies and skills, because that challenge is one that we are willing to accept, one we are unwilling to postpone, and one which we intend to win, and the others, too.

Extract from the *Moon Speech* delivered by John F. Kennedy (1962)

In your concluding paragraph, make sure to restate the thesis, summarize the main points, and end by reflecting on the thesis and making a memorable statement. Also, remember that your conclusion is to be read aloud—it will, after all, be part of a speech—so adjust your writing style to reflect this (i.e., use short clauses that can be said in one breath, avoid passive voice, and use inclusive "we" where appropriate).

Compare your paragraph with that of a peer's. The actual ending to Kennedy's speech can be seen in the answer key for this unit.

5.1.3. Referencing

As noted above, some forms of argument require support from outside voices, opinions, statistics, and arguments made by other people. Writers do this by referencing these outside sources. Referencing is not only important to give credit to others' ideas, research, and specific words, but it also helps writers to avoid plagiarism.

Plagiarism, Paraphrasing, and "Patch-Writing"

Plagiarism can be a difficult concept to define and there are often significant differences between how students and teachers view plagiarism and respond to it (Bowen & Nanni, 2021). Historically, plagiarism has been defined as a kind of theft—the word *plagium* is Latin for "kidnap," and similar negative connotations exist in Eastern languages: Chinese has 抄襲 ("lift"/"steal") and 剽窃 ("pirate"), and Thai has ขโมยความคิด ("steal thoughts").

Some people also see plagiarism as more than just stealing the language choices, structures, and ideas of others. In their view, plagiarism crosses the boundaries of intellectual property and assumes ownership of another's "voice." Others—mainly educators working in second language settings—view plagiarism as a necessary developmental stage and classify it as a form of "textual borrowing" (Barks & Watts, 2001) or "nontransgressive intertextuality" (Borg, 2009). From this perspective, students are merely attempting to learn a new form of social practice—a form of practice that will allow them entry into a specialized discourse community once they master it by learning how to properly cite other people's work and thus to avoid plagiarism.

Regardless of these views, it is your job—as a student and an ethical person—to be honest and open about where the ideas and/or words that you put into your essay have come from. For instance, if you directly copy the words of someone else (or from a previous essay you have written), then you must put these words in between quotation marks and reference where the quote is from (as I have done throughout this book). Otherwise, you are plagiarizing the work of others or self-plagiarizing, which is equally frowned upon.

Similarly, if you use an AI chatbot like ChatGPT to generate content, or an AI paraphraser like InstaText to rewrite sections of text, the resultant language choices and ideas are not your own. Therefore, you should appropriately cite or acknowledge any AI-generated or AI-modified text to avoid being accused of plagiarism. Indeed, these forms of plagiarism are now picked up by the kinds of text matching software used in most educational institutions (e.g., *Turnitin*), and if you are found guilty of plagiarizing by such software, then you will probably get a failing grade for your essay or have to redo it.

Such software is also very good at picking up "patch-writing," which is when a writer takes a quote and simply substitutes a few words for close synonyms and/or makes small adjustments to sentence structure. At this point, you may be thinking, "but isn't patch-writing just a form of paraphrasing?" Technically, they are two very different things. When you paraphrase, you are putting something into your own words through your own perspective and way of expressing things. This often involves simplifying the original text and/or presenting it in alternative way. If you have simply changed a few words and a bit of syntax (word order or other aspects of grammar), then you have not really shown any in-depth understanding or interpretation of the original text. Patch-writing is a "quick-and-dirty" shortcut that results in text that is recognizably close to the words of the source from which it has been taken—too close to be considered your own original wording.

Thus, in the eyes of your teacher and other readers, patch-writing is a poor writing strategy, while paraphrasing is a valuable writing skill demonstrating that you truly understand the material and have absorbed it into your own way of thinking and communicating. Nevertheless, whether you have patch-written something or paraphrased it, you need to give a reference to the source, as the original idea was not your own.

Referencing Styles

There are many different styles of referencing. Some of the better-known ones include the APA (American Psychological Association), Chicago, Harvard, and MLA (Modern Language Association) styles. Each one is usually associated with a different discipline and/or subject area—although some are simply tied to certain institutions or organizations. Your teacher should be able tell you which one is appropriate, or they will ask you to use a specific one. Either way, it is then your job to find out what the detailed formatting requirements are for that particular style guide.

Regardless of which style guide you need, choose, or are told to use, they all require two fundamental elements in order to build a reference to an outside source:

→ A REFERENCE LIST ITEM, which includes enough information so that an interested reader can find the original source themselves;

→ AN IN-TEXT CITATION, which acts as a place marker within your essay, and effectively tells the reader "this part of my essay comes from this source, which I have included in my reference list at the end of this essay."

In other words, a reference list item points the reader to an outside source, whereas an in-text citation points the reader to the reference list item inside your essay.

The exact formatting of these two elements differs among style guides, and there is not enough space here to cover them all. Therefore, I will only introduce one of the most popular ones here: *APA 7ᵗʰ Edition*.

The definitive source for information about APA 7th Edition style guidelines is their website (https://apastyle.apa.org/). On this site, you can find out how to reference all manner of sources, from textbooks, to journal articles, to websites and online podcasts. You can also find out how to caption figures, use appropriate colors in images, format data tables, and label titles and headings.

Reference List Items

To build a reference list item using the APA 7th Edition style guide, you need to include the information shown below, and each element (author name, book title, etc.) needs to follow the exact format shown. For instance, note how the titles of the books in the examples are in lower case other than the first word, even though the actual books probably have a capitalized title in print. Note also that if the book has a subtitle, it follows a colon (:) and starts with a capital letter on the first word. Also, make note of what is italicized and what is not, how all the author's initials are included (with spaces between them), and how the reference list item is formatted using a hanging paragraph indent. This can be done in most word processing programs using the paragraph formatting option: Simply highlight the reference list item in your document and change the paragraph formatting from "first line indented" to "hanging indent."

REFERENCING A BOOK

Author A. A. (Copyright Year). *Title of the book* (#th ed.). Publisher. DOI or URL if available

Bowen, N. E. J. A. (2022). *Essential skills and knowledge for essay writing: A practical guide for ESL and EFL undergraduates*. Equinox.

REFERENCING A CHAPTER IN AN EDITED BOOK

Author, A. A., & Author, B. B. (Copyright Year). Title of the book chapter. In A. A. Editor (Ed.), Title of the book (pp. #–#). Publisher. DOI or URL if available

Oswald, M. E., & Grosjean, S. (2004). Confirmation bias. In R. F. Pohl (Ed.), *Cognitive illusions: A handbook on fallacies and biases in thinking, judgement and memory* (pp. 79–96). Psychology Press.

270 ESSENTIAL KNOWLEDGE AND SKILLS FOR ESSAY WRITING

REFERENCING A JOURNAL ARTICLE

Author, A. A., & Author, B. B. (Copyright Year). Title of the article. *Name of the Journal, volume number.* (issue number), #–#. https://doi.org/xxxx

Bowen, N. E. J. A. (2021). Hybrid discourse and the emergence of context in BBC's Question Time. *Discourse and Interaction. 14*(2), 41–60. https://doi.org/10.5817/DI2021-2-41

As you can see, there are a number of subtle differences between referencing a book and referencing an article. These include what details you need to include, what to capitalize (e.g., capitalize the abbreviation Ed. for *editor*, but not ed. for *edition*), what to put in italics, and where to place certain punctuation marks. Also, note the use of the en dash and not a hyphen for a page range (e.g., 1–15). Pay attention to these small details. They are what separate a mediocre reference list from a very good one, and your teacher may even deduct marks for reference list items that are incorrectly formatted or missing small details. Ultimately, you need to learn to closely follow the style guide that you are required to use, so you will not lose marks over little things that are relatively easy to get right. For other types of reference list items, see the APA style guide website.

In-Text Citations

In-text citations come in two formats: narrative and parenthetical. They are further differentiated in terms of whether they require page numbers (direct quotes) or not (paraphrased text), as shown below:

NARRATIVE IN-TEXT CITATION FOR A PARAPHRASED ITEM

Bowen and Nanni (2021) found significant differences between how students and teachers view plagiarism and respond to it.

NARRATIVE IN-TEXT CITATION FOR A QUOTED ITEM

Bowen and Nanni (2021) found "a clear difference between students' and teachers' views on plagiarism and the academic practices surrounding it" (p. 11)

PARENTHETICAL IN-TEXT CITATION FOR A PARAPHRASED ITEM

> There are often significant differences between how students and teachers view plagiarism and respond to it (Bowen & Nanni, 2021).

PARENTHETICAL IN-TEXT CITATION FOR A QUOTED ITEM

> A recent study found "a clear difference between students' and teachers' views on plagiarism and the academic practices surrounding it" (Bowen & Nanni, 2021, p. 11)

The APA format in its most recent edition (7th) also requires us to shorten the in-text citation if there are three or more authors. For example:

→ Bowen, Satienchayakorn, Teedaaksornsakul, and Thomas (2021) becomes Bowen et al. (2021);

→ Bowen, Satienchayakorn, Teedaaksornsakul, and Thomas (2022) becomes (Bowen et al., 2022).

This requirement varies among referencing styles, so check the one you are using.

5.1.4. Methods of Argument

As noted in the previous section, a good argument contains a reasonable assertion (claim) that is supported by relevant evidence (grounds) and logical reasons (warrants). Moreover, so far in this book, you have used the five-paragraph essay approach to write descriptions, narratives, and expositions. There should be no surprise then that you can also apply it to argumentation, and that you can have the same components that you have had before: (a) an introductory paragraph; (b) three body paragraphs that incorporate evidence and may include discussion of opposing views; and (c) a concluding paragraph. However, for longer essays based on issues that are more complex, you need to make a more complete argument in support of your assertions/claims. Essays that incorporate empirical research or reviews of published literature, for example, will almost certainly be more than five paragraphs long.

In constructing an argument, you may come across the terms, *Classical/Aristotelian*, *Rogerian*, or *Toulmin argument*, which I referred to at the start of this unit. These are three well-established frameworks for structuring arguments. Their classification of components can help writers develop and organize their ideas and to build an argument in a systematic way. Each framework is useful for considering the structure of an argument and breaking an argument down into its component parts, so that the writer and the reader can decide how effectively those parts contribute to the whole. Using these frameworks, writers can determine if there are any missing elements that they need to build a good argument or any extra information that is not relevant and can therefore be left out. While there are some overlaps in what they cover—there are only a finite number of elements in an argument—they differ with regard to who your audience is and what you are trying to do in your argument.

A ***Classical/Aristotelian*** argument aims to inspire an audience to action. It is made up of five components (Young et al., 1970):

1. **Exordium** – introduction that appeals to an audience in a given moment (*Kairos*).
2. **Narratio** – a viable context (setting) where your argument is situated.
3. **Proposito & Partitito** – three to four sentences (in an essay) that assert the claim and briefly outline how your argument will support this claim.
4. **Confirmatio & Refutatio** – confirm your claim(s) and refute counterclaim(s).
5. **Peroratio** – the conclusion and a call to action.

This is the most direct and aggressive of the three frameworks. Here, the element of power in the relationship between speaker/writer and audience/reader plays a key role in its production and reception. This type of argument is most useful when your audience already knows and respects you, or you have some standing over them.

A ***Rogerian*** argument aims to establish a compromise position between opposing opinions. It is made up of six components (Young et al., 1970):

1. **Introduction** – presents the issue as a problem to be solved.
2. **Opposing position** – accurately and objectively states the counterclaim.
3. **Context for opposing position** – acknowledges that the counterclaim has merit in some specific contexts, but perhaps not others.
4. **Your position** – accurately and objectively states your view/claim.
5. **Context for your position** – describes how your view/claim has merit in some specific contexts, but perhaps not others.
6. **Benefits** – appeals to your opponents by outlining how they will benefit from your position.

A Rogerian argument takes the middle ground as it seeks to establish compromise. It is therefore seen as a useful framework when your audience has power over you, and/or do not relate to you or your views. It is also useful when the audience is overly sensitive to a topic or the topic is a PARSNIP one. However, it may not be very useful if you are arguing to decide an important issue, or if you need to convince the majority of the audience that your claim is clearly the strongest.

The third type of argument is the ***Toulmin Method***, developed by the philosopher, Stephen E. Toulmin in *The Use of Argument* (Toulmin, 2003/1959). Like the Rogerian argument, it consists of six parts:

1. **Grounds (data)** – evidence or facts used to support a claim.
2. **Claim** – statement(s) of the assertion being argued for.
3. **Warrants** – general, hypothetical statements that link the grounds to the claim.
4. **Backing** – additional support given to the warrant (typically some form of example or reference to published literature).
5. **Qualifier** – helps limit the claim.

274 ESSENTIAL KNOWLEDGE AND SKILLS FOR ESSAY WRITING

6. **Rebuttal** – acknowledgment of other valid assertions on the same issue.

This method is useful when dealing with objective information that you want to put at the forefront of your argument. It is thus useful when your audience expects data and other forms of reliable information together with transparent logic, such as those who follow the scientific method of inquiry. For these reasons, I will focus mainly on the Toulmin Method for the rest of this unit.

5.2. THE TOULMIN METHOD

In addition to being useful when you want to put the evidence at the forefront of your argument, the Toulmin method can be used to construct any kind of argument, since it only specifies the components and not the order of the argument nor its expected outcome. Second, as for the other models of argument described above, it can be used to achieve the following goals:

- Develop and organize your ideas in a systematic way.
- Break an argument down into its component parts, so that you can decide how effectively those parts contribute to the whole.
- Ascertain any missing elements that you need to add in order to build a good argument.
- Identify any extra information that is not relevant and can therefore be left out.

5.2.1 Elements of the Toulmin Model

Figure 5.1 outlines the six component parts of the Toulmin Method in more detail. Notice how everything in the diagram feeds into the claim. This is because a writer typically makes a claim based on available evidence (grounds) and warrant (e.g., logical reasoning) + any backing (supporting details). It would be unwise to establish a claim and then look for evidence to support it. For example, you would not claim someone was guilty of a crime and then look for evidence to support this claim. You would look at all the evidence (grounds [data]), and then decide what supports a claim of guilty and what supports a claim of innocent.

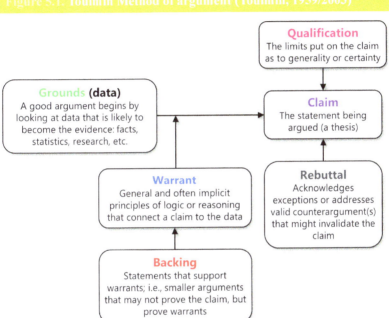

Figure 5.1. Toulmin Method of argument (Toulmin, 1959/2003)

In many cases, it is also unwise to make a claim without some kind of qualification limiting its generality or your certainty about it. You might also consider possible counterarguments and give rebuttals that seek to show why opposing views are not correct, truthful, valid, or valuable, and why your view is the stronger one.

The next section breaks down the Toulmin Method into each of its component parts.

Grounds (Data)

A good argument begins with exploring data that is likely to become the proof in an argument—an argument starts from the ground up, thus the term grounds for an argument or claim. The grounds are effectively the data that support a claim. As you build up an argument, you (re)examine the data, ask questions based on the data, and look for data that is likely to become good evidence in an argument. As Hillock (2011) notes, the beginning of an argument starts with "the examination of data, not the invention of a thesis statement [claim] in a vacuum" (p. xxii).

During the researching/planning stage of your argument essay, it may be a good idea to formulate a question statement (or writing prompt) related to your topic and then make a list of pros (evidence that supports your initial view) and cons (evidence that opposes your initial view). By doing this, you get to visualize the amount and type of data on each side and can make an informed judgement to stick with your initial view or change it.

Claim

The *claim* is the most central component of an argument. It is the statement being argued or asserted (thesis statement). The claim is written after you have looked at all the available data and considered possible warrants and counterclaims. Generally speaking, there are three types of claim that are commonly found in short argument essays: claim of fact, claim of value, and claim of policy.

Claim of fact – something was, is, or will be true or false, correct or incorrect, or valid or invalid. For instance, Abortions were one of the safest medical procedures in England in 2022; The Irish Wolfhound is the tallest breed of dog; The Tesla Plaid will be the fastest electric vehicle on sale in America in 2023. Claims of fact are quantifiable, which means they draw heavily on empirical data that is measurably observable and objective. When making a claim of fact, it is important that you use factual evidence that is appropriate, reliable, and sufficient. This type of claim is the most suited to the Toulmin argument.

Claim of value – something has or does not have worth. For example, *Abortion is morally wrong; Corgis are the most beautiful breed of dog; Tesla cars are the best electric cars on the market.* It is often difficult to support value claims with empirical evidence as they tend to be of a qualitative nature (i.e., they are often more subjective than objective). Nevertheless, you should still strive to base as much of your argument as possible on good evidence; and if the evidence is not very substantial, then consider using a different method of argumentation such as the Rogerian argument, as opposing viewpoints are often difficult to reconcile when debating value claims.

Claim of policy – something should or should not be done about something. In other words, an existing policy, method, or state of being is flawed and/or inadequate and it needs to be changed. For example, *Abortion should be legalized in the Philippines*; *Dogs should only be fed fresh meat; Tesla cars should be more affordable*. The key word in most claims of policy is *should*. Claims of policy draw on both claims of fact (highlighting the need for change) and claims of value (highlighting the desirability of making the change), and they are often well suited to the Classical/Aristotelian argument method.

Warrant

A *warrant* is an underlying principle that guides reasoning. It allows the writer to make an inferential connection between the grounds and the claim. Warrants can be explicit explanations of how and why the data you present supports the claims you are making, or they can be—and typically are—implicit and unstated rules that people accept as generally true. For instance, if I am in America, I drive on the right-hand side of the road; if I am in the UK, I drive on the left. My decisions are premised on the evidence alone: I see everyone driving on the same side of the road in each country, and it is obvious to me that if I do not, I will cause an accident. Whether they are explicit or implicit, warrants can be common-sense rules that most people follow, or they can be laws, scientific principles, or logical relationships that are well-established and widely accepted. In other words, warrants connect the grounds for an argument to a claim through societal or scientific conventions, or through logical reasoning.

Warrants are perhaps the most difficult part of the Toulmin Method to grasp. This is because they are, as noted above, often

278   ESSENTIAL KNOWLEDGE AND SKILLS FOR ESSAY WRITING

implicit and thus not included in the wording of an argument. However, one way to clarify the concept is to draw analogies with the use of syllogisms in classical logic, which most people are familiar with.

A *syllogism* derives a conclusion from a set of statements called premises, or to put it another way, a premise offers evidence, justification, or a reason for the conclusion. Thus, there is little debate that Toulmin's concept of grounds is directly relatable to a premise (Hitchcock, 2006), as shown in the following example:

Major premise	*All humans are mortal.* [grounds]	
Minor premise	*I am a human.* [grounds]	
Conclusion	*Therefore, I am mortal.* [fact claim]	

In the above example, the link between the two premises and the conclusion is relatively straightforward. The conclusion follows from an *implicit rule of logical reasoning*. Thus, there is no need to provide any warrants—most people will be capable of making the inferential leap between the grounds (categorical statements of fact) and the claim. However, there may be instances when you need to explicitly state the link between a premise (grounds) and a conclusion (claim). In such instances, providing a warrant further strengthens your argument by giving clearer justification and/or reasons for why the premise (grounds) can be linked to the conclusion (claims). Consider the following examples, which show simple arguments supported through different kinds of warrants.

ARGUMENT BASED ON GENERALIZATION assumes that what is true for a representative sample or from the weight of evidence in the past will be true for a larger sample or future experience:

Major premise	*So far, I have liked all the units in this course.* [grounds (data)]
Inferential rule	*Based on the consistency of my experience up to now I expect the same going forward.* [warrant for generalization-based claim]
Conclusion	*Thus I will probably enjoy this final unit.* [qualifier + value claim]

An issue with this type of warrant is how representative the sample of experience is and what the factors are that could change the pattern—such as, in this case, finding the topic or focus of this unit less interesting or more difficult than the previous ones.

ARGUMENT BASED ON ANALOGY is another form of generalizing, but instead of making links between similar samples from the same population or same event, it makes links between similar populations or events. In the example below, the warrant provides an explicit inferential link between the two premises (grounds) and the conclusion (claim).

Major premise	*Chimpanzees lose weight when they take Strippomol.* [grounds]
Minor premise	*People share 98.8% of their genetic makeup with chimpanzees.* [grounds]
Inferential rule	*When two sets of animals share this amount of DNA, then biological reactions in one should be seen in the other.* [warrant for analogy-based claim]
Conclusion	*Therefore, I should lose weight if I take Strippomol.* [claim]

An issue with this type of warrant is how strong the analogical connection is and what the factors are that could give a different result. In this case, those factors might include individual genetics, lifestyle, and diet.

ARGUMENT VIA A SIGN OR CLUE is another frequently found form of logical reasoning. It follows the logic that if there is A, then B usually follows. In the following example, the warrant provides an explicit link between A and B for anyone who does not know what smoke usually means:

Major premise	*I see smoke.* [grounds]
Inferential rule	*Smoke usually signals that something is on fire.* [warrant for sign/cue-based claim]
Conclusion	*Therefore, something is on fire.* [fact claim]

An issue with this type of warrant is how reliable something is as a sign or cue of something else. In this case, the connection of smoke to fire is very strong, but note that putting out a fire often

280 ESSENTIAL KNOWLEDGE AND SKILLS FOR ESSAY WRITING

generates a great deal of smoke, and that smoke sometimes indicates a chemical reaction rather than something burning. Thus this claim would need to be qualified accordingly (more on this below).

ARGUMENT FROM PRINCIPLE is a form of reasoning that applies to good morals or ethics:

Major premise	*Some people do not make enough money to be able to put any into savings.* [grounds]
Inferential rule	*It is fair that everyone should be able to save some money.* [warrant for principle-based claim]
Conclusion	*We should raise the minimum wage so that everyone can afford to start saving.* [policy claim]

An issue with this type of warrant is how universal or generally accepted the principle is. In this case, there is very little doubt that most people would agree that everyone should have a living wage. However, there may be some people who would not accept that everyone should be paid enough so they could save money.

There are many other types of reasoning that you can invoke, but there is no space to consider them all here. If you are interested in further reading, I recommend looking at the books by Toulmin (1959/2003) and/or Young et al. (1970).

Backing

Backing consists of statements that support warrants—they back up your reasoning to make it stronger. These statements do not typically support the main claim, but they do support the warrant. As Verheij (2006) notes, "the difference between backing and warrant: backings can be categorical statements of fact just like data, while warrants always are general bridge-like statements" (p. 193). Backing can consist of real-world examples, references to published literature, statistical reports, statutes and acts of law, and references to taxonomical systems. For instance, in the argument based on analogy example above, the backing might consist of an appeal to the result of experiments, such as the following:

> When two sets of animals share this amount of DNA, biological reactions in one should be seen in the other. [warrant] Indeed, a substantial number of drugs that were initially tested on monkeys have proven effective in humans (Friedman et al., 2017). [backing]

As Toulmin (1959/2003) emphasizes, backing is often field-dependent, meaning that the type of claim being made and the area within which it is being made determines what can be considered an acceptable form of backing. For instance, when dealing with arguments based on judgement (value claims) or policy (policy claims), extended legal definitions can be considered an acceptable and useful form of backing, as they can help to bolster an argument involving abstract or ambiguous concepts. For example, when claiming that something constitutes hate speech (a value claim), a legal definition of exactly what the term "hate speech" refers to will probably be needed, and it might be a good idea to situate this definition in relation to the concept of "freedom of speech."

Qualification

When you make a claim or a statement, it is not wise to make it a 100% certainty or to suggest that it applies in every circumstance. Any such claim is usually easy to refute (i.e., disprove). Therefore, writers *qualify* (or soften) claims using language such as modal verbs, mood adjuncts, and comment adjuncts. For instance, writers can choose words or phrases such as *might, may, probably, possibly, most likely, in most cases, it seems/appears, in my view*, etc. In addition to these forms of qualification, writers can also qualify their claims by adding information that indicates the specific circumstances in which they apply. For example, they might limit themselves to one location, group of people, or time period. By qualifying a claim through such language choices or additional information, writers acknowledge that there are valid counterclaims and that perhaps their claim is not valid in every context. Essentially, writers qualify a claim or statement so that their argument becomes more manageable in terms of its scope.

Rebuttals

A *rebuttal* addresses any potential exceptions or opposing arguments that might invalidate your argument. A rebuttal can be something as simple as offering exceptions to a claim, or it can be more complex, such as identifying a valid counterargument, arguing against it with sufficient, accurate, and credible evidence, and then reaffirming your argument through further constructive proof.

The following table includes some transitional phrases that are useful when setting up a rebuttal (i.e., it includes concessionary relationships that introduce other viewpoints).

Table 5.2. Concession starters / transitional phrases for rebuttals

Even though	Nevertheless	All the same
Admittedly	On other hand	An alternative viewpoint
While it is true that	In contrast	Be that as it may

When writing your argument essay, you should (a) anticipate any exceptions or counterarguments to your argument, and (b) include your own rebuttal against these exceptions or counterarguments. It is a good idea to include rebuttals in your essays, as they show that you are aware of opposing views and can counter them, and they further strengthen your side of the argument in the process. Providing a rebuttal also helps to clarify your position, making it seem more balanced and fair. However, remember that a rebuttal is not the same as a refutation. A refutation is "the repelling, contradicting, tearing down of an argument of another" (Smith, 1964, p. 130), whereas rebuttal is refutation *plus* reinforcement of one's own argument through additional support and constructive evidence. Thus, a rebuttal is more than just countering the other side's argument: it is also highlighting your own argument's strengths (see Example 5.3 in section 5.2.3 if you are unsure what this means).

5.2.2. Putting the Toulmin Method into Action

The relationships between the six elements of the Toulmin Method are succinctly demonstrated by Karbach (1987), who provides useful diagrams with respect to different forms of reasoning (i.e., using different types of warrants such as those provided in the syllogisms above). In Figure 5.2 I draw upon one of his examples to clarify further the elements (I have simplified Karbach's wording where appropriate).

Figure 5.2. Toulmin Argument in action via a concept map

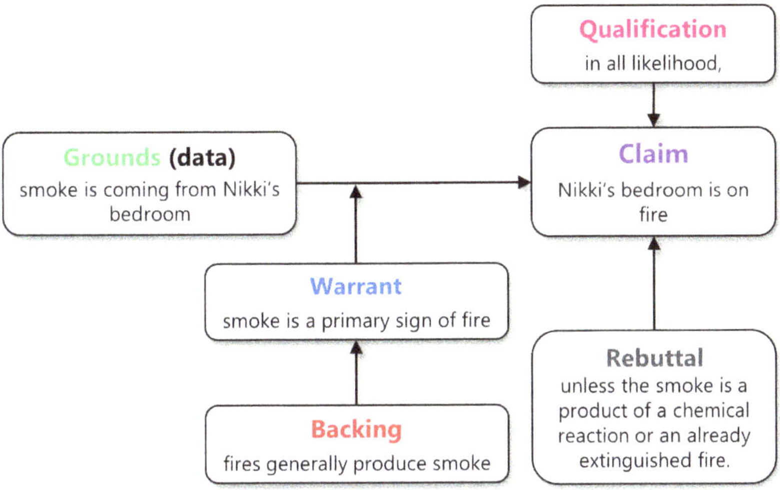

The full argument developed in our concept map (Figure 5.2) can be stated as follows:
- → *Smoke is coming from Nikki's bedroom.* [grounds (data)]
- → *Because smoke is a primary sign of fire, since fires generally produce smoke,* [warrant + backing]
- → *in all likelihood, Nikki's bedroom is on fire* [qualifier + claim]
- → *unless the smoke is a product of a chemical reaction or an already distinguished fire.* [rebuttal]

These bullet points can now be combined to form the following paragraph:

It seems that smoke is coming from Nikki's bedroom *[grounds]*. Therefore, because smoke is a primary sign of fire *[warrant]* and fires generally produce smoke *[backing]*, in all likelihood *[qualifier]*, Nikki's bedroom is on fire *[claim]*—unless the smoke is a product of a chemical reaction or from an already extinguished fire *[rebuttal]*.

In Exercise 5.9 you will further familiarize yourself with the elements of the Toulmin Method of argumentation. Specifically, you will practice generating claims based on evidence (data), establish warrants to support your claims, and consider any rebuttals or qualifications needed. The inspiration for the exercise comes from Hillocks (2011), while the material for the task was created by Lawrence Treat and appeared in *Crime and Puzzlement 2: More Solve-Them-Yourself Picture Mysteries, a book of picture mysteries* (Treat, 1982). I have modified the original task so that you cannot simply google the answers.

In the exercise you are to <u>assume the role of a lawyer in the trial of Queenie Volupides</u>, who is pictured in Figure 5.3 standing over her dead husband's body. This picture was taken by one of her friends as they arrived back at her house after a night out at the country club.

Figure 5.3. Queenie discovering her dead husband (Treat, 1982, p. 10)

At five-feet-six and a hundred and ten pounds, Queenie Volupides was a sight to behold and to clasp. When she tore out of the house after a tiff with her husband, Arthur, she went to the country club where there was a party going on. She left the club shortly before one in the morning and invited a few friends to follow her home and have one more drink. They got to the Volupides house about ten minutes after Queenie, who met them at the door and said, "Something terrible happened. Arthur slipped and fell on the stairs ... he's dead. Oh, dear—what shall I do?" The autopsy conducted later concluded that Arthur had died from a wound on the head and confirmed that he'd been drunk.

Extract from *Slip or Trip* by Lawrence Treat (Treat, 1982, p.11)

Credit: Lawrence Treat, "Slip or Trip?" from Crime and Puzzlement 2: More Solve-Them-Yourself Picture Mysteries, illustrated by Kathleen Borowik, page 10. Copyright © 1982 by Lawrence Treat. Illustrations copyright © 1982 by Kathleen Borowik. Reprinted with the permission of The Permissions Company, LLC, on behalf of David R. Godine, Publisher, Inc., www.godine.com.

ARGUMENT/OPINION WRITING   285

Your goal is to write a closing statement for the jurors in Queenie's murder trial. Your statement will be based on the available evidence, Figure 5.3 and the information in the extract below. You are to include the following: an overall claim plus any necessary qualifiers, grounds (evidence), warrants, backing, and rebuttal(s). Your claim should answer the question: "Is Queenie innocent or guilty in the death of her husband?"

Exercise 5.9. Slip or trip?

Using the information in Figure 5.3 and the extract (above), answer questions 1–4 individually. Then, working in pairs, complete the tasks that follow.

1. Examine the evidence presented in the crime scene pictured in Figure 5.3. Question the evidence in light of any inconsistencies between what you see and what Queenie said happened. List three questions in the spaces below and answer these questions with warrants and backing that reflect upon the data (grounds). Remember to qualify your conclusions/claims where necessary. I have provided you with an example question, grounds for an argument, and accompanying mini-argument as a guide.

Q. Why does Arthur's nightgown and clothing look so neat?

Grounds   *Arthur's clothes look too neat and tidy.* [grounds]

Warrant   *When people fall down the stairs, their clothes usually end up being messy, disheveled, or torn;* [warrant]

Backing   *since a person usually bumps into things and clothes get pulled out of shape.* [backing]

Claim   *Therefore, Queenie may be lying about Arthur falling down the stairs.* [qualifier + claim]

Qi)

   Grounds

   Warrant

   Backing

   Claim

286 ESSENTIAL KNOWLEDGE AND SKILLS FOR ESSAY WRITING

Qii)

Grounds
Warrant

Backing

Claim

Qiii)

Grounds
Warrant

Backing

Claim

2. Examine the evidence presented in the text extract. Question this evidence in light of any inconsistencies between what it says and what Queenie said happened. List three questions in the spaces below and answer these questions with warrants and backing that reflect upon the data (grounds). Remember to qualify your claims where necessary.

Qi)

Grounds
Warrant

Backing

Claim

Qii)

Grounds
Warrant

Backing

Claim

Qiii)

Grounds
Warrant

Backing

Claim

3. Is it possible that something else happened?

4. Is Queenie telling the truth?

In pairs, follow the steps below and make detailed notes as you do so. Draw upon your answers to the previous questions where relevant. You may also want to use a concept map, like the one in Figure 5.2, if it will help clarify your thoughts.

1. **Examine the data** in detail—both the statement and the image. With your partner, critically examine any peculiar or contradictory evidence. List the evidence in two columns: one column that supports a claim of guilty and one column that supports a claim of innocent.

2. **Make a claim** based on your interpretation of the data— namely, what you can infer from the timeline of events, the autopsy conducted by the medical examiner and Queenie's statement, as well as any relevant information in the image. In other words, answer the question, "Is Queenie guilty of murdering her husband or did he simply fall down the stairs?"

3. **Provide warrants and backing** for how the data supports your claim. Here, you can draw on the mini-arguments that you created above as well as create any more that come to mind.

4. **Sequence your argument** by listing the data and their accompanying warrants and backing from most important (strongest) to least important (weakest).

288 ESSENTIAL KNOWLEDGE AND SKILLS FOR ESSAY WRITING

5. **Address any potential counterarguments** to the data/warrants/backing on your list. In other words, provide rebuttals where necessary that address any opposing viewpoints while also shoring up your own argument.
6. **Summarize your argument** in a 250–350 word paragraph that can be read out at trial. Do not forget to qualify your claims where needed.

5.2.3. Sequencing a Toulmin Argument

In the previous section you created a number of mini-arguments based on your observations (grounds), which were linked to conclusions (claims) through logical reasoning (warrants + backing). You did this in pursuit of an answer to the question, "Is Queenie innocent or guilty in the death of her husband?". However, as you probably discovered when it came to writing your paragraph, stringing together a set of mini-arguments to form a larger argument is not as simple as just sequencing them in a list-like fashion.

To convert a series of mini-arguments into a cohesive, unified, and fully-developed argument, you can group your mini-arguments in terms of shared conclusions (claims). These can then become the basis for individual paragraphs. For instance, in the "Slip or trip?" exercise, you should have noticed two emergent themes from your conclusions (individual claims): (a) Arthur may not have fallen down the stairs; and (b) Queenie was exhibiting some strange behaviors. These two emergent themes would make good topic sentences for two body paragraphs. These paragraphs could then be fleshed out / built up with the grounds, warrants, and backing that you outlined in your investigation.

As already noted, when writing your body paragraphs, you should start with the strongest piece of evidence (grounds) that supports your topic sentence (individual claim). Then provide warrants that link this piece of evidence to (a part of) that topic sentence and thus, by default, to your thesis statement (overall

ARGUMENT/OPINION WRITING   289

claim). You should provide backing where warrants are perhaps not that strong, which can take the form of findings from empirical studies, authorative voices, historical precendents, and other kinds of reliable support/evidence.

In a complex argument, you will need to elaborate on your warrants by expanding the amount of backing and evidence you present, as well as provide rebuttals where necessary. Consider the following paragraph that expands the earlier argument by analogy example, which focused on claims surrounding a fat loss supplement. Note that "Strippomol" is a made-up product for the purposes of this example as is the parenthetical citation to "(Smith, 2022)". The rest of the argument is factual. As you read the example, note how the middle of the paragraph (in italics) is actually a rebuttal. I have chosen to put this in the middle of the paragraph to preempt any counterclaims before I get into the bulk of my own argument—the grounds have an obvious flaw: monkeys and humans are not identical.

5.3   Sequencing a Toulmin argument in a paragraph

Although there is no quick and easy way to lose weight, there are weight loss supplements that can help [topic sentence]. For instance, non-human primates have been shown to lose weight when they take Strippomol (Smith, 2022) [grounds]. *Technically, this drug has not been proven in humans yet* [counterclaim]*, but people share 98.8% of their genetic makeup with chimpanzees* [grounds for rebuttal]*. When two sets of animals share this amount of DNA, then biological reactions in one should be seen in the other* [warrant for rebuttal]*. Indeed, a substantial number of drugs that were initially tested on monkeys have proved effective in humans (Friedman et al., 2017)* [backing for rebuttal]. Moreover, non-human obese primates given the drug Adipotide, which has many of the same chemical compounds as Strippomol, showed an 11% decrease in bodyweight over a 28-day period (Barnhart et al., 2011) [grounds]. It has also shown promise in human trials (Kumar, 2019) [grounds]. Therefore, you <u>could</u> lose weight if you take Strippomol [qualified claim].

290 ESSENTIAL KNOWLEDGE AND SKILLS FOR ESSAY WRITING

> **References**
>
> Barnhart, K. F., Christianson, D. R., Hanley, P. W., Driessen, W. H., Bernacky, B. J., Baze, W. B., Wen, S., Tian, M., Ma, J., Kolonin, M. G., Saha, P. K. Do, K-A., Hulvat, J. F., Gelovani, J. G., Chan, L., Arap, W., & Pasqualini, R. (2011). A peptidomimetic targeting white fat causes weight loss and improved insulin resistance in obese monkeys. *Science Translational Medicine, 3*(108), 1–20. https://doi.org/10.1126/scitranslmed.3002621
>
> Friedman, H., Ator, N., Haigwood, N., Newsome, W., Allan, J. S., Golos, T. G., Kordower, J. H., Shade, R. E., Goldberg, M. E., Bailey, M. R., & Bianchi, P. (2017). The critical role of nonhuman primates in medical research. *Pathogens & Immunity, 2*(3), 352–365. https://doi.org/10.20411/pai.v2i3.186
>
> Kumar, M. S. (2019). Peptides and peptidomimetics as potential antiobesity agents: overview of current status. *Frontiers in Nutrition, 6*(11), 1–12. https://doi.org/10.3389/fnut.2019.00011

Overall, there are many ways that you can sequence an argument, and the above example is but one suggestion. The important thing is that you include the necessary components and order them in a logical way that your reader will be able to follow and that cumulatively builds your argument to a strong conclusion.

5.2.4. Rhetorical Structure of a Toulmin-Based Essay

Because of the complexity of argument structures, there are many ways that you might structure an argument essay. For instance, you might organize a five-paragraph argument essay based on the Toulmin Method in the following way:

Introduction	Paragraph 1	CONTENT: INTRODUCE YOUR ARGUMENT **Hook**. Grab your reader's attention with something memorable. **Establish the territory**. Set up the background and/or context for the upcoming argument by introducing the topic in a general way. **Establish importance**. Why should the reader care about your topic? **Present thesis**. (claim) with accompanying qualification.
	Paragraph 2	CONTENT: MINI-ARGUMENT 1 **Topic sentence**. Grounds + Warrant (+ backing). Grounds + Warrant (+ backing). Grounds + Warrant (+ backing). **Concluding sentence** (*can also be used as a link to the next paragraph).

		CONTENT: MINI-ARGUMENT 2
Body paragraphs	Paragraph 3	**Topic sentence**. Grounds + Warrant (+ backing). Grounds + Warrant (+ backing). Grounds + Warrant (+ backing). **Concluding sentence** (*can also be used as a link to the next paragraph).
	Paragraph 4	CONTENT: INTRODUCE COUNTERARGUMENT(S) + PROVIDE REBUTTAL(S) **Outline counterargument 1**. Rebuttal to counterargument 1 (refutation + reasons why your claim is stronger). **Outline counterargument 2**. Rebuttal to counterargument 2 (refutation + reasons why your claim is stronger). Depending on your word limit and the complexity of your topic/claim, you may want to extend your counterargument to include further rebuttals.
Conclusion	Paragraph 5	CONTENT: CONCLUDE YOUR ARGUMENT **Restate thesis**. Remind the reader what your central claim was and reiterate why the topic is important. **Summarize**. Review the main points of your argument. **Final thought**. Address or reflect upon your thesis statement and/or topic in a memorable way.

Yet, as Example 5.3 highlighted, the structure of an argument often depends on the argument itself, and thus you should expect to modify its structure as you draft and redraft your essay. The important thing is that your argument builds in strength and is unified (anchored to your thesis statement throughout), cohesive (well-sequenced and organized), and fully developed (supported by good evidence [grounds], logical reasoning [warrants], and sufficient backing).

5.3. WRITING AN ARGUMENT ESSAY

5.3.1. Writing the First Draft

Stage 1. Choosing a Topic

For this task, I am going to give you a topic so that you can pool your research efforts as a class and discuss the complexities surrounding the argument. Once you have done this, you will then work with a partner to plan, outline, draft, and revise an argument essay. Your resulting paired essay will be distinct from those of your peers, but it nonetheless should reach a similar conclusion, as you have used much of the same evidence.

In this task, you will be writing about the general topic of conspiracy theories. Your specific topic will be flat earth theory. This specific topic concerns the fact that a growing number of people believe the earth is flat, despite all the scientific evidence that points to the earth being a globe. These people are often referred to as "Flat Earthers": A community of people who believe the earth is not a globe but is actually a disk covered by a firmament (glass dome). They also believe that mankind will not fall off the edge of this disk because it is surrounded by an ice wall. This is classified as a "conspiracy theory" because Flat Earthers, like other conspiracy theorists, believe that there has been a conspiracy by "The Establishment" (in this case, the scientific community; in other cases, the government or other powerful people) to withhold true information and mislead people with false information.

In this paired writing assignment, you will develop an argument essay to convince the reader that Flat Earthers are not stupid, but that there are other (logical) explanations as to why they so strongly believe in their theory. Your essay should be 800–1000 words long excluding the reference list. You will explore the reasons why beliefs like these are still held among educated people, and are in fact becoming more popular—even though the internet has enabled more access to information than ever before. You will be arguing that people who hold such beliefs are not misguided or silly, but that such beliefs fulfill certain psychological and sociological drives, mechanisms, and needs.

Stage 2. Pre-Writing Activity: Doing Research

To help familiarize yourself with the topic, watch the Netflix documentary, *Beyond the Curve* (Clarke, 2018) and/or search YouTube or other internet sites for the countless videos and other information related to Flat Earthers. As you watch the video(s), look for examples of the following:

BOOMERANG EFFECT

When you throw a boomerang, it whizzes away from you on an arc and then circles back toward you. This analogy is the basis of the socio-psychological process known as the ***boomerang effect***. The boomerang effect occurs when you throw facts, statistics, and evidence at someone in order to break down their viewpoint (i.e., you attempt to refute their position), but instead of listening to you, they go on the defensive and frantically reject everything you say. It often occurs when your opponent has become so attached to their ideas that they see them as a part of who they are. Thus, your effort to refute their point of view threatens their very sense of being and identity. It can also occur if you present your refutation in such a way that it is seen as aggressive or controlling—in order to regain control, your opponent will reject everything that you have said in an attempt to restore their own sense of freedom (see Steindl et al., 2015, for more on this issue). Ultimately, the boomerang effect causes your refutation to miss its target, turn around, and head straight back to you with negative consequences. For further reading on this topic see Byrne and Hart (2009).

CONFIRMATION BIAS

When you confirm something, you reinforce it and make it stronger. When you have a bias against something, you have a prejudicial view for or against it. Put these two processes together and you get ***confirmation bias***. Confirmation bias is when an individual processes information through a filter that prioritizes an existing set of beliefs. Fundamentally, this (usually implicit, unintentional) filter functions by blocking out any inconsistent or opposing evidence or viewpoints while allowing evidence that confirms existing beliefs to pass through unimpeded. Confirmation bias thus effects how we process, collect, and even recall evidence, viewpoints, and information in general. No doubt, you have encountered it many times in your life, and it may have led you to think of someone as stubborn, "pig-headed" (unwilling to change strong opinions), or even plain stupid. However, confirmation bias is a natural tendency that we all have. Thus, when building an argument, it is important to be mindful of it in yourself and in others—especially if dealing with emotionally charged topics. For further reading on this topic see Heshmat (2015) or Oswald and Grosjean (2004).

DUNNING-KRUGER EFFECT

The ***Dunning-Kruger effect*** is a type of cognitive bias in which people believe that they are smarter and more capable than they really are (Kruger & Dunning, 1999). For example, have you ever watched a YouTube influencer or Instagrammer give advice about something like they are a seasoned professional, but you have found yourself looking on in amazement at the fact that they are barely out of high school and have not accomplished anything in life besides creating a social media page? If yes, then you may have been witnessing an example of the Dunning-Kruger effect. For further information on this topic see Kruger and Dunning (1999) or Dunning (2011).

Here are some other readings that will be useful for this task:

Aupers, S. (2012). 'Trust no one': Modernization, paranoia and conspiracy culture. *European Journal of Communication*, *27*(1), 22–34. https://doi.org/10.1177/0267323111433566

Hall, K. (2014). Create a sense of belonging: Finding ways to belong can help ease the pain of loneliness. *Psychology Today*. https://www.psychologytoday.com/us/blog/pieces-mind/201403/create-sense-belonging

Maslow, A. H. (1943). A theory of human motivation. *Psychological Review*, *50*(4), 370–396. https://doi.org/10.1037/h0054346

To shore up your argument, you must collect additional evidence that relates to the general topic of conspiracy theories and the specific topic of Flat Earth believers. This evidence should take the form of facts, statistics, and opinions from expert sources.

You must correctly cite these sources in your text and use APA 7th edition formatting in your reference list. The definitive guide to formatting references following APA style can be found at https:// apastyle.apa.org/style-grammar-guidelines/references

Once you have a better understanding of the general topic area (conspiracy theories) and the specific topic area (main reasons why people believe the earth is flat), consider the following questions:

- What is my exact topic and why should my reader care about it?
- Who is my reader and what might they know or not know about my topic?
- What is my purpose in writing this essay?
- What do I want my reader to do with the information I am giving them?

Stage 3. Outlining

Once you think that you have sufficient grounds (data), warrants (reasoning), and backing for a reasonable claim (or series of claims), then choose a suitable outlining technique. Populate your outline with your chosen elements and consider any counterarguments to your claim(s). Remember that your finished essay should be 800–1000 words long excluding references, so plan the length of your paragraphs with this word limit in mind. As a rough guide, you should give your introductory and concluding paragraphs about 135–150 words each for an essay of this projected length, with the remaining words allocated to your body paragraphs.

At this stage, it is also a good idea to clarify your thoughts before you begin writing. Once you have completed your outline, answer the following questions:

- What am I trying to prove?
- Why do I feel the way I do about this topic? Have I exhibited any biases?
- What kind of proof do I have? Is it relevant and reliable?
- Have I fully considered opposing viewpoints?

296 ESSENTIAL KNOWLEDGE AND SKILLS FOR ESSAY WRITING

Stage 4. Drafting

When you are happy with your outline, start drafting your essay. To save time, I have provided you with the first part of an introductory paragraph below. It was written by one of my students, Iwarin Suprapas. It is missing a thesis statement, so you need to write your own. Also, feel free to adapt this introductory paragraph to suit your own vision of an introduction to your essay. To clarify, you must write the title, thesis statement, body paragraphs, concluding paragraph, and reference list yourselves.

When drafting your essay, the body paragraphs should achieve the following aims:

- Clearly present the *grounds* (data or evidence) that support your overall claim (thesis statement).
- Explore *warrants* that show how the grounds are logically connected to your claim(s).
- Offer valid and reasonable *backing* that supports warrants where necessary;
- *Rebut* (not refute) one counterargument—be sure that you know the difference between rebut and refute (see the explanation earlier on in the unit if need be).

Your concluding paragraph, meanwhile, should achieve the following aims:

- Restate why the topic is important.
- Review the main points of your argument.
- Address and/or reflect upon your thesis statement.
- Provide a memorable final point.

Give your draft a title that is imaginative and captures the essence of your essay. Set the line spacing, paper size, margins, and font type and size according to the instructions given by your teacher or as specified in your assigned style guide. Do not forget to cite your sources in your text where needed and to include page numbers for direct quotes.

ARGUMENT/OPINION WRITING   297

> **5.4   Start of an introductory paragraph for your argument essay**
>
> The Earth is a sphere. Over four thousand years ago, Aristotle believed that the earth was round. Through rigorous scientific testing and mathematical proofing, many people have no issue with the Earth being a ball. Nonetheless, there are still people who believe in a flat Earth. They identify themselves as Flat Earthers, and their chosen conspiracy became popular in late 2013. Since then, their numbers have spiraled over the last few years, reaching unbelievable heights. Since Flat Earthers stoically believe that the earth is flat—despite the scientific evidence—many people judge them as stupid, insane, or both. … [Your thesis statement should go here]…
>
> Extract from *It is not Crazy to Believe the Earth is Flat* by
> Iwarin Suprapas

5.3.2. Writing the Second Draft

Stage 5. Post-Writing Activity: Collaborative Peer Review

After you and your partner have completed your first joint draft, swap your draft with another paired team in your class. Ask them to check what you and your partner have written in your draft. Check their draft in return. For added feedback, use the scoring rubric at the end of this unit (Appendix 5A) to grade the other team's drafts. At the very minimum, the feedback you give (and receive) should answer the following questions:

1. Is the essay 800–1000 words excluding references?
2. Is it formatted consistently and correctly to APA 7th style guidelines?
3. Are there any examples of wordiness? If so, circle them and suggest a way for the other team to fix the problem.
4. If they have modified the introduction, does it still include the following items?

☐ A hook.

☐ The territory (general–specific topic area).

☐ The importance of the topic (why should the reader care?).

☐ A strong thesis statement.

298 ESSENTIAL KNOWLEDGE AND SKILLS FOR ESSAY WRITING

5. Do the body paragraphs include the following elements?
- [ ] Topic sentence summarizing the entirety of the points the paragraph covers.
- [ ] Topic sentence that in some way links to the thesis statement.
- [ ] Relevant and reliable facts, statistics, evidence, and examples.
- [ ] At least one reference in each paragraph to an outside source.
- [ ] Reasonable and logical warrants that connect the evidence to the claim.
- [ ] Transitions so that the ideas flow together in a logical order.
- [ ] Concluding sentence summarizing the paragraph or linking to the next one.
6. Does the rebuttal paragraph do the following things?
- [ ] Clearly introduce one valid counterargument.
- [ ] Outline the major evidence that supports the counterargument.
- [ ] Refute the counterargument using relevant and reliable evidence + warrants.
- [ ] Explain why their argument is stronger than that of the counterargument.
7. Does the conclusion do the following things?
- [ ] Summarize the argument(s) without simply repeating things;
- [ ] Not introduce new information (such as another supporting point);
- [ ] Remind the reader why they should agree with the writers' position;
- [ ] Give the reader something to think about at the end.

Stage 6. Edit and Revise Your Draft

When your peers return your combined draft (and possible score), read their feedback. Then reread, rethink, and rewrite your own draft in your paired team. As you revise your draft, incorporate the feedback from your peers and add any new ideas that may have come to you as you read their draft. Check your edits against the scoring rubric for argument writing at the end of this unit to see if you can identify the strong and weak points of your essay.

Stage 7. Let Your Revised Draft Sit a While and Then Proofread It Carefully

Before your final proofread, give yourself a break from your revised draft. Also, before proofreading, it is usually a good idea to reread the instructions for the assignment or task rubric and/or look at the grading criteria or scoring rubric again. This will help to ensure that you have not gone off task or missed something important during the revision process.

---------------------- SUBMIT FINAL DRAFT ------------------------

300 ESSENTIAL KNOWLEDGE AND SKILLS FOR ESSAY WRITING

APPENDIX 5A.
SCORING RUBRIC FOR ARGUMENT WRITING

MICRO-LEVEL MISTAKES

→ One point deducted for every 5 micro-level mistakes: _____ divided by **5** =

INTRODUCTION _____ out of **10** (2.5 points per item)

→ Title is imaginative and reflects the essay's content

→ Hook creatively grabs reader's attention

→ Linking sentences clearly introduce the topic

→ Introduction indicates what type of argument the essay will be

THESIS _____ out of **10** (2 points per item)

→ Offers a thought-provoking idea

→ States why the topic is important to write about

→ Is clear, concise, and well-placed

→ Claim is qualified appropriately

→ Topic is not too general or too broad

DEVELOPMENT/SUPPORT _____ out of **35** (7 points per item)

→ Appropriate topic sentences start each body paragraph

→ Thoroughly covers the main points of the argument

→ Body paragraphs provide sufficient examples and evidence

→ Content is interesting and supported with references where needed

→ Supporting details are relevant and tied to thesis

ORGANIZATION/STRUCTURE _____ out of **15** (5 points per item)

→ Transition words and phrases effectively link sentences and paragraphs

→ Essay exhibits sophistication in structure and is not merely a list of points

→ Information is well placed in terms of importance

GRAMMAR / STYLE _____ out of **20** (5 points per item)

→ Variety of sentence lengths and sentence beginnings

→ Complete sentences throughout (no run-ons or fragments)

→ Observes the conventions of plain language usage

→ Exhibits correctly used advanced punctuation—colon, dashes, etc.

CONCLUSION _____ out of **10** (5 points per item)

→ Thesis not merely restated

→ Summarizes content and ends with a memorable point

Total _____ out of **100**

ARGUMENT/OPINION WRITING 301

APPENDIX 5B. UNIT 5 ANSWER KEY

Exercise 5.1
1. The student will gain marks for effort, <u>in all likelihood.</u>
2. Marks will <u>most likely</u> not be given for effort.
3. <u>No doubt,</u> the teacher will award some points for effort.
4. Effort will <u>presumably</u> not be rewarded.

Exercise 5.2 (suggested answers).

1. *typically,* **2.** *As a matter of fact,* **3.** *characteristically* **4.** *would*
5. *probably* **6.** *could* **7.** *most likely* **8.** *predictably*
9. *wrongly* **10.** *unjustifiably* **11.** *obviously* **12.** *Sadly*
13. *truly* **14.** *may* **15.** *For my part,*

Exercises 5.3 and 5.4
Answers will vary so consult with your peers or teacher.

Exercise 5.5
1. The writer established the territory by giving four infamous examples in which celebrities' privacy rights have been violated.
2. The writer established the importance of the topic via the following sentence: Such invasions of privacy violates celebrities' rights, sabotages their career and health, and can even take away their lives.
3. The thesis statement is not a particularly good one as it merely states an opinion. The reader is not given any indication of what the content of the essay will be, nor is any caveat given as to the other side of the argument.

Exercise 5.6

Questions of relevance
1. All of the the sources except source A are relevant and might help to explore both sides of the issue. Any difference in relevancy here would come down to which side of the argument

302 ESSENTIAL KNOWLEDGE AND SKILLS FOR ESSAY WRITING

you are supporting through each individual source. For instance, sources C, E, and F would be relevant to claiming that cell phones are a health risk, whereas sources B and D would be relevant to the other side of the argument.

2. Source A is the least relevant as it does not specifically focus on health risks, but only on how cellphones and electromagnetic radiation work. It would therefore not be very useful in a short essay. However, it might be useful for establishing the territory section of an introduction in a longer essay.

Questions of reliability

3. Sources A (high school textbook) and B (public info text) can be ranked "1" as the most reliable/trustworthy sources. Source A would have been very carefully vetted for authoritativeness and reliability, and it presents information that is not controversial in neutral academic terms. Source B would be highly authoritative. The public info text is a credible source that has probably had a lot of money invested into researching the topic; it also seems somewhat more balanced than the other sources that debate the health hazards of cellphones.

4. Source F (newspaper article) is the least reliable and should be ranked "4," as it is simply one person's opinion; it is also likely to be based on emotion rather than objective logic. Rather than being used as evidence, it could be used to develop an opening anecdote as a "hook" at the start of the essay. This hook could illustrate a prevalent point of view about cellphone use which the writer might argue for or against.

5. Source C merits a ranking of "2" for reliability/trustworthiness since it is not an academic journal but does cite research. It is also written by a research reporter, who would be expected to review the evidence carefully and to be neutral. Source D could also be given a "2" for reliability as the writer is an authority, but it may deserve a "3" because a phone industry engineer has a vested interest in arguing the side of the issue that supports the cellphone industry. Source E can be given a "3" for reliability because the writer is not an authority

ARGUMENT/OPINION WRITING   303

(though they do cite research) and the tone of the argument is emotional.

6. Answers will vary, but you should have mentioned sources such as reports from government entities and professional standards organizations (e.g., the World Health Organization), empirical research articles published in peer-reviewed journals, and suitable "gray literature" (publications by practitioners rather than academics).

Exercise 5.7

1. Yes, but this does not appear until the middle of the paragraph, with the statement: *The invasion of celebrities' privacy can indeed handicap their fundamental rights, as well as disrupt their careers and trigger mental illness.*

2. The three cited in number 1 above.

3. Through the statement: *After exploring both sides of the issue it is practical to say that celebrities should be able to fend off most privacy violations.*

4. It is an appeal to the reader in the form of a call to action: *Therefore, it is for us, the devourers of media to stop allowing a celebrity's privacy to be raided only just to feed our curiosity. After all, they are only human, just like we are.*

Exercise 5.8

Here is the ending to Kennedy's speech:

> Many years ago the great British explorer George Mallory, who was to die on Mount Everest, was asked why did he want to climb it. He said, "Because it is there." Well, space is there, and we're going to climb it, and the moon and the planets are there, and new hopes for knowledge and peace are there. And, therefore, as we set sail we ask God's blessing on the most hazardous and dangerous and greatest adventure on which man has ever embarked. Thank you. (Kennedy, 1962)

How does this compare to the conclusion you wrote?

304 ESSENTIAL KNOWLEDGE AND SKILLS FOR ESSAY WRITING

Exercise 5.9

1. There are a lot of inconsistencies and peculiarities that you could have mentioned with regard to Figure 5.3. Here are some of my observations:

    Why is the glass still in Arthur's hand if he fell down the stairs?

    Grounds *I can see that the glass is still in Arthur's hand.*

    Warrant *When people fall down the stairs, they usually drop whatever it is they are holding,*

    Backing *so that they can use their hands to try and stop or protect themselves from the fall.*

    Claim *Someone probably put the glass in Arthur's hand.*

Why is Arthur lying on his back and not on his front or side?

Grounds *I can see Arthur lying on his back with his heels on the steps.*

Warrant *When people go down stairs or walk anywhere, they typically face forward.*

Backing *This is because they need to see where they are going and place their feet accordingly.*

Claim *It seems unlikely that Arthur would land on his back with his heels on the steps if he fell when walking down the stairs.*

How did the mirror and candlestick holders remain fixed to the wall?

Grounds *Nothing seems to be disturbed by Arthur's fall.*

Warrant *When people fall down a narrow staircase, such as Arthur did, anything hanging on the walls of said staircase is typically disturbed.*

Backing *This is because during the fall, a person would be trying to stop himself or herself from falling and reach out to a wall or banister.*

Claim *It seems unlikely that Arthur fell down the stairs.*

ARGUMENT/OPINION WRITING   305

Why is Queenie cooking if she just found her husband dead?

Grounds   *I can see a steaming frying pan on the stove.*

Warrant   *When a person finds a dead body, the last thing on their mind is food.*

Backing   *People would more likely be in shock and call emergency services.*

Claim   *In all likelihood, there is an ulterior motive for why Queenie is cooking.*

2.   There are also quite a few inconsistencies in the information provided in the extract. Here is what I noticed:
Why did Queenie invite friends back to her place and then travel home alone?

Grounds   *I am told that Queenie's friends arrived ten minutes after she did.*

Warrant   *When you invite friends back to you place late at night, it is customary to travel back together.*

Backing   *This is particularly true if the invitee is a young woman on her own.*

Claim   *Queenie may have had an ulterior motive for inviting her friends back.*

Why did Queenie not call for an ambulance before her friends arrived?

Grounds   *Over the course of ten minutes, Queenie did not call an ambulance.*

Warrant   *Upon discovering a dead body, most people would immediately call the emergency services*

Backing   *because they want help as soon as possible and they have no idea how to deal with the situation by themselves.*

Claim   *It seems likely that something stopped Queenie from calling the emergency services.*

What exactly did Arthur hit his head on to cause such a deadly blow?

Grounds   *I cannot see anything that Arthur could hit his head on except for the floor.*

Warrant   *The kind of fall that would cause death from a head injury is usually quite severe.*

Backing   *Yet Arthur's body position, the glass in his hand, and pristine nature of his clothes, the rug, and the decorations on the stairwell does not indicate this.*

Claim   *It is quite possible that something else caused his head injury.*

3.   One possible interpretation is that during their fight, Queenie hit Arthur over the head with the frying pan. He fell to the floor and did not get back up. Queenie, thinking that he was just unconscious, escaped to the party before he regained consciousness. When it was time to go home, she was scared that Arthur might still be mad because he had not come to the party. Therefore, she invited her friends back, believing that she would be safe in their company (not realizing that he was in fact dead). Queenie rushed home to let Arthur know that their friends were on their way, so as not to surprise him by turning up with a bunch of friends. However, upon arriving home, she discovered Arthur in the exact same position as she had left him in. Namely, on the kitchen floor with the frying pan covered in blood and laid beside him. In a panic, she moved Arthur's body to make it look like he had fallen down the stairs. As a small woman, she did not have the strength to roll his body over, but she could drag him across the floor. She straightened up his clothes, put the glass back in his hand to highlight that he had been drinking, and placed the frying pan on the stove to burn away any trace of his DNA on the bottom of it. By the time she had done all of these things, her friends had arrived, and so she did not have time to call the emergency services.

ARGUMENT/OPINION WRITING   307

4. As you can see from my answer above, Queenie may not be telling the truth. However, to prove this in a court of law would require a lot more than circumstantial evidence. Indeed, you may have convincingly argued her innocence, as there was no right or wrong answer—only what you can claim based on the evidence.

References

Adams, D. (1981). *The restaurant at the end of the universe*. Pan Books.

American Cancer Society. (2017, December 15). *Living as a stomach cancer survivor*. https://www.cancer.org/cancer/stomach-cancer/after-treatment/follow-up.html

Bacon, F. (2009). *The essays or counsels, civil and moral, of Francis Ld. Verulam, Viscount St. Albans* (W. C. Hazlitt, Ed., & C. Cotton, Trans.). Project Guttenberg. https://www.gutenberg.org/files/575/575-h/575-h.htm (Original work published 1597)

Barks, D., & Watts, P. (2001). Textual borrowing strategies for graduate-level ESL writers. In D. Belcher & A. Hirvela (Eds.), *Linking literacies: Perspectives on L2 reading-writing connections* (pp. 246–267). University of Michigan Press.

Barthes, R. (1975). An introduction to the structural analysis of narrative (L. Duisit, Trans.). *New Literary History*, *6*(2), 237–272. https://doi.org/10.2307/468419

Bazerman, C. (1997). The life of genre, the life in the classroom. In W. Bishop & H. Ostram (Eds.), *Genre and writing: Issues, arguments, alternatives* (pp. 19–26). Boynton/Cook Publishers.

Biber, D., Johansson, S., Leech, G., Conrad, S., & Finegan, E. (1999). *Longman grammar of spoken and written English*. Longman.

Bennett, R. E., Zhang, M., Deane, P., & van Rijn, P. W. (2020). How do proficient and less proficient students differ in their composition processes? *Educational Assessment*, *25*(3), 198–217. https://doi.org/10.1080/10627197.2020.1804351

Bordwell, D., & Thompson, K. (2020). *Film art: An introduction* (12th ed.). McGraw-Hill.

Borg, E. (2009). Local plagiarisms. *Assessment & Evaluation in Higher Education*, *34*(4), 415–426. https://doi.org/10.1080/02602930802075115

REFERENCES 309

Bowen, N. E. J. A. (2019). Unfolding choices in digital writing: A functional perspective on the language of academic revisions. *Journal of Writing Research, 10*(3), 465–498. https://doi.org/10.17239/jowr-2019.10.03.03

Bowen, N. E. J. A., & Nanni, A. (2021). Piracy, playing the system, or poor policies? Perspectives on plagiarism in Thailand. *Journal of English for Academic Purposes, 51*, 100992, 1–13. https://doi.org/10.1016/j.jeap.2021.100992

Bowen, N. E. J. A., & Thomas, N. (2020). Manipulating texture and cohesion in academic writing: A keystroke logging study. *Journal of Second Language Writing, 50*, 100773, 1–15. https://doi.org/10.1016/j.jslw.2020.100773

Bowen, N. E. J. A., & Van Waes, L. (2020). Exploring revisions in academic text: Closing the gap between process and product approaches in digital writing. *Written Communication, 37*(3), 322–364. https://doi.org/10.1177/0741088320916508

Bowen, N. E. J. A., Satienchayakorn, N., Teedaaksornsakul, M., & Thomas, N. (2021). Legitimising teacher identity: Investment and agency from an ecological perspective. *Teaching and Teacher Education, 108*, 103519, 1–11. https://doi.org/10.1016/j.tate.2021.103519

Bowen, N. E. J. A., Thomas, N., & Vandermeulen, N. (2022). Exploring feedback and regulation in online writing classes with keystroke logging. *Computers & Composition, 63*, 102692, 1–30. https://doi.org/10.1016/j.compcom.2022.102692

Brontë, C. (1998). *Jane Eyre: An autobiography*. Project Guttenberg. https://www.gutenberg.org/files/1260/1260-h/1260-h.htm (Original work published 1847)

Browning, R. (1842). *Dramatic lyrics*. Edward Moxon.

Burton, T. (Director). (2005). *Willy Wonka and the chocolate factory* [Film]. The Zanuck Company; Plan B Entertainment; Village Roadshow Productions; Theobald Film Productions.

Byrne, S., & Hart, P. S. (2009). The boomerang effect: A synthesis of findings and a preliminary theoretical framework. *Annals of the International Communication Association, 33*(1: Communication Yearbook 33), 3–37. https://doi.org/10.1080/23808985.2009.11679083

Camus, A. (1946). *The stranger* (S. Gilbert, Trans.). Alfred A. Knopf. (Original work published 1942)

Carroll, L. (2008). *Alice's adventures in Wonderland*. Project Guttenberg. (Original work published 1865) https://www.gutenberg.org/cache/epub/11/pg11-images.html

310 ESSENTIAL KNOWLEDGE AND SKILLS FOR ESSAY WRITING

Chauvet, J-M., Deschamps, E. B., & Hillaire, C. (1996). *Dawn of art: The Chauvet Cave (the oldest known paintings in the world)*. H. N. Abrams.

Chekhov, A. P. (2004). The dependent. In *The cook's wedding and other stories by Anton Pavlovich Chekhov* (C. Garnett, Trans.). Project Guttenberg. https://www.gutenberg.org/ebooks/13417 (Original work published 1886)

Clark, D. J. (Director). (2018). *Behind the curve* [Documentary film]. United States: Delta-V Productions.

Crossley, S. A. (2020). Linguistic features in writing quality and development: An overview. *Journal of Writing Research*, *11*(3), 415–443. https://doi.org/10.17239/jowr-2020.11.03.01

de Montaigne, M. (2006). *Essays of Michel de Montaigne, complete* (W. C. Hazlitt, Ed. [1877], & C. Cotton, Trans. [1685–6]). Project Guttenberg. https://www.gutenberg.org/files/3600/3600-h/3600-h.htm (Original work published 1580)

Dickens, C. (1994). *A tale of two cities*. Project Guttenberg. https://www.gutenberg.org/cache/epub/98/pg98-images.html (Original work published 1859)

Dickens, C. (2009). *David Copperfield*. Project Guttenberg. https://www.gutenberg.org/files/766/766-h/766-h.htm (Original work published 1869)

Dickens, C. (1998). *Great expectations*. Project Guttenberg. https://www.gutenberg.org/files/1400/1400-h/1400-h.htm#chap02 (Original work published 1867)

Dickens, C. (1992). *A Christmas carol in prose; being a ghost story of Christmas*. Project Guttenberg. https://www.gutenberg.org/files/46/46-h/46-h.htm (Original work published 1843)

Dickinson, E. (2004). *Poems: Three series, complete* (M. L. Todd & T. W. Higgins, Eds). Project Guttenberg. https://www.gutenberg.org/files/12242/12242-h/12242-h.htm (Original work published 1890)

Dostoyevsky, F. (1996). *Notes from the underground* (C. Garnett, Trans.). Project Guttenberg. https://www.gutenberg.org/cache/epub/600/pg600-images.html (Original work published 1864)

Dunning, D. (2011). The Dunning–Kruger effect: On being ignorant of one's own ignorance. In M. Zanna & J. Olson (Eds.), *Advances in experimental social psychology* (Vol. 44, pp. 247–296). Academic Press. https://doi.org/10.1016/B978-0-12-385522-0.00005-6

Fitzgerald, F. S. (2021). *The great Gatsby*. Project Guttenberg. https://www.gutenberg.org/files/64317/64317-h/64317-h.htm (Original work published 1925)

Foster Wallace, D. (1996). *Infinite jest*. Little, Brown and Company.

Freeman, D. (2004). *Creating emotion in games: The art and craft of emotioneering*. New Riders. https://doi.org/10.1145/1027154.1027179

Galbraith, D., & Baaijen, V. M. (2018). The work of writing: Raiding the inarticulate. *Educational Psychologist*, *53*(4: Conceptualizing Writing), 238–257. https://doi.org/10.1080/00461520.2018.1505515

Gardner, S., & Nesi, H. (2013). A Classification of genre families in university student writing. *Applied linguistics*, *34*(1), 25–52. https://doi.org/10.1093/applin/ams024

Graham, S., & Harris, K. R. (2018). An examination of the design principles underlying a self-regulated strategy development study. *Journal of Writing Research*, *10*(2), 139–187. https://doi.org/10.17239/jowr-2018.10.02.02

Halliday, M. A. K., & Matthiessen, C. M. I. M. (2014). *Introduction to functional grammar*. Routledge. https://doi.org/10.4324/9780203431269

Hayes, J. R. (2012). Modeling and remodeling writing. *Written Communication*, *29*(3), 369–388. https://doi.org/10.1177/0741088312451260

Hemingway, E. (2012). *The old man and the sea*. Project Gutenberg. https://gutenberg.ca/ebooks/hcmingwaye-oldmanandthesea/hemingwaye-oldmanandthesea-00-h.html (Original work published 1952)

Hemingway, E. (2016). Hills like white elephants. In E. Hemingway (Ed.) *Men without women* (reprint of first edition). Project Guttenberg. https://gutenberg.ca/ebooks/hemingwaye-menwithoutwomen/hemingwaye-menwithoutwomen-00-h.html (Original work published 1927)

Heshmat, S. (2015, April 23). What is confirmation bias? *Psychology Today*. https://www.psychologytoday.com/us/blog/science-choice/201504/what-is-confirmation-bias

Hillock, G. (2011). *Teaching argumentative writing*. Heinemann.

Hitchcock, D. (2006). Good reasoning on the Toulmin Model. In D. Hitchcock & B. Verheij (Eds.), *Arguing on the Toulmin Model: New essays in argument analysis and evaluation* (pp. 203–218). Springer. https://doi.org/10.1007/978-1-4020-4938-5

Huang, Y., & Zhang, L. J. (2020). Does a process-genre approach help improve students' argumentative writing in English as a foreign language? Findings from an intervention study. *Reading & Writing Quarterly*, *36*(4), 339–364. https://doi.org/10.1080/10573569.2019.1649223

Jackson, P. (Director). (2001). *The lord of the rings: The fellowship of the ring* [Film]. New Line Cinema; Wingnut films.

Jackson, W., Luske, H., & Geronimi, C. (Directors). (1950). *Cinderella* [Film]. Walt Disney Productions.

312 ESSENTIAL KNOWLEDGE AND SKILLS FOR ESSAY WRITING

Karbach, J. (1987). Using Toulmin's model of argumentation. *Journal of Teaching Writing*, *6*(1), 81–92.

Keles, U., & Yazan, B. (2020). Representation of cultures and communities in a global ELT textbook: A diachronic content analysis. *Language Teaching Research*, OnlineFirst, 1–22 https://doi.org/10.1177/1362168820976922

Kennedy, J. F. (1962). *Address at Rice University, Houston, Texas, 12 September 1962* [Reading copy of speech]. John F. Kennedy Presidential Library and Museum. https://www.jfklibrary.org/asset-viewer/archives/JFKPOF/040/JFKPOF-040-001

King James Version. (1989). *The King James version of the Bible*. Project Guttenberg. https://www.gutenberg.org/cache/epub/10/pg10-images.html (Original work published 1611)

Kinneavy, J. L., & Warriner, J. E. (1993). *Elements of writing*. Holt, Rinehart, and Winston.

Kruger, J., & Dunning, D. (1999). Unskilled and unaware of it: How difficulties in recognizing one's own incompetence lead to inflated self-assessments. *Journal of Personality and Social Psychology*, *77*(6), 1121–1134. https://doi.org/10.1037/0022-3514.77.6.1121

Labov, W., & Waletzky, J. (1967). Narrative analysis. In J. Helm (Ed.) *Essays on the Verbal and Visual Arts* (pp. 12–44). University of Washington Press.

Martin, J. R., & Rose, D. (2008). *Genre relations: Mapping culture*. Equinox.

Melville, H. (2001). *Moby Dick*. Project Guttenberg. https://www.gutenberg.org/files/2701/2701-h/2701-h.htm (Original work published 1851)

Morrison, B. (1999, September 25). How to hook them from the start. *Independent*. https://www.independent.co.uk/arts-entertainment/how-to-hook-them-from-the-start-5382385.html

Orwell, G. (1949). *Nineteen eighty-four*. Sacker & Warburg.

Orwell, G. (1968). Extracts from a manuscript note-book. In S. Orwell & I Angus (Eds.), *The collected essays, journalism, and letters of George Orwell: In front of your nose, 1945–1950* (Vol. 4). Secker & Warburg. (Original work published 1949)

Oswald, M. E., & Grosjean, S. (2004). Confirmation bias. In R. F. Pohl (Ed.), *Cognitive illusions: A handbook on fallacies and biases in thinking, judgement and memory* (pp. 79–96). Psychology Press.

Poe, E. A. (1854). *The raven and other poems*. Wiley and Putnam.

Propp, V. (1968). *Morphology of the folktale* (L. Scott, Trans., 2nd ed.). University of Texas Press. (Original work published 1928)

Racelis, J. V., & Matsuda, P. K. (2013). Integrating process and genre into the second language writing classroom: Research into practice. *Language Teaching*, *46*(3), 382–393. https://doi.org/10.1017/S0261444813000116

REFERENCES 313

Rosário, P., Núñez, J. C., Rodríguez, C., Cerezo, R., Fernández, E., Tuero, E., & Högemann, J. (2017). Analysis of instructional programs in different academic levels for improving self-regulated learning SRL through written text. In R. Fidalgo, K. R. Harris & M. Braaksma (Eds.), *Design principles for teaching effective writing* (pp. 201–230). Brill. https://doi.org/10.1163/9789004270480_010

Shakespeare, W. (1994). *The Complete works of William Shakespeare*. Project Guttenberg. https://www.gutenberg.org/files/100/100-h/100-h.htm (Original work published 1623)

Smith, R. W. (1964). "Refutation" and "rebuttal". *American Speech, 39*(2), 124–130. https://doi.org/10.2307/453114

Steindl, C., Jonas, E., Sittenthaler, S., Traut-Mattausch, E., & Greenberg, J. (2015). Understanding psychological reactance. *Zeitschrift für Psychologie, 233*(4), 205–214. https://doi.org/10.1027/2151-2604/a000222

Swales, J. (1990). *Genre analysis: English in academic and research settings*. Cambridge University Press.

Tardy, C. M. (2009). *Building genre knowledge*. Parlor Press.

Thompson, H. S. (1972). *Fear and loathing in Las Vegas*. Random House.

Todorov, T. (1977). *The poetics of prose* (R. Howard, Trans.). Cornell University Press. (Original work published 1971)

Tolkien, J. R. R. (1968). *The lord of the rings*. George Allen and Urwin.

Tolstoy, L. (2001). *War and peace* (L. Maude & A. Maude, Trans.). Project Guttenberg. (Original work published 1869) https://www.gutenberg.org/files/2600/2600-h/2600-h.htm

Toulmin, S. E. (2003). *The uses of argument* (updated edition). Cambridge university press. (Original work published 1958)

Treat, L. (1982). *Crime and puzzlement 2: More solve-them-yourself picture mysteries*. David R. Godine Publisher.

Verheij, B. (2006). Evaluating arguments based on Toulmin's scheme. In D. Hitchcock, & B. Verheij (Eds.), *Arguing on the Toulmin Model: New essays in argument analysis and evaluation* (pp. 181–203). Springer. https://doi.org/10.1007/978-1-4020-4938-5_12

Wilde, O. (1994). *The picture of Dorian Gray*. Project Guttenberg. https://www.gutenberg.org/cache/epub/174/pg174-images.html (Original work published 1890)

Yarmolinsky, A. (1954). *The unknown Chekhov: Stories and other writings hitherto untranslated by Anton Chekhov*. Noonday Press.

Young, R. E., Becker, A. L., & Pike, K. L. (1970). *Rhetoric: Discovery and change*. Harcourt, Brace, and World.

Sources for Images

All figures and tables were produced by the author unless explicitly stated on the page where they occur. The image of a teacher working with students, which is shown at the top right-hand side of the exercise boxes, is an author produced photograph. The original sources for all other photographs used throughout the book are listed below.

Unit 1

PAGE 50

"Boats on a jetty" photograph by Nan Ingraham. (2017). *Several boats on dock*. Unsplash. https://unsplash.com/photos/mNuLRRjLwjA

Unit 2

PAGE 79

Image 1 photograph by Norbert Braun. (2022). *Sales boats at a floating market*. Unsplash. https://unsplash.com/photos/Wf6K4YvZYcc

Image 2 photograph by Frida Aguilar Estrada. (2017). *Heavy traffic*. Unsplash. https://unsplash.com/photos/_ffkj8TnuGo

PAGE 81

Image 1 photograph by Igor Kyryliuk. (2020). *Palm tree shot in Los Angeles, California*. Unsplash. https://unsplash.com/photos/sK6vKcIOqsw

Image 2 photograph by Wolfgang Hasselmann. (2020). *Pink and white trees under blue sky during daytime*. Unsplash. https://unsplash.com/photos/kPYG-BgN1l0

Image 3 photograph by Kata Urban. (2020). *Green plant in white ceramic pot on brown wooden table*. Unsplash. https://unsplash.com/photos/zULz6c6-uf8

PAGE 93

"Hallway" photograph by User 5460160. (2018). *Vestibule hall door*. Pixabay. https://pixabay.com/images/id-3542790/

SOURCES FOR IMAGES   315

PAGE 102

Image 1 photograph by Prince Akachi. (2018). *Woman holding her collar standing near wall*. Unsplash. https://unsplash.com/photos/J1OScm_uHUQ

Image 2 photograph by Jimmy Fermin. (2018). *Woman staring directly at camera near pink wall*. Unsplash. https://unsplash.com/photos/bqe0J0b26RQ

Image 3 photograph by Yonas Bekele. (2020). *Man in blue crew neck shirt wearing gold necklace*. Unsplash. https://unsplash.com/photos/UgVbUMQrmjY

Image 4 photograph by Jurica Koletić. (2017). *Man wearing Henley top*. Unsplash. https://unsplash.com/photos/7YVZYZeITc8

Image 5 photograph by Nartan Büyükyıldız. (2021). *Man in black crew neck shirt*. Unsplash. https://unsplash.com/photos/wYEpS2XGWb4

Image 6 photograph by Josh Scorpio. (2021). *Man in grey suit jacket*. Unsplash. https://unsplash.com/photos/H3Tuh0hwYQk

Image 7 photograph by Frank Holleman. (2018). *Man in blue collared top*. Unsplash. https://unsplash.com/photos/GdhPy1cwtGE

Image 8 photograph by Tim Snurderl. (2021). *Woman in black and red tank top*. Unsplash. https://unsplash.com/photos/JvBd3vlPj8E

Image 9 photograph by Kate Bezzubets. (2021). *No tile*. Unsplash. https://unsplash.com/photos/UJbqowk5fso

Image 10 photograph by Darshan Patel. (2018). *Man wearing eyeglasses and blue shirt inside coffee shop*. https://unsplash.com/photos/QJEVpydulGs

Image 11 photograph by Joseph Gonzalez. (2017). *Man wearing V-neck shirt*. Unsplash. https://unsplash.com/photos/iFgRcqHznqg

Image 12 photograph by Christian Buehner. (2019). *Men's blue and white button-up collared top*. Unsplash. https://unsplash.com/photos/DItYlc26zVI

Image 13 photograph by Connor Wilkins. (2019). *Woman in gray jacket*. https://unsplash.com/photos/2crxTr4jCkc

Image 14 photograph by Gabriel Silvério. (2018). *Woman wearing pink spaghetti strap dress*. Unsplash. https://unsplash.com/photos/QJCtd5KGI9Y

Image 15 photograph by Ghaly Wedinly. (2019). *Woman wearing tribal dress*. Unsplash. https://unsplash.com/photos/K07jvi25Qxg

PAGE 110

Main image by Brian Lundquist. (2020). *Swag*. Unsplash. https://unsplash.com/photos/KVAZCI2nrj4

316 ESSENTIAL KNOWLEDGE AND SKILLS FOR ESSAY WRITING

PAGE 111

Image 1 photograph by Yann Allegre. (2018). *The ghost house*. Unsplash. https://unsplash.com/photos/PblvRWusYWA

Image 2 photograph by Guillaume Issaly. (2018). *Gray concrete lighthouse*. Unsplash. https://unsplash.com/photos/ane7j9URy8c

Image 3 photograph by Joshua van der Schyff. (2019). *Brown and white house*. Unsplash. https://unsplash.com/photos/g1_qduahbDg

PAGE 124

Main image by Lynn Greyling. (n.d). *At the bloodbank*. Public Domain Pictures. https://www.publicdomainpictures.net/en/view-image.php?image=89787&picture=at-the-bloodbank

Image 1 photograph by Maskmedicare Shop. (2021). *No title*. Unsplash. https://unsplash.com/photos/zCsup0tF-q4

Images 2, 3, and 4 by Author (Neil Evan Jon Anthony Bowen).

Image 5 photograph by Hush Naidoo Jade Photography. (2018). *Person injecting syringe*. Unsplash. https://unsplash.com/photos/Zp7ebyti3MU

Image 6 Band Aid Flat Icon Vector by Videoplasty.com. Wikimedia Commons CC-BY-SA 4.0. https://commons.wikimedia.org/wiki/File:Band_Aid_Flat_Icon_Vector.svg

Unit 3

PAGE 149

Image 1 photograph by Juan Rumimpunu. (2018). *Gray monkey in Bokeh*. Unsplash. https://unsplash.com/photos/nLXOatvTaLo

Image 2 photograph by Andy Beales. (2015). *Running in an airport*. Unsplash. https://unsplash.com/photos/BjcGdM-mjL0

Image 3 photograph by Emily Rudolph. (2018). *Tea time (2)*. Unsplash. https://unsplash.com/photos/-m0xspcr6Xw

Image 4 photograph by Jan Canty. (2020). *Brown lioness on green grass field during daytime*. Unsplash. https://unsplash.com/photos/rud1eTeykNg

Image 5 photograph by Sammie Chaffin. (2018). *Don't look down*. Unsplash. https://unsplash.com/photos/Zdf3zn5XXtU

Image 6 photograph by Mwangi Gatheca. (2018). *Person laying down on white surface*. Unsplash. https://unsplash.com/photos/xViKfocA-Uc

Image 7 photograph by Renji Desh. (2022). *No title*. Unsplash. https://unsplash.com/photos/yi8e4hZtVXs

Image 8 photograph by Ikwuegbu, E. (2021). *Man in black crew neck t-shirt using black laptop computer*. Unsplash. https://unsplash.com/photos/tpTFuvXLNFI

SOURCES FOR IMAGES   317

Unit 4

<u>PAGE 215</u>

"Amphibian" photograph by Wallace Heng. (2020). *Poisonous blue frog*. Unsplash. https://unsplash.com/photos/njsOI5hXeRQ

"Fish" photograph by Rachel Hisko. (2018). *Nemo*. Unsplash. https://unsplash.com/photos/rEM3cK8F1pk

"Mammals" photograph by Brian Mann. (2015). *Two baby monkeys on gray tree branch*. Unsplash. https://unsplash.com/photos/aXqlZFeVFrU

"Birds" photograph by Joey Smith. (2021). *Lorikeets sitting on a bench*. Unsplash. https://unsplash.com/photos/0r99iaOh3tc

"Reptiles" photograph by Lisa Yount. (2020). *Alligator*. Unsplash. https://unsplash.com/photos/POKb4uUOizU

Author Index

Adams, Douglas 155
American Cancer Society 234

Baaijen, Veerle M. 6
Bacon, Francis 10
Barks, Debbie 266
Barthes, Roland 137–138
Bazerman, Charles 7
Becker, Alton L. 272–273, 280
Bennett, Randy E. 57
Biber, Douglas 30
Bordwell, David 138
Borg, Erik 266
Bowen, Neil E. J. A. 2, 13, 26, 266, 269–271
Brontë, Charlotte 141–143
Browning, Robert 80
Burton, Tim (Director), 171
Byrne, Sahara 294

Camus, Albert 155
Carroll, Lewis 144, 146, 147
Cerezo, Rebeca 57
Chauvet, Jean-Marie 138
Chekhov, Anton P. 100–101
Clark, Daniel J. (Director) 292
Conrad, Susan 30
Crossley, Scott A. 5

de Montaigne, Michel 10

Deane, Paul 57
Deschamps, Eliette B. 138
Dickens, Charles 107, 142, 151, 160
Dickinson, Emily 82
Dunning, David 294

Fernández, Estrella 57
Finegan, Edward 30
Fitzgerald, F. Scott 91–92
Foster Wallace, David 80
Freeman, David 170

Galbraith, David 6
Gardner, Sheena 5
Geronimi, Clyde (Director) 175
Graham, Steve 57
Greenberg, Jeff 293
Grosjean, Stefan 269, 294

Halliday, Michael A. K. 19–20, 88–90, 249, 251–252
Harris, Karen R. 57
Hart, Philip S. 294
Hayes, John R. 6
Hemingway, Ernest 106–107, 146
Heshmat, Shahram 294
Hillaire, Christian 138
Hillock, George 276, 284
Hitchcock, David 278
Högemann, Julia 57

AUTHOR INDEX

Huang, Yu 2

Jackson, Peter (Director) 258
Jackson, Wilfred (Director) 175
Johansson, Stig 30
Jonas, Eva 293

Karbach, Joan 282, 283
Keles, Ufuk 3
Kennedy, John F. 265–266, 303
Kinneavy, James L. 247
Kruger, Justin 294

Labov, William 172, 173
Leech, Geoffrey 30
Luske, Hamilton (Director) 175

Martin, Jim R. 5, 7
Matsuda, Paul K. 2
Matthiessen, Christian M. I. M.
    19–20, 88–90, 249, 251–252
Melville, Herman 103–104,
    143–144, 151–152, 155
Morrison, Blake 156, 159, 161

Nanni, Alexander 266, 270–271
Nesi, Hilary 5
Núñez, José C. 57

Orwell, George 101, 155
Oswald, Margit E. 269, 294

Pike, Kenneth L. 272–273, 280
Poe, Edgar A. 82
Propp, Vladmir 167

Racelis, Juval V. 2
Rodríguez, Celestino 57

Rosário, Pedro 57
Rose, David 5, 7

Satienchayakorn, Natakorn 271
Shakespeare, William 26, 81–82
Sittenthaler, Sandra 293
Smith, Robert W. 282
Steindl, Christine 293
Swales, John 7

Tardy, Christine M. 4–5
Teedaaksornsakul, Mareeyadar 271
Thomas, Nathan 2, 13, 26, 271
Thompson, Hunter S. 155
Thompson, Kristen 138
Todorov, Tsvetan 173
Tolkien, John. R. R. 167
Tolstoy, Leo 144–145
Toulmin, Stephen E. 273, 280–281
Traut-Mattausch, Eva 293
Treat, Lawrence 284
Tuero, Ellian 57

van Rijn, Peter W. 57
Van Waes, Luuk 2
Vandermeulen, Nina 2, 26
Verheij, Bart 280

Waletzky, Joshua 172–173
Warriner, James E. 247
Watts, Patricia 266

Yarmolinsky, Avrahm 105
Yazan, Bedrettin 3
Young, Richard E. 272–273, 280

Zhang, Lawrence J. 2
Zhang, Mo 57

Subject Index

active voice 12, 14, 32, 125
AI 267
alliteration 82, 150
argument types
    Classical/Aristotelian 256, 272, 277
    Rogerian 256, 272–273, 277
    Toulmin Method 256, 272–290
argument/opinion writing
    definition 246–248
    general guidelines 254–265

backing (of warrant) 247, 273–291
block method 197–198, 221, 232–233

cause–effect essay 194–195
cause–effect writing
    definition 225
    general guidelines 226–230
chain
    of events 162–164, 174, 181
    of reasoning 226
    reference chain 36, 50
    sequence chain 125, 127
characterization 139, 145, 166–170
    flat, static, rounded, dynamic
      roles 168
    through dialogue 106,
      138–141, 145–148

cherry-picking (of evidence) 261
choosing a topic
    for argument essay 254–255
    for cause–effect essay 226–228
    for classification essay 215–216
    for compare/contrast essay
      202–207
    for narrative essay 153–154
    general guidelines 58
circumstantial element 86–91
citation 268, 270–271
    see also referencing
claim (in an argument essay)
    274–277, 281
classification essay 194
classificatory writing
    definition 214–215
    general guidelines 215–218
cliché 83
climax (of narrative) 138–140, 154,
    162, 164, 174, 177
cohesion 18, 36, 50–51
comma splice 23
    see also punctuation, comma
comment adjunct 230, 249,
    251–254, 281
compare/contrast essay 194
compare/contrast writing
    general guidelines 202–206
concept map 111–112, 127, 222, 283

SUBJECT INDEX   321

concession starters
    see transitional phrases for
        rebuttals
conjunctive adjunct 17–20, 197, 230
constant theme 14
coordinating conjunction 17–19, 23,
    25, 139

description
    general guidelines 75–76
dialogue tag 146–147

evidence (for argument) 246–247,
    260–261, 271, 273–278, 282

falling action (of narrative) 89, 164,
    174–177
flash-back 180
fragment 11, 17–18
frame 180, 230
    see also timeframe
fused sentence 21

golden details 151–153
grounds 247, 260, 271, 273–279, 283

hook 47, 60, 155–157, 216
hyperbole 80

linear theme 14

metaphor 77, 81–84, 151
modal verb 230, 249–250, 253–254,
    281
mood adjunct 230, 249–251, 253,
    281

narration 91, 138, 140–145
    first-person perspective
        141–144

second-person perspective
    143–144
third-person perspective
    144–145
narrative writing
    definition 138
    general guidelines 139

onomatopoeia 80
opening
    in narrative essay 140,
        143–144, 155, 159–160
    in opinion essay 248
    see also hook
opinion
see argument/opinion writing
outlining template
    for cause–effect essay 232–233
    for classification essay 221
    for compare/contrast essay 198,
        200
    for descriptive essay 128
    for describing a process
        (explaining) 119
    for five-paragraph essay 60
    for narrative essay 184
    for Toulmin argument 290–291

paragraph development
    see also cohesion
    concluding sentence 44, 49,
        166, 259
    supporting sentence 36, 43–44,
        47–49, 228
    topic sentence 35–44, 47–50,
        158, 166, 206, 259–260,
        288–289
    see also unity
paraphrasing 266–268
passive voice 12–14, 42

322 ESSENTIAL KNOWLEDGE AND SKILLS FOR ESSAY WRITING

patch-writing 266–268
peer review (instructions for) 61–62
personification 82–83
plagiarism 266–267
planning 57
plain language 32, 88
plot 138–140, 143, 154, 166–169, 177, 179–181
plotline 153
point-by-point method 197, 200
punctuation
    colon 25–27, 269
    comma 17–18, 21–23, 25, 31, 146
    em dash 23–25, 146
    en dash 23–25, 270
    hyphen 23–26, 270
    semicolon 19, 22–23, 25

qualification (of claim) 275, 281
quest (in narrative) 167, 174

readability 31
rebuttal (of argument) 275, 282
referencing 266–271
    style 268–269
    list item 269–271
resolution (of narrative) 138–139, 154, 164–165, 174–177, 180
rhetorical structuring 50, 55, 58, 140, 177, 180
    see also block method
    see also point-by-point method
rising action (of narrative) 139, 174, 176–183

sequential and causal connectors
    see transition, of time or cause
setting the scene (for narrative) 139, 141, 161, 175–177
show, don't tell 76, 101, 105–106, 109, 139, 148, 167
simile 80–81, 83–84, 151
subject–verb agreement 29–30

thesis statement
    for argument essay 256–258, 260, 264, 276, 291, 296
    for cause–effect essay 227–228, 235
    for classification essay 221
    for compare/contrast essay 204–206, 208
    for descriptive essay 98
    general guidelines 5, 7, 48–51
    for narrative essay 158
timeframe 28
transition 36, 44, 50, 114, 166, 197, 207, 259
    expository and exemplifying 219
    of time or cause 122
    spatial 95
    transitional phrases for rebuttals 282

unity 35, 37, 50–53, 55

Venn diagram 203, 209

warrant 275, 277–280

www.ingramcontent.com/pod-product-compliance
Ingram Content Group UK Ltd.
Pitfield, Milton Keynes, MK11 3LW, UK
UKHW021502030725
460355UK00001B/3